Praise for *Preventing Ministry Failure*

"Michael Todd and Brad have lived in the world they write about. Their passion is enabling called-out men and women to succeed without stepping on the land mines that haunt clergy everywhere. Devour their book and live the life they prescribe. It will become a win-win."

H. B. London Jr., Vice President, Church & Clergy, Focus on the Family

"Nothing ignites my passion more than instructing and encouraging fellow ministers through our Timothy Barnabas conferences. As one who has ministered to thousands of pastors struggling with the demands of ministry, *Preventing Ministry Failure* is as instructive as it is encouraging for the minister dealing with the daily challenges of ministry responsibility—including the important need for intentional boundaries to protect the minister's calling, family and personal integrity. This book promotes something I've been encouraging ministers to do for over fifteen years: to develop relationships with other pastors that they may serve as support to one another. If you're serious about having a lifelong and fruitful ministry, *Preventing Ministry Failure* is for you."

Dr. Johnny M. Hunt, Senior Pastor, First Baptist Church of Woodstock, Georgia, and Founder, Timothy Barnabas Ministries

"It has long been time for us ministers to become honest with ourselves and break the silence surrounding the myth, 'It won't happen to me.' I work with countless ministers every year who believed the same lie yet found themselves in one of our Faithful & True workshops—burned out on life and ministry from an affair, Internet pornography use or some other pattern of sexual indiscretion. Moral and ministry failure can happen to any of us and it happens all the time. *Preventing Ministry Failure* is a book for ministers who are willing to admit 'There, but for the grace of God, go I.' Those with honest humility will see this book as a godsend—a systematic and practical tool for proactive maintenance in the minister's life."

Mark Laaser, Founder, Faithful & True Ministries, and author of *Healing the Wounds of Sexual Addiction*

"ShepherdCare is a wonderful ministry to help pastors keep their hands to the plow and finish well. This book is a must-read for all ministers . . . a resource they will go to again and again as they strive to serve the Lord, their families and their churches with integrity."

Michael Catt, Senior Pastor, Sherwood Baptist Church, Albany, Georgia

"*Preventing Ministry Failure* is most timely and appropriate. Covering a wide range of challenges facing pastors today, it provides insightful and practical suggestions for avoiding ministry failure. Also, as the authors point out, long-term effectiveness in ministry isn't just about the pastor, it's also about the pastor's family as well. There is little point in building a great church while your own family disintegrates or your children turn against you and God—which is what occurs more often than we acknowledge publicly. With suggestions for self-care, having an accountability group, boundary setting and a host of other important issues essential to finishing well in ministry, this book is the most comprehensive I have yet seen. I recommend it as a textbook for every seminary."

Archibald D. Hart, Ph.D., FPPR, Senior Professor of Psychology and Dean Emeritus, Graduate School of Psychology, Fuller Theological Seminary

"*Preventing Ministry Failure* is a first of its kind package that is sure to have deep and broad impact for those committed to shepherding ministries. This resource is the result of collaborative efforts of pastors and professionals empirically deriving seven areas of concern for force-terminated ministers. These findings have been provided for us now in a workbook format for establishing and applying preventative self-care plans that are theologically and psychologically sound. Thank you, Michael Todd and Brad, for providing a text that I am eager to implement at our seminary."

C. GARY BARNES, THM, PHD, LICENSED PSYCHOLOGIST AND ASSOCIATE PROFESSOR, DALLAS THEOLOGICAL SEMINARY

"In a day where senior pastors and ministers alike are reading, collecting and gathering materials from books, CDs and seminars for the benefit of someone else, Brad Hoffmann and Michael Todd Wilson have written an excellent self-help book for the minister himself. These seven reasons why ministers struggle with, resign from or are forced out of ministry have been identified and analyzed, and a course of action recommended for the health and happiness of the minister's home and family. The book moves beyond the theory to the practical. Trust me, these two have been there, done that and bought the shirt."

KEN WHITTEN, SENIOR PASTOR, IDLEWILD BAPTIST CHURCH, LUTZ, FLORIDA

PREVENTING MINISTRY FAILURE

A ShepherdCare Guide for Pastors,
Ministers and Other Caregivers

Michael Todd Wilson
and Brad Hoffmann

With contributions from
members of CareGivers Forum

IVP Books

An imprint of InterVarsity Press
Downers Grove, Illinois

InterVarsity Press
P.O. Box 1400, Downers Grove, IL 60515-1426
World Wide Web: www.ivpress.com
E-mail: email@ivpress.com

InterVarsity Press® is the book-publishing division of InterVarsity Christian Fellowship/USA®, a student movement active on campus at hundreds of universities, colleges and schools of nursing in the United States of America, and a member movement of the International Fellowship of Evangelical Students. For information about local and regional activities, write Public Relations Dept., InterVarsity Christian Fellowship/ USA, 6400 Schroeder Rd., P.O. Box 7895, Madison, WI 53707-7895, or visit the IVCF website at <www.intervarsity.org>.

All Scripture quotations, unless otherwise indicated, are taken from the Holy Bible, New International Version®. NIV®. Copyright © 1973, 1978, 1984 by International Bible Society. Used by permission of Zondervan Publishing House. All rights reserved.

Design: Cindy Kiple

Images: Kenneth Sponsor/iStockphoto
      Architectural sketch (p. 139): Gregory Deddo

ISBN 978-0-8308-3444-0

Printed in the United States of America ∞

Library of Congress Cataloging-in-Publication Data

Wilson, Michael Todd.
  Preventing ministry failure: a ShepherdCare guide for pastors,
  ministers and other caregivers/Michael Todd Wilson & Brad
  Hoffmann: with contributions from members of CareGivers Forum.
     p. cm.
  Includes bibliographical references.
  ISBN 978-0-8308-3444-0 (pbk.: alk. paper)
  1. Caring—Religious aspects—Christianity.   2. Helping
  behavior—Religious aspects—Christianity.   3. Pastoral care. I.
  Hoffmann, Brad, 1963-   II. Caregivers Forum. III. Title.
  BV4647.S9W54 2007
  253'.2—dc22
                        2007021665

| P | 23 | 22 | 21 | 20 | 19 | 18 | 17 | 16 | 15 | 14 | 13 | 12 | 11 | 10 | 9 | 8 | 7 | 6 | 5 | 4 | 3 | 2 | 1 |
| Y | 27 | 26 | 25 | 24 | 23 | 22 | 21 | 20 | 19 | 18 | 17 | 16 | 15 | 14 | 13 | 12 | 11 | 10 | 09 | 08 | 07 |

CONTENTS

Getting the Most from This Workbook

Great ministers don't just happen; great falls from ministry don't just happen either. Successful ministry isn't just about today's leadership meeting or tomorrow's revival or mission trip; it's also about daily faithfulness to our calling along the journey. A variety of problems can lead to removal from ministry—some caused by the minister, some caused by a dysfunctional organization and some caused by both. We would like all of us to be spared the agony others had to endure. This workbook is about becoming aware of the common pitfalls in ministry and learning to build a strong foundation on such knowledge.

Long-term effectiveness in ministry isn't just about the minister; it's also about a minister's spouse, children, grandchildren, congregants and ministry partners. It even affects all those who reside in the surrounding community and their close relationships. The carnage that accompanies a forced removal from ministry has a ripple effect on everyone. Even the pastor of a small congregation can, through indiscretion, easily do spiritual harm to thousands. It happens every day.

Great ministers don't just happen; great falls from ministry don't just happen either.

This isn't meant to be frightening. More than anything, our heart's desire is that ministries will be enhanced and strengthened. We've designed this workbook to deliver a positive message: we *can* have a fruitful and long-standing ministry for the kingdom of God, as long as we are willing to learn from those who have gone before us.

WHO IS SHEPHERDCARE?

Brad understands the unique struggles of being a minister because of his own experience as a pastor. Prior to cofounding ShepherdCare, Brad worked in central Florida with a ministry known as Antioch Affection, a residential program that serves ministers removed from ministry. He is currently senior pastor of Memorial Baptist Church in Baytown, Texas.

During his time in central Florida, Brad contacted Michael Todd to provide professional counseling for those in the Antioch residential program. As a Christ-centered licensed professional counselor with a heart for those in ministry, Michael Todd was eager to help.

One day, the two of us sat down to reminisce about those we'd worked with who were removed from ministry, grouping them by reason for termination. We discovered seven areas of consistent failure: (1) lack of genuine intimacy in relationships with God, spouse and others; (2) a distorted sense of calling; (3) inadequate stress-management skills; (4) lack of appropriate boundaries; (5) failure to prioritize re-creation; (6) insufficient people skills; and (7) underdeveloped leadership skills.

From this simple exercise, the vision of ShepherdCare was born. God called us to redirect our energy from reparative work with removed ministers to *preventative* work with those still functioning in ministry. In 2003 we began ShepherdCare from a desire to provide ministers with resources to sustain long-term effectiveness in their ministry calling, to help them avoid the heartache and destruction that results when ministers prematurely quit, burn out or morally fail.

At the October 2003 gathering of the CareGivers Forum (www.CareGiversForum .org) we shared with those in attendance our experience regarding the seven areas of concern and our plans to create a curriculum to address them. Many of the participants were intrigued and offered to share their stories and unique experiences of helping hurting ministers. The CareGivers Forum is an association of retreat centers, counseling ministries and resource organizations that assist ministers and their families. Some of the participants in CareGivers have worked in the area of ministerial renewal for twenty to thirty years or more. Members meet annually to share and encourage each other from the wealth of their experience.

Lack of intimacy is the biggest factor for ministry burnout and failure.

These caregivers have backgrounds as counselors, psychiatrists, pastors and Christian retreat directors. Together, they've sat with thousands of hurting pastors, missionaries and other full-time Christian workers:

- Some have provided crisis counseling after a minister was inappropriately forced to resign by lay leadership.

- Some have offered telephone encouragement to ministers who weren't sure they had the emotional energy to preach another sermon.

- Some have wept with wounded ministry couples in an intensive retreat setting as they shared stories of affairs and pornography addiction.

This workbook is the first of its kind: the collaborative wisdom of more than a dozen pioneers in their field, professionals in the area of ministering to hurting ministers. It's intended as a source of encouragement for the dedicated ministers who give day after day after day in their places of ministry.

Since this workbook is the collective experience not only of the authors but also its contributors, the pronoun *we* will predominantly be used throughout our journey together. We'll identify ourselves individually when one of us (Michael Todd and Brad) has a particular story or principle to relate. Members of the CareGivers Forum will be identified in the context of their individual stories.

We ask for the reader's grace ahead of time for any unintentional missteps, theologically or otherwise. While we feel confident that our views are solidly in the mainstream, a particular reader may hold a different view from the authors here or there. Though we may have our "disputable matters," we must not allow Satan, our common enemy, to deceive us: removal from ministry is a risk we all face, no matter our differing theological viewpoints.

As mentioned previously, the seven areas of concern were empirically derived from our years of ministering to force-terminated ministers. Because we want to encourage those in ministry to safeguard against such pitfalls, we will discuss these topics in terms of the need for a *preventative self-care plan*—a set of practical skills uniquely designed by each minister to both promote their personal best and to safeguard against ministry failure. We firmly believe that putting these principles into practice is foundational to a fruitful and long-standing ministry. Therefore, we will refer to them as "foundation stones" for establishing a successful and long-standing ministry.

GAINING MAXIMUM BENEFIT FROM THIS WORKBOOK

While this workbook is intended for use in a variety of contexts, we strongly recommend that it be used in relationship with another human being. The reason is simple: lack of intimacy is *the* biggest factor for ministry burnout and failure. When we isolate ourselves and withdraw from deep relationship with others for whatever reason—feeling misunderstood, fear of exposure, feelings of superiority, being too busy, not wanting to "air our dirty laundry"—the slope into ministry failure becomes very slippery. In isolation, we more easily gloss over the more difficult parts of our daily experience, thereby "overriding" the gentle whisper of the Holy Spirit. As fearful as it may sound, processing this material (along with your answers, journal entries and action plans) alongside another human being is one of the best sources of prevention for ministry failure.

Some ministers have asked, "Why can't I simply process my answers in my intimate relationship with God?" While our relationship with God is critical, God also designed us to exist in community with like-minded people of faith. Practically speaking, a brother or sister in Christ who truly has our best interest at heart won't be afraid to challenge us in our areas of needed growth—especially if we've given them specific permission to do so. Because of our humanity, discounting the Holy Spirit's speaking through a caring friend or mentor is more difficult for most of us than discounting the Holy Spirit's speaking from within our own conscience.

Here, then, are a few possibilities for how this workbook might best be used:

Small Groups of Ministers

Our dream is to have groups of ministers around the country willingly setting aside their fears and bravely encouraging one another in ways that only other ministers can. Those who find a way to gather in a small group of three to six ministers to journey through this workbook together will derive maximum benefit from this material:

- They will relate to the experiences of the other group members.

- They will feel supported and encouraged in their common struggles and experiences of ministry.

- The group will also promote deepening friendships within ministry—a valuable and helpful resource for many of us.

The biggest reason some initially shy away from this idea is their fear that if other ministers knew their weaknesses and insecurities, such knowledge could find its way out of the group and into the religious rumor mill. Regrettably, there have been just enough instances of this actually happening to fan the flame of worry.

However, truth is still truth: the factor causing more downfalls than anything in Christian ministry is our isolation from genuine relationship with others. Such relationships hold up a mirror for us to see ourselves as others do. We need input from others to see ourselves as we really are.

Agreeing to strict confidentiality among such a group will promote an atmostphere of honesty and sincerity. Otherwise there will be a tendency toward "intellectualizing" the material, which defeats the purpose of the study. Intellectualizing is the default mode for many ministers, so purpose ahead of time to not let this happen.

Studying this workbook with a small group of ministers is the riskiest way, for sure. However, it is by far the method of greatest potential benefit.

With an Accountability Group

This workbook is also suitable for study alongside an accountability group. The group may include other ministers, elders, board members or lay leaders with whom you have closer relationships. It can be formal or informal, designed to hold accountable all its members (as in a peer-support group) or merely to hold yourself accountable (in, for example, a process of restoration). The benefits of this type of group are similar to the small group of ministers: a built-in support network, greater understanding and the potential for real ongoing relationships.

With a Ministry Coach, Mentor or Protégé

For ministers fortunate enough to have a ministry coach or mentor, this book can be an ideal tool. Younger ministers without a coach might use this as a reason for finding one. The real-world experience of a seasoned mentor can make studying this material a rich experience.

If you feel called to mentor someone but don't currently have a protégé, you can prayerfully invite a younger or less-seasoned minister to join you in this study. It would be a great way to start a mentoring relationship with someone who could benefit from your years of wisdom and experience.

A PEEK AT THE FOUNDATION'S BLUEPRINT

Preventing Ministry Failure is organized to be useful in regular and systematic study over an extended period of time—ideally six months to one year. This allows adequate time for processing the material and exercises within the context of one or more real-world relationships. Following the introductory chapter, there are seven core chapters, one for each of the seven foundation stones. Each stone has between four and seven sections that progressively discuss various facets of a particular topic.

While each reader should determine the best method for their situation, we recommend one of the following two methods: (1) complete one section weekly or (2) complete one foundation stone monthly, with the introductory material completed as the first monthly assignment. Either method should allow plenty of time for meditation on the principles and (more important) how they may be applied to a unique ministry setting.

Resist the temptation to complete one section daily unless you are on sabbatical or are being led through the material under professional care. Even then, however, be aware that such a fast pace might encourage intellectualization of the material, leaving less time for reflection and for the Holy Spirit to accomplish deeper heart transformation.

Throughout each foundation stone, you'll have plenty of opportunity to personalize the material being discussed. We've left room in the margins for you to take notes along the way, and at the end of each stone, space will be given for synthesizing a few final thoughts about the topic. It's all designed to help you be intentional about personal application—making the main goal your own personalized self-care plan.

WHAT IS A SELF-CARE PLAN?

Ministers are quite skilled at helping others live balanced, more effective lives. Yet many times we fail to practice what we preach. As stewards of our bodies, time, talents, relationships and resources, we must find ways to apply to our own lives the good advice we often find ourselves giving to others.

For example, how might you advise a young father of a family of five to steward his family over the long term? An emergency savings account, life insurance, regular time invested with his wife and children, and a plan to set aside funds for retirement—all are good suggestions and represent *proactive* steps for preventing family failure in the future. They of course don't *guarantee* prevention of such calamity, yet such a family-care plan can go a long way toward health, stability and long-term provision.

In a similar manner, a minister's self-care plan is a comprehensive, preventative plan designed not only to prevent ministry failure but also to give the minister every opportunity for deep satisfaction, significant influence and long-term effectiveness in ministry. Ministers who are proactive and intentional about their personal lives are far more likely to see deeper and more lasting results from all their endeavors, both personally and professionally.

A FINAL WORD OF ENCOURAGEMENT

Ministers read lots of books. Yet rarely is such reading about improving the quality of personal ministry; more often it's about better ways to communicate a particular spiritual truth or implement the latest program du jour. However, healthy ministers have personally experienced the great truth and promise of 2 Corinthians 1:3-5: "The God and Father of our Lord Jesus Christ, the Father of compassion and the God of all comfort, . . . comforts us in all our troubles, so that we can comfort those in any trouble with the comfort we ourselves have received from God." To be effective in our ministry to others, we must first be ministered to.

As we walk this journey together, resist the temptation to look for great material to pass along in an upcoming sermon, newsletter or blog. Instead, ask God for focus in hearing his voice speaking directly to you about enhancing your relationships, strengthening your boundaries, improving your ability to manage stress, and managing and leading those under your care. As you do so, God's healing light will shine on you, exposing all that needs attention in the deep places of your heart. You can then relax in his arms, experiencing him as the lover of your soul, who will take great delight in you, quiet you with his love and rejoice over you with singing (Zephaniah 3:17). We pray that each will genuinely and humbly seek to be all the Father intends you to be—*first* as his child, then as his called minister.

INTRODUCTION

Why Preventing Ministry Failure
Is So Important

D o you remember the old Looney Tunes cartoon where Foghorn Leghorn tries to "mentor" the young (and much more intelligent) widow hen's son? When the brainiac youngster draws an equation on paper to "prove" something, Foghorn reluctantly confesses to his protégé, "I know, boy. Figures don't lie!"

1. Ministry in America Today

Try the following quiz to see how well you understand the "figures" regarding your fellow ministers:

_____ have been forced out of or fired from a ministry at least once.[1]
□ 5%o   □ 10%   □ 15%   □ 25%   □ 35%

_____ feel inadequately trained to cope with ministry demands.[2]
□ 10%   □ 20%   □ 50%   □ 70%   □ 90%

_____ believe that pastoral ministry affects their families negatively.[3]
□ 20%   □ 40%   □ 60%   □ 80%   □ 95%

_____ say they've experienced depression or burnout to the extent that they needed to take a leave of absence.[4]
□ 35%   □ 40%   □ 45%   □ 50%   □ 55%

_____ have serious conflict with a church member at least once a month.[5]
□ 20%   □ 30%   □ 40%   □ 50%   □ 60%

---

[1]ChristianityToday.com <www.christianitytoday.com/leaders/newsletter/cln00712.html>, accessed February 26, 2007.
[2]Fuller Theological Seminary, survey of pastors, Pasadena, California, 1991.
[3]Ibid.
[4]H. B. London Jr. and Neil B. Wiseman, *Pastors at Greater Risk* (Ventura, Calif.: Regal), p. 172.
[5]Fuller Theological Seminary, survey of pastors.

_____   admit to having an affair while in the ministry.[6]
         ☐ 5%   ☐ 10%   ☐ 15%   ☐ 20%   ☐ 25%

_____   admit that Internet pornography is a *current* struggle.[7]
         ☐ 10%   ☐ 22%   ☐ 37%   ☐ 47%   ☐ 62%

_____   do not have someone they consider a close friend.[8]
         ☐ 30%   ☐ 40%   ☐ 50%   ☐ 60%   ☐ 70%

Answers for these questions can be found on page 31.

Which statistics surprise you most and why?

Which do you identify with most and why?

THE UNIQUE CHALLENGES OF BEING CALLED "MINISTER"

Vocational ministry is more difficult than most laypeople realize. Only those in ministry truly appreciate the daily struggles associated with it. We each answered God's call to ministry with zeal and excitement because we had dreams of touching lives for God's kingdom. We energetically attended seminary or Bible college and soaked up everything we could. We entered our first pastorate, chaplaincy or ministry position, ready to save the world.

Then reality set in! The theoretical world of ministerial training programs often fails to reflect the real life of a typical minister: working with demanding board members, trying to please everyone (and being polite about it!), learning to lead experienced volunteer staff, meeting all the challenges of a one-minister organization, getting along with other staff in a larger church or parachurch ministry, and coordinating our calling with the other professionals in our organization. At times, being a minister can be overwhelming.

Think back to your days in seminary, Bible college or other related training. What did you assume ministry life would be like?

---

[6]Save America Ministries, "The State of Ministry Marriage and Morals," <www.saveus.org/docs/factsheets/ state of ministry2003.pdf>, accessed February 26, 2007.

[7]Christianity Today Library, <www.ctlibrary.com/le/2001/winter/12.89.html>, accessed February 26, 2007.

[8]Save America Ministries, "The State of Ministry Marriage and Morals."

Which of these assumptions did you discover to be untrue or idealistic once you entered your first ministry post?

Looking back, what advice might you give a young seminary student or minister seeking their first ministry position?

The statistics at the beginning of this section are where the average minister lives today. It's easy to see how this common path could ultimately lead to burnout or moral compromise. Couple this with the fact that most ministers live isolated lives—a trait common to corporate executives and other leaders but further complicated by the special role ministers play among those we lead. The dynamic isn't new: it's been at work since the days of judges and kings.

THE PEOPLE ASK FOR A KING

The disgruntled Israelites wanted a king like the pagan nations around them. Despite God's raising up strong judges to lead the tribes, time and again "the Israelites did evil in the eyes of the LORD" (see, for example, Judges 3:12). The book of Judges ends with this revealing yet haunting verse: "In those days Israel had no king; all the people did whatever seemed right in their own eyes" (Judges 21:25 NLT).

The prophet Samuel in his later years appointed his sons as judges, but they were not righteous men, so the people pressured Samuel to give them a king: "Now appoint a king to lead us, such as all the other nations have" (1 Samuel 8:5). God told Samuel not to take their grumbling personally; it was simply evidence that their wayward hearts were rejecting God's leadership in their lives.

Israel had a history of desiring a physical manifestation of God they could see and touch. When the Israelites thought they'd lost Moses, they created a golden calf, an image of God to pacify their insecurities that God had abandoned them. Both the Old (Exodus 32:1-6) and New Testaments (Romans 1:21-25) acknowledge a tendency among God's people to place their trust in the created rather than the Creator.

Wayward hearts trouble God's people still today. Ministries and congregations in many ways treat their ministers like gods. The average parishioner would likely deny such "worship," but their actions sometimes demonstrate a misplaced sense of trust (not to mention pressure). Why else would they become so upset when we don't measure up to their unspoken expectations of perfection? Why else would so many leave—not just an organization but their faith altogether—when a minister is exposed for moral indiscretion? No longer are we seen as human beings with feet of clay who have a special calling to lead or preach the gospel. No, for some the minister has become a god, placed high on a pedestal. This is a great danger in ministry.

Where have you observed this "give us a king" perspective in previous ministry settings?

To what extent might you notice it occurring in your current ministry setting?

HOW MINISTERS SOMETIMES ADD FUEL TO THE FIRE

Unfortunately, that's only half the problem. Take a trip with us down memory lane, back to our first ministry placement. There we were, fresh out of training and ready to impact the world. In the statistics we read earlier, we learned that most ministers feel ill-equipped for the job. But it would be inappropriate to admit such weakness when those we lead place such trust in us, right?

So we put on an air of confidence, even though on the inside we're fearful of letting them down. We know we don't deserve their accolades, but even if it's not quite true, it does make us feel good about ourselves for a while. So we redouble our efforts to front a good image. We give 110 percent of our time and energy toward serving and encouraging others, unaware that part of our unconscious motivation is to maintain their appreciation and acceptance.

Of course, significant effort is required to present such a "perfect" public image. We begin letting our guard down in our private life, with our spouse and our children—and most of all, when we're alone. More imperfections surface in these private areas. Though we may be unaware of this slow transformation, those closest to us notice and may even comment about our increased moodiness, temper, lack of presence or decreased energy.

When have others (spouse, family, coworkers, close friends) expressed concern that you were splitting into a "public" life that appears perfect and a "private" life that is deteriorating?

Those working with ministers who've been forced from ministry have seen it time and again. If we don't get our innermost needs met in our personal relationship with God and with our spouse and close friends, we'll inevitably begin to crave praise from those we lead. This all-too-common pattern results in what we call the "god complex": we begin to play the role of God in the lives of those to whom we minister. We start believing what we hear from them day in and day out.

This two-edged sword—our ministry's unrealistic expectations of us and our own unmet self-esteem needs—is a big part in why ministers sometimes fail in ministry.

Consider to what extent you might be functioning with a "god complex" in your present ministry. Ask your spouse or a trusted friend for their thoughts—but don't ask unless you really want an honest opinion! Use the space below to write down any feedback you receive from others.

Ask the Holy Spirit to give you insight into any "god complex" in your life. Ask him to restore within you a broken and contrite heart (Psalm 51:17). Use the space below to write such a prayer or to process any response you receive from him.

2. Resolving the "God Complex"

The "god complex" plagues many ministers, but it doesn't have to be this way. Ministers who get into this syndrome have forgotten a significant fact that keeps us grounded in reality: *It's God's ministry, not ours!*

When we begin playing the role of God in the lives of others, we find ourselves thinking it's our program, our building campaign, our ministry's growth, our success or failure in evangelism. This kind of thinking is toxic and will eventually poison any ministry. Sure, playing God will help us grow a ministry, and our people will love us all the way—until we disappoint them by showing our humanity. Likewise, ministering under a "god complex" can set us up for a fall through our own unreasonable internal expectations of ourselves—especially when our efforts aren't as successful as we had planned or as others had anticipated. Many a minister has been irreparably wounded from such a fall.

What accomplishments in your ministry are you most proud of?

What was God's role in these accomplishments?

What prevents you from allowing God to use you in whatever way he sees fit, whether or not you receive any material blessings or recognition as a result?

RIGHT PERSPECTIVE IS EVERYTHING

Ultimately, any accomplishments we experience in ministry are due to God's blessing. The glory belongs to him for whatever he chooses to accomplish through his chosen instruments. On the flip side, discouragement is a normal human emotion, but to contemplate exit from full-time ministry or become bitter from our suffering is to take our ministry out of his hands. It's God's ministry, not ours. God has the divine authority to give and take whatever he chooses for his own purposes, and he might not share with us the reasons why.

Accomplishments and failures in ministry aren't necessarily an accurate measure of either faithfulness or sin in our life. There are many instances in Scripture where God blessed the less-than-perfectly faithful (King David) and withheld material blessings from those who were quite faithful (Jeremiah). Jesus told his disciples that the man born blind was not blind due to anyone's sin but merely that the power of God might be perfectly demonstrated through his weakness (John 9:1-3). The same was true of Paul's "thorn in the flesh" (2 Corinthians 12:7-10). It's not always about us, but it is always about *him*.

A humble

understanding

of ourselves

will prevent us

from performing

for the crowd and

instead encourage

us to play to an

audience of One.

HUMILITY IN MINISTRY

Scripture describes God as our Good Shepherd (John 10:1-18). He is the One who tends the flock, ensures the sheep have new fields to graze and clean water to drink. He oversees their safety in the middle of the darkest night and comforts them with his rod and staff (Psalm 23:4). We serve a similar function in the lives of those we lead. However, this position is to be served in humility and with full recognition of our place under the authority of the Good Shepherd. Any authority we have is not inherently ours, but rather given to us by God. Instead of playing God, we do well to remember one of the most beloved titles we hold: *under-shepherd.*

Consider the exchange between Jesus and Peter in John 21:15-19. Peter had just demonstrated the weakness of his own humanity by his denial of Christ—not once but three times—during Jesus' trial. When the rooster crowed, Peter was reminded that Jesus predicted his betrayal just after Peter had boldly proclaimed he would fight to the death on Jesus' behalf.

Peter was so broken over his betrayal that he apparently went back to his career as a fisherman. Jesus finds him after the resurrection in a state of disillusionment. But he pulls Peter aside and reinstates him to ministry—no longer as an arrogant disciple but now as a humble servant. And what does Jesus ask him to do?

> Feed my sheep. I tell you the truth, when you were younger you dressed yourself and went where you wanted; but when you are old you will stretch out your hands, and someone else will dress you and lead you where you do not want to go. (John 21:17-18)

Through his humility and brokenness, Peter was able to lay down his "god complex." He'd been restored by the Good Shepherd and was given the ministry of an under-shepherd. He was to care for the sheep God entrusted to him, all the while remembering that he himself needed the constant care and attention of the Good Shepherd.

Dennis Siebert tells this personal story about his weakness being used by God:

> Early in my pastoral ministry, there were two particular occasions I recall getting up to preach and halfway through the message feeling like it was a total failure. What had made good sense in the office seemed to be coming out total confusion. I wanted to walk off the stage but knew I couldn't do that. So, in the middle of the message, I prayed, "Lord, this feels like a total failure. If you can use it in any way in someone's life, please do so for Your glory." In both cases, someone thanked me for the message during the following week and pointed to a specific comment from the message that had been so useful for a problem they were facing.

A humble understanding of ourselves is necessary to have a right view of our calling as ministers. Such understanding will prevent us from performing for the crowd and instead encourage us to play to an audience of One (Galatians 1:10). Only then can we help the sheep entrusted to us to see our proper role in their lives and encourage them to keep their gaze on God, their true Shepherd and King.

What comes to mind when you hear the title "under-shepherd"?

What role do you feel humility plays in ministry? Practically speaking, what does it look like?

Describe a time you saw God use your weakness for his glory.

In what ways do you struggle to "boast all the more gladly about my weaknesses, so that Christ's power may rest on me" (2 Corinthians 12:9)?

Ask God to give you a fresh spirit of humility. Ask him to give you a vision for being a faithful under-shepherd to the flock he's entrusted to you. Use the space below to jot down any thoughts or insights from your prayer time.

3. The Process of Restoration: The Journey Back Home

There are times when we all drift off course. Even ministers stumble into sin, falling short of God's mark of perfection (Romans 3:23). Some sins result in dismissal from ministry or even legal prosecution. Others, however, go undetected by others.

Before we can begin our exploration into preventing ministry failure, we first need to seek restoration for any areas of known brokenness in our lives and ministries to this point. As we boldly approach God's emergency room, the Great Physician waits to bring healing to our broken lives. Once restored, we will be more able to put into practice the "prescriptions" he gives us as preventative measures for maintaining our vitality.

It's easy to see how the process of restoration applies to ministers who have been removed from their positions of leadership. Yet this biblical prescription applies to every believer. All Christians are fallen image-bearers of God who still reflect the light of his glory—albeit dimly at times. These principles of restoration apply equally to broken ministers who have been removed from their positions of authority as they do to the rest of us in ministry. We do well to remember with humility, "There, but for the grace of God, go I."

Regardless of the nature of our sins or their consequences, the process of restoration remains the same. Restoration of our broken self involves confession, repentance, reconciliation, restitution, accountability and a renewing of the mind.

CONFESSION AND REPENTANCE

Every process of restoration begins with an admission to God and (when appropriate) to others the exact nature of our wrongs. This is biblical *confession*. We are all fallen humans who have inherited an inner predisposition toward rebellion and sin. If we aren't able to admit to ourselves before God that we've sinned, we will forever remain in denial and our heart will become calloused to future sins of the same variety. Admission of sin is the pre-requisite for calling the Great Physician for healing.

Generally speaking, confession to others needs to be public only to the extent that the sin was in the public arena. Godly counsel from those who intimately know both us and the situation can be invaluable in determining what the exact nature of confession should be for a particular situation.

Restoration isn't simply a matter of agreeing with God about our situation. We must also *repent*, changing our future course. We refuse to continue moving away from God and instead turn back to him, committing to what is right. This doesn't mean we'll never sin in the same way again. However, by changing our course and surrendering ourselves fully to God we will make ourselves available to his power the next time we're tempted in this way.

Which is typically more difficult for you: confession or repentance? Why do you think this is so?

RECONCILIATION AND RESTITUTION

Confession and repentance result in the *reconciliation* of our vertical relationship with God. However, we may need to apply this same process to our horizontal relationships to bring about a similar reconciliation with our spouse, family, friends or those within our ministry. While reconciliation with God may be relatively easy for some, it can be anything but easy when it comes to reconciling with others. Yet reconciliation of our horizontal relationships is the only way to expect our vertical relationship to function as God intended (Matthew 5:23-24; 18:21-35).

What others do or refuse to do in light of our confession isn't the point. Our part on the road to reconciliation is simply to confess and repent.

Does forgiveness play a role in reconciliation? Scripture doesn't actually encourage us to "ask" for forgiveness from those offended by our sin. While the Bible does call the offender to confess, extending grace and mercy is the task of the offended. Although God always forgives, others may take a long time to come to such a place—or may never extend forgiveness.

An offender who asks to be forgiven runs a great risk of either rejection or "premature forgiveness." Particularly when the offender is someone with power, the request for forgiveness can serve to manipulate the offended, who mouths words that sound like forgiveness but are void of the very mercy that evidences genuine forgiveness.

When we have offended another, we should not solicit their forgiveness. What others do or refuse to do in light of our confession isn't the point. Our part on the road to reconciliation is simply to confess and repent.

Is it more difficult for you to confess and repent before God or before people? Why do you think this is true?

What lesson(s) do you see taught in Matthew 5:23-24 and 18:21-35?

To fully reconcile our horizontal relationships, some form of *restitution* may be needed. In this context, restitution is the act of returning something to as near an original condition as possible. That is, we may have offended someone, misappropriated money, not given someone credit where it was due, neglected to fulfill a promise, deceived someone or taken something that didn't belong to us. Whatever the situation, corrective action may be required to either actually or symbolically "restore" what was lost as a result of our wrong actions. For example, if we misappropriated money in the ministry, we could confess it, repent of it and seek to reconcile our relationships with those inside the ministry. But that would all be meaningless if we didn't also replace the stolen money.

A desire for restitution is a natural byproduct of genuine repentance. Such action was originally sanctioned by God as a part of the Mosaic Law (Exodus 22:1-15, for example). It was also demonstrated by Zacchaeus (Luke 19:1-10). There are many cases, however, where direct restitution isn't possible. A son or daughter whom we failed on a promise to attend a school play or championship soccer game cannot be directly repaid. The opportunity to attend that particular event has gone forever. The fallout from an affair can never be made to go back the way things were with either the other party's spouse or our own. The damage cannot be undone. Restitution in such cases will be limited to some type of symbolic repayment, such as a letter of apology to our daughter for missing her soccer game, taking our son someplace special when we've missed his play or seeking post-affair marital counseling. Genuine repentance and reconciliation will also result in an ongoing pattern of restitution, making a habit out of such healthy actions.

The societal concept of incarceration for lawbreakers was established as a symbolic restitution for certain crimes against society. Being removed from ministry—either temporarily or permanently—is sometimes a reasonable action for more consequential sins, both as an act of symbolic restitution and as a way of preventing additional damage from repeated action in the future.

Making restitution is often a neglected component in the process of restoration. Think back over your life and ministry. List any wrongs that may still require restitution, along with the name of the person who was hurt and the act of restitution you might consider. If you're unsure how to make restitution in a particular case, place a question mark next to the person's name.

Some offenses cannot be directly made right. Perhaps those with question marks require some type of symbolic restitution. If you're unsure how best to make restitution, consider asking the advice of a close friend or mentor. Others not as close to the situation may have a clearer perspective and might offer helpful suggestions. Who could you ask for such godly advice?

STAYING ON THE RIGHT ROAD: ACCOUNTABILITY AND RENEWING THE MIND

Our old human nature constantly pulls us in the direction of sin. The more habitual a sin has become, the more need there is for an ongoing system of *accountability*—a set of internal and external constraints established to help prevent future inappropriate behaviors.

Most people associate accountability almost exclusively with relationships, but external constraints are both relational and nonrelational. In an accountable relationship, we might give a close friend, ministry associate or spouse permission to directly ask us tough questions about our area of struggle. We agree to be completely honest in our answers. Some ministers have formal accountability relationships, where the purpose of the meeting or phone call is only to discuss the issues. Others have informal arrangements, where each periodically asks the other how things are going. Still others simply have an agreement that they can call or meet to request prayer or advice if they begin struggling again in that particular area.

External constraints may also be nonrelational in nature; that is, things outside ourselves that increase the likelihood we won't fall to temptation. Examples might be a necklace that has symbolic meaning, a pertinent Scripture posted on the bathroom mirror, or an Internet filter on the home or office computer.

Internal constraints serve a similar purpose to external constraints. The only difference is that they exist inside us. Meditating on a mental image of Christ, making the choice to call an accountability partner before we slip or finding an alternate route home from work to avoid the allure of our favorite fast-food restaurant are all examples of internal constraints. A common internal constraint related to sexuality is committing to never go anywhere alone with a member of the opposite gender besides our spouse. Ministers who struggle with same-gender sexual temptation might commit similarly to avoiding alone time with anyone of the same gender for whom they feel a strong erotic attraction.

We will consider more ideas related to accountability in the foundation stones on intimacy and boundaries. For now, consider any sins you've been struggling with lately that you already know would be easier to deal with if you added some form of accountability to your spiritual discipline. Whether large or small, list these areas of struggle in the left column on the next page.

For each one listed, consider an accountability measure you could implement: Start an accountability relationship? Put an external constraint into place? Create an internal constraint? Write specific ideas in the right column next to each area of struggle. Devote prayer to this list and take action as God gives you insight.

Area of Struggle   *Proposed Accountability Measure*

Renewing the mind (changing our thinking) to better match God's viewpoint is a helpful part of any attempt at changing behavior. When Scripture speaks of the "heart" it's referring to the very core of who we are, which includes our inmost thoughts and feelings. If we are going to bring lasting change, we must also change how we think and feel about our areas of struggle internally: "For from the heart come evil thoughts, murder, adultery, all sexual immorality, theft, lying, and slander. These are what defile you" (Matthew 15:19-20 NLT).

Considering the list you just created, what Scriptures might help align your thinking with God's point of view?

RESTORATION IN DAILY LIVING

The twelve-step community has been a source of encouragement and hope for millions around the world. While it's true that some who follow their model for sobriety have watered down its message over time, the original twelve steps envisioned by Bill W. were remarkably spiritual and derived from the gospel itself. In twelve-step traditions not only is there an initial point in time where restoration takes place, there is to be an ongoing process of regular restoration characterizing a person's daily experience.

Practicing the process of restoration in our daily life will significantly contribute to our long-term health in ministry by taking care of things the moment we recognize something needs attention. Like practicing the disciplines of the faith, practicing self-care as an undershepherd will keep us spiritually healthy so we will have what it takes to respond to each assignment God gives us. Prioritizing self-care using the seven foundation stones helps keep us and our ministry at maximum effectiveness.

What might a plan for ongoing restoration look like for you?

4. The Seven Foundation Stones for Effective Long-Term Ministry

The only thing better than experiencing the process of restoration after removal from ministry is not falling in the first place. By learning from the major reasons for burnout and moral failure over the past few decades, we've created a model for not only preventing such damage but for strengthening and enhancing pastoral ministry for the hundreds of thousands who currently serve as Christian ministers. These seven foundation stones can ground us in skills to help ensure long-term effectiveness for us and our ministry.

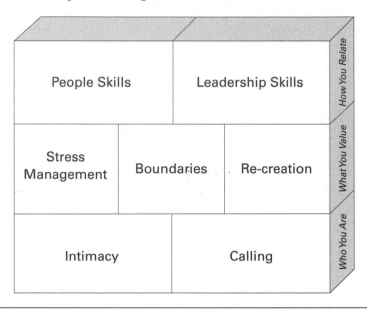

Figure 1. Wall of foundation stones.

The foundation stones are divided into three categories. Intimacy and calling are about promoting *who we are*. Stress management, boundaries and re-creation are about protecting *what we value*. People skills and leadership skills are about practicing *how we relate*.

In God's economy,

there are three

primary venues for

genuine biblical

intimacy: with God,

with others and with

a spouse.

WHO WE ARE

The most foundational of the seven stones have to do with who we are at the core of our being. Whether we're a full-time missionary, plumber, part-time interim music director or businessperson, intimate relationships are central to who we are and what we were created for. Our unique vocational calling into Christian ministry is also a fundamental part of that identity.

Intimacy

We were created for intimacy. Unfortunately the word *intimacy* has been so overused and misused that some people cringe when they hear it. A pastor once told us, "When I hear that word, I assume you're talking about sex." Such misunderstanding is common, influenced as we are by the secular media and our culture. In God's economy, there are three primary venues for genuine biblical intimacy: with God, with others and with a spouse.

Intimacy with God is the real and vibrant relationship each of us has been invited to enjoy with our Creator. It's only from the context of this relationship that other intimate relationships derive their meaning. God also created us to have intimacy within the context of community—that is, with like-minded brothers and sisters in the faith. And while God calls some of us to lifelong celibacy for greater kingdom focus, he calls many more toward intimacy with a believing spouse.

Although the word *intimacy* can refer to sexual relations, it is only used this way in its euphemistic sense. But even within the context of marriage, sex was never meant to be experienced apart from intimacy of the soul. Each intimate relationship requires nurturing and protection if we are to enjoy lifelong fulfillment in our ministry calling.

How would you have most likely defined intimacy before today?

Based on this overview, draft a working definition of genuine biblical intimacy.

Calling

As with intimacy, our calling is central to who we are. While all Christians are called to minister, relatively few are called into the ministry. We received a unique and special call by God when he set us apart for the ministry. Such a calling is cause for humility, gratitude and even a bit of healthy fear that we should be called in such a way.

> *To be called to something is also to be not called to many other things.*

Unfortunately, some in the ministry today serve under a false calling. It is extremely important to be certain our calling is from God and not by some other means. Great damage can be done when those who aren't truly called attempt to lead without spiritual empowering.

It is also important to distinguish between the different types of callings in Christian ministry. To be called to something is also to be *not called* to many other things. A minister shouldn't feel "called" to be all things to all people. This is not only an impossible demand, it's also inconsistent with the idea of being called to something in the first place.

To what extent are you certain of your calling by God for vocational ministry?

As far as you understand your calling at this point in your ministry career, to what type of ministry have you been uniquely called?

WHAT WE VALUE

What matters most in our lives are those things related to our intimate relationships (God, friends and spouse) and to our calling. Three foundation stones help us protect these things.

Stress Management

Stress is a reality of life in the modern world. We can't make it go away, nor would we really want to. Stress is actually the impetus that motivates humans toward accomplishment. It's not the amount of stress we're under that causes problems in our lives. Rather, it's the *inability to manage stress* that will cause us to call it quits on ministry. Therefore, the goal isn't to find a stress-free job but to learn to manage the stress we will confront in an effective manner.

Unfortunately, many ministers have turned to a variety of unhealthy substances and behaviors in attempts to cope with stress. Examples include unregulated prescription drugs, compulsive entertainment, workaholism (under the guise of "serving Christ") and explosive anger. The presence of these or similar behaviors in our life will serve as feedback that our coping with stress isn't going so well.

On a scale of 1 (poor) to 10 (excellent), how effective do you feel at managing stress?

What would you say are the two or three biggest stressors in your life right now?

What action could you take that might reduce your overall stress level?

Boundaries

The other two foundation stones that help protect what we value are actually specific tools of good stress management. The first is learning to set good boundaries. Just like the physical boundaries around our home, personal boundaries serve to protect the things we value most. For example, if we're going to say "yes" to accomplishing one thing, we must necessarily say "no" to other things.

Being called to some things necessarily means being "not called" to others. Boundaries are the tools that help us differentiate the one from the other. Boundaries also help us prioritize the more important of two legitimate callings (such as family needs versus ministry needs). If something must be neglected, clear boundaries help ensure it's the lesser calling that gets neglected rather than the truly more important one. They protect that which matters most to us according to our values.

Is there a boundary you know you need to put into place but haven't for some reason? What is it?

What's the biggest reason you've hesitated putting this boundary into place?

Re-creation

The other foundation stone that's an outgrowth of healthy stress management is the priority of re-creation. No, this is not a typo! We *are* talking about recreation, but the real meaning of the word has (like intimacy) been watered down. For too long the church has gone without a theology of re-creation. It's not just about having fun, wasting time or finding an enjoyable hobby. These are byproducts of re-creation and should not be confused with its purpose. Re-creation is supposed to be a purposeful activity to restore and regenerate us so that we can better pursue our calling and intimate relationships. To neglect re-creation is to potentially resign ourselves to a foreshortened tenure in ministry.

What are your favorite forms of re-creation?

What is your most common excuse for neglecting re-creation?

HOW WE RELATE

Now we come to the last of the three categories for the foundation stones. We've already looked at who we are and what we value. Now let's examine how we relate, especially with those in our family and sphere of ministry.

People Skills

Ministers are called into the people business. Because what we work with most in our vocation is people, it's critical that we have excellent people skills. Countless Christian leaders have been removed from ministry due to their deficiency relating with others.

Recall a Christian leader you feel was deficient in people skills. What were some of the consequences of their deficiency? How do you think they could have handled their relationships more effectively?

Each person has their own personality, style and quirkiness. Fortunately, God in his wisdom has helped us by creating categories of people with similar personalities and giftedness. This allows us to classify people, not for the purpose of discriminating against them but for the purpose of better understanding them. Understanding that certain personalities are easy for us to get along with while others rub us the wrong way is a critical first step toward working well with all types of people.

Recall someone whose personality has been particularly difficult to bear in your ministry. How would you characterize the nature of the difficulty? Was it their quirkiness, unusual ideas, physical mannerisms?

What impact did these relational challenges have on your effectiveness in ministry?

In what ways was their personality significantly different from yours? To what extent were your personalities similar?

Additionally, we'll want to have in our tool bag the ability to truly listen and (when necessary) assertively respond. Such skills not only allow us to make others feel at home as we minister to them but also enable us to handle our detractors and naysayers with repose and confidence.

Leadership Skills

Like people skills, leadership skills are an important component for effective ministry. While we will naturally gravitate toward certain styles of leadership, others we may have to cultivate. Different leadership skills will be required at various stages throughout our ministry years to accomplish what's needed for a particular challenge. Similarly, effective leadership styles will vary based on the culture of our ministry setting and that of our ministry's surrounding community.

Effective leaders are transformative leaders—that is, they are willing to continuously be remade from the inside out by the power and direction of the Holy Spirit. They are humble learners open to God's instruction and shaping in their own personal lives.

On a scale of 1 (poor) to 10 (excellent), how teachable are you as a minister?

What do you believe is the greatest reason you are sometimes not teachable?

Before setting out on the rest of this journey, consider the following prayer:

> Father, I humbly ask you to shine the light of your Holy Spirit into my heart to expose where improvements are needed in my life and ministry. Please enable me to be painfully honest with myself and with you as I consider my responses and as you reveal my shortcomings and areas of weakness. I desire to be moldable, teachable and open to what you have for me. Keep me from reading with someone else in mind that "needs it more." I know it's me that you desire to change through this process. Most of all, help me to remember it's not my ministry, but yours. Amen.

There is great power in ministry where we have first been personally transformed by the One in whose name we minister. Only then will we be able to serve out of the overflow of what God has first poured into us.

■　■　■

Below are the answers to the quiz at the beginning of this chapter.

Of ministers in the United States:

25 percent have been forced out of or fired from their ministry at least once.

90 percent feel inadequately trained to cope with ministry demands.

80 percent believe that pastoral ministry affects their families negatively.

45 percent say they've experienced depression or burnout to the extent that they needed to take a leave of absence.

40 percent have serious conflict with a church member at least once a month.

20 percent admit to having an affair while in the ministry.

37 percent admit that Internet pornography is a current struggle.

70 percent do not have someone they consider a close friend.

1

INTIMACY

Connecting to the Heart of Successful Pastoring

If you're sharing this journey with others in a small group, exchange brief answers to the following questions:

- Where are you from originally?

- What is your spouse's name? What are the names/ages of your children/grandchildren (if applicable)?

- Where did you receive your ministry training (formal or informal)?

- In what types of ministry settings have you served (including presently)?

Once each person has a chance to share their answers to the above questions, try the next set:

- What is your favorite spectator sport, sports team or athlete?

- What is your favorite hobby or pastime?

- If you could live out your latter years anywhere in the world, where might you want to live and why?

Finally, share with the group brief answers to the final set:

- What have you found most challenging about being a minister?

- Share an experience in which God clearly demonstrated his faithfulness to you.

- What is the most significant thing you'd like to accomplish in the next five to ten years?

Sharing with the group may have become increasingly difficult with each set of questions. The first set simply requests facts, whereas the second requests opinions, and the final set requires sharing very personal concerns and passions. Answers to questions like this final set offer the opportunity for others to know more about the real us.

Some may have found this to be the first time in quite a while they've been asked to share parts of their genuine self.

What was this experience like for you?

1. What Intimacy Really Is

There is great misunderstanding about the real definition of intimacy among most people. Take a look at the following definitions of *intimate/intimacy* from the *Merriam-Webster* and *Collins English* dictionaries and compare them with your definition back on page 27:

- "Close or warm friendship or understanding; personal relationship" *(Collins English Dictionary)*
- "Marked by very close association, contact, or familiarity" *(Merriam-Webster Dictionary)*
- "Marked by a warm friendship developing through long association" *(Merriam-Webster Dictionary)*
- "Of a very personal or private nature" *(Merriam-Webster Dictionary)*
- "A euphemism for sexual relations" *(Collins English Dictionary)*

Intimate relationships are those in which others truly understand us, even if they don't agree with us. Their warmth and closeness demonstrate that they care about us as a person. We matter to them. They are familiar with our strengths, weaknesses and idiosyncrasies, and they still desire our relationship. They know the more private details about our life, the things we are passionate about and what makes us fearful—things that most aren't aware about us. They know the real us that exists below the mask we wear when we're "on-stage" in ministry. They know our hurts, our struggles, our private victories and the things at the top of our prayer list.

There's a reason why intimacy has become a euphemism for sexual relations. Sex enjoyed within marriage is a beautiful illustration of what intimacy really is: two committed people who are completely naked and unashamed before one another—completely known and accepted with nothing hidden. The physical nakedness and vulnerability of the sexual relationship is symbolic of the very essence of genuine intimacy. Because many in our society are uncomfortable speaking of sex directly, our culture has largely adopted *intimacy* as a substitute word, to the exclusion of intimacy's broader and richer meaning. Therefore, a simple but effective way of describing intimacy might be "any relationship where we know another fully and where we are also fully known."

What relationships do you currently have which you would characterize as intimate on a personal and emotional level?

WHY INTIMACY IS SO IMPORTANT

Human beings were never intended to function in isolation. From creation, we learn that God's plan for us was to exist within the context of community. God declared that it was "not good for the man to be alone" (Genesis 2:18). This passage is most often taught to demonstrate God's blessing on marital union, and it certainly applies to this. However, at an even more basic level, this passage is a commentary that we were not designed to live without others who understand us and can share our load (Galatians 6:2-5). In fact, the existence of the divine Trinity and our being created in God's image are compelling evidence of God's priority on relationships and community. God is a relational being and humans were created in God's image. Therefore, it comes as no surprise that we were also designed as relational beings.

All of us have the same need for intimate connection with others. Ministers are no different in terms of their need for real relationships, especially their need for both mentors and friends. The pastor is the only person in a church who doesn't have a pastor,[1] and because of our positions within the community of faith, we have more difficulty creating close peer relationships than the average believer (we'll discuss this unique difficulty a bit later). But if we choose to believe that somehow the blueprint for humanity doesn't apply to us—that we have no need for intimate relationships—we will tend to redirect our intimacy needs into all kinds of unhealthy alternatives to fill the void.

Think back over your preparation for ministry. What were you told by professors or other mentors about your need (or lack of need) for intimate rela-

---

[1] Gary L. Pinion, *Crushed: The Perilous Journey Called Ministry* (Springfield: 21st Century Press, 2006), p. 130.

tionships? What intimate relationships were encouraged? If it was never mentioned, why do you suppose it was overlooked?

Rate the quality of your intimacy in the following relationships as well as your level of investment (such as time and emotional investment) on a scale from 1 (neglected) to 10 (rich):

	Quality	Investment
God	_____	_____
Good friendships	_____	_____
Spouse (if applicable)	_____	_____

Take a look at your lowest-scoring relationship(s). If this is not satisfactory, what do you think are the biggest factors holding it back?

2. The Consequences of Avoiding Intimacy

Sin was a destructive gift given us by our earliest parents, Adam and Eve. The result of their introduction of the human race to sin was intimacy lost—both with God and with one another. Whereas Adam and Eve enjoyed perfect intimacy before sin entered the human experience, immediately following their removal from Eden we find the first couple reaching out to one another through sexual union in an effort to intimately reconnect (Genesis 4:1). For the first time, Adam and Eve experienced loneliness, a condition for which no amount of intimate connection in the arms of the other would ever again completely satisfy.

THE SABOTAGE OF INTIMACY

We find four significant results of humanity's fall into sin and loss of Paradise: fear, shame, hiding and blaming. As they were evident in Adam and Eve's rebuttal of God's confrontation (Genesis 3:9-13), these same tendencies are no less evident in our own lives.

I Was Afraid . . .

The immediate effect of sin was fear. We are fearful of others seeing our flaws, our weaknesses and our insecurities because we believe if they really knew who we were they would reject us. "If my colleagues knew how insecure I am, they would fire me." "If people in my organization knew my secret sins, the gossip would ruin my reputation." "If the lay leadership of my ministry knew how uncertain I was about how to pull off this new campaign, they wouldn't follow my leadership." It's the fear we've all lived under since the Fall.

John Eldredge in his book *Wild at Heart* uses the term *poser* to refer to someone who pretends to be something they're not.[2] We feel fake in a world of people who seem to have it all together. We fear that becoming real will jeopardize our standing in the eyes of the people around us, or that their reaction to the real us will hurt. Perhaps they might be so disgusted with us they would no longer want anything to do with us—the ultimate form of rejection.

Isn't that our fear deep down? We put on a great game face to prove to others, and sometimes even to ourselves, that it isn't so. But deep inside we sense the burning question: "Do I really have what it takes? Will I ever be found out?"

Because I Was Naked . . .

Our fear originates from the shame of our "nakedness." Where once our nakedness was pure and without sin (Genesis 1), now our nakedness seems to expose our every weakness and imperfection, leading to feelings of deep inadequacy and shame (Genesis 3). Yet such shame is distinct from its cousin, guilt. Guilt is what Scripture refers to as the "godly sorrow [that] brings repentance that leads to salvation and leaves no regret" (2 Corinthians 7:10). This can be illustrated by the phrase, "I've *done* something bad." The Holy Spirit uses guilt to expose where we've made an error in behavior, encouraging us toward confession, repentance, reconciliation and restitution. He calls us out of darkness and into the light of God's love and forgiveness, as well as into Christian community for help in making things right again.

Contrast this with shame, or what Scripture calls "worldly sorrow [that] brings death" (2 Corinthians 7:10). It can be illustrated by the phrase "I *am* bad." Notice the focus is no longer on behavior but rather on who we are at the core of our being. We feel worthless, unworthy of love and support. We believe God hates us and everything about us. We feel unable to change no matter how hard we try, leading us toward isolation from both God and community for letting God and others down.

---

[2]John Eldredge, *Wild at Heart,* new ed. (Nashville: Nelson, 2006).

So I Hid . . .

Fear and shame are what we experience as the result of intimacy lost. Hiding is a common response to these feelings and becomes a further block to real intimacy. We hide to protect ourselves from being exposed and harmed by others. Hiding sometimes becomes the only tool we know for holding it all together.

Some hide by physical isolation. Others attempt to prevent exposure by hiding behind elaborate "fig leaves" such as moralism, perfectionism, a relational mask, a forced smile—anything that serves to hide the real us from exposure. It's all an attempt to get others to think better of us than we do of ourselves. The more important a particular person is to us, the more likely our hiding will be.

The Woman You Put Here with Me . . .

When we're unsuccessful at avoiding pain, when the "real us" starts peeking out from behind our mask, we might shift the focus from our weakness to someone else's weakness. Like Adam with Eve and like Eve with the serpent, the blame game becomes our attempt to "save face" to avoid the rejection of God and others.

In what ways do you tend to sabotage intimacy in your relationship with

> *God?*
>
> *Your spouse?*
>
> *Friends?*

What is it about these relationships that might trigger such a response?

The ongoing effects of the Fall are feelings of fear and shame. Our attempts to hide and blame are often primary tools we use in an effort to escape the rejection we believe will occur if we are exposed. But we still have a deep internal desire for intimacy—that "knowing and being known" that assures us that we're accepted for who we are, imperfections and all. When we reject intimacy with God and like-minded believers, our need for it doesn't go away. It merely goes underground.

Consider the remarkable technology of nuclear energy. When used properly, radioactive material can power an entire city. However, when buried underground and disposed inappropriately, stories of toxic waste leaking its way into nearby streams and playgrounds make front-page news. Like radioactive material, our desire for intimacy is a powerful resource. When handled properly, it provides a full life—a vibrant relationship with God and meaningful relationships with key friends, and a healthy respect for the covenantal nature of erotic love. Burying this desire for intimacy, however, will eventually contaminate every aspect of our lives.

Ask God, your spouse and your closest friends to help you recognize the potential symptoms of a lack of intimacy in your life.[3]

- Having difficulty reaching out to begin new or deeper relationships

- Tending toward passivity and detachment from others

- Frequently seeing yourself as a victim

- Denying or keeping your feelings, both positive and negative, to yourself

- Using addictions or other dysfunctional behaviors to numb your feelings

- Being reluctant to ask for help

- Maintaining an unrealistic workload

- Keeping your thought processes private

- Expecting influence or favors in return for your caring for others

- Basing your self-esteem on your ability to care for others

- Minimizing or discounting other people's feelings

- Bringing ulterior/sexual motives to your physical touch

- Struggling with honesty in relationships with friends, spouse and God

- Avoiding conflict

- Using anger to control others

- Avoiding direct communications

- Refusing to take risks or try new things

- Taking yourself too seriously

- Rarely laughing

- Having few or no hobbies (unless they are compulsive, competitive or income-producing)

- Having a limited idea for how to enjoy the people in your life

When we reject intimacy with God and like-minded believers, our need for it doesn't go away. It merely goes underground.

---

[3]Adapted from Mark Laaser's *Faithful and True* (Nashville: Lifeway, 1996), pp. 63-65.

What are other difficulties you have experienced that might also be related to missing intimacy?

BROKEN CISTERNS

When we refuse God's offer of intimate relationships, he often allows us to attempt to fill the resulting "God-shaped hole" with everything but God (Romans 1:21-32). Jeremiah reminds us of the choice we make in following our own way rather than God's: "My people have committed two sins: they have forsaken me, the spring of living water, and have dug their own cisterns, broken cisterns that cannot hold water" (Jeremiah 2:13).

Which of these behaviors might exist in your life as an unconscious attempt to satisfy unmet intimacy needs?

___Excessive TV watching, Internet use or other isolating activities (perhaps even reading or studying) as an "escape from reality"

Even "good"

behaviors could be

unhealthy based on

the reason we choose

for doing them.

___Compulsive hobbies

___Overeating

___Oversleeping

___Angry outbursts

___Chronic bitterness

___Workaholism

___Emotional or physical infidelity

___Use of pornography

___Other sexually compulsive behaviors

___Drug or alcohol use

___Other:

There are as many different "broken cisterns" as there are fallen people. Anything that's an attempt to get our intimacy needs met without engaging in genuine relationship becomes a broken cistern. Even "good" behaviors could be unhealthy based on the reason we choose for doing them. For example, studying Scripture is a wonderful thing. However, if we're studying in an attempt to stroke our ego or avoid time with our family, we might be doing little more than unconsciously numbing emotional pain. It's more about the heart behind the behavior than the behavior itself. While right behavior is a big part of a life pleasing to God, we also need to ask ourselves *why* we choose to do certain things.

If such behaviors are masking real intimacy needs, we will continue to be frustrated by their ultimate ineffectiveness. This will result in either the addition of other unhealthy behaviors or an increase in the time invested in the ones we already use. Eventually exhaustion sets in, leading to emotional burnout, addictions and even suicidal thinking.

How might greater intimacy in your relationship with God, Christian friends or your spouse counteract unhealthy patterns currently present in your life?

How might you clear any obstacles that might prevent you from seeking genuine connection with Christian friends and with your family?

How could your peer group members, mentor, spouse or close friends assist you in correcting any problems you discovered?

"Search me, O God, and know my heart; / test me and know my anxious thoughts. / See if there is any offensive way in me, / and lead me in the way everlasting."

PSALM 139:23-24

Satan's lie will say we can't afford the risk of exposure involved in sharing our problems with someone else. But we and our ministry can't afford not to clear this toxic waste from our life. Every day that intimacy needs are mishandled may be doing serious damage to us, our family and our ministry. Yet we are promised that we can boldly approach God and his grace for help in our time of need (Hebrews 4:16). This is where it can all begin to change.

3. Intimacy with God

The most miserable people in the world are Christian leaders whose intimacy with God has gone cold. And it's so easy to let that happen by becoming consumed with the "rituals" of our duties. We can delude ourselves into thinking we're experiencing intimacy with God by virtue of our busyness for him. In reality, we may only be experiencing religious activity.

Many believers think of intimacy with God as a set of behaviors: Bible study, prayer, worship attendance, fasting, evangelism and so on. These were never intended to be the end goal of a relationship with God but merely some of the means by which such a relationship might be experienced. Adam and Eve walked intimately with God in the Garden of Eden (Genesis 3:8), and Enoch was commended because he walked with God (Genesis 5:24).

What do you think it means to walk with God?

Look back at the definitions of intimacy presented on page 34. How do these definitions shape your understanding of intimacy with God?

What words would you use to describe your current relationship with God? How is it different from the way it used to be?

What do the following passages add to your understanding about the importance of intimacy with God?

   Matthew 6:6-13:

   Luke 15:11-27:

   Romans 8:15:

What practices and resources have you tended to turn to in your pursuit of intimacy with God? How are you currently using (or not using) these resources in your regular routine?

How would you rate your current level of satisfaction with them?

How might you improve your overall level of satisfaction?

There is a tendency among Christian leaders to mistake our investment in preparing sermons, ministry newsletters, Bible studies and the like with our pursuit of intimacy with God. They are not the same. Nevertheless, inviting God to meet with us as we do our preparation and asking the Holy Spirit to instruct us in how we should apply its truths to our own lives can revolutionize such times of preparation. Simply asking, "Lord, how does this apply to my life, my family, my work, my relationship with you?" *before* applying it to those to whom we minister can transform a "burden" of ministry into a fountain of blessing.

Depending on how neglected our own spiritual life has become by our own busyness, we may have to take on fewer projects to make space. However, what we lose in quantity we will gain back many times over in quality and depth in our ability to minister to the hurting people around us. In doing so, we may also discover that the newsletters and sermons we've been preparing *about* the love of God have been a subconscious attempt to earn God's approval. Being made to both love and be loved by God, we can find peace in simply *experiencing* God through the mundane tasks of our daily routines.

How might the Holy Spirit help you to change the way you approach specific work tasks?

What impact might this have, both positive and negative, on your productivity at work?

How might you initiate a conversation about your need for time with God with your employer, board or supervising body?

Nothing is more essential as ministers than our vibrant personal relationship with the One who both called us and sustains us. Without it, we have nothing to offer of any real value to anyone.

4. Intimacy Through Close Friendships

The movie *K-19: The Widowmaker* tells the true story of Captain Alexei Vostrikov (played by Harrison Ford), commander of a state-of-the-art Soviet nuclear submarine during the politically tense 1960s. The nuclear reactor on the submarine was leaking and in imminent danger of explosion. This would not only take the lives of the men aboard but also destroy a nearby American military vessel. The Americans would likely misinterpret such events as a hostile act, sparking a nuclear war between the two superpowers.

Some of the sailors on board sacrificed their lives to repair the reactor breach and averted the calamity. However, the severity of the radiation levels on board still caused the boat to be evacuated. Captain Vostrikov was almost forced to surrender to the American destroyer, which led to false allegations of treason by the Communist party. Due to the secrecy of their mission and the embarrassment of its outcome, those involved were not even allowed to speak of the incident until the fall of Communism some twenty-eight years later.

At a remembrance gathering of the crew on the twenty-eighth anniversary of the event, Captain Vostrikov made a toast to honor the dead:

> For their courage, I nominated these men for the title "Hero of the Soviet Union." But the committee ruled that, because it was not wartime and because it was merely an accident, they were not worthy of the title "hero." What good are honors from such people? These men sacrificed not for a medal but because when the time came it was their duty—not to the Navy or to the State, but to us, their comrades.

"And so," as he lifted his glass in a toast, "to comrades!" The crew vigorously responded with raised glasses, "To comrades!"

We all need intimate friendships with others, comrades alongside us throughout life's journey. God created us for such community, ministers included. We need friends who know us deeply and with whom we can share our hopes and dreams as well as our fears and concerns—a place to be ourselves without mask or façade. Men need intimate connections with other men, and women need intimate connections with other women. Safe relationships—not just golfing or shopping buddies—are among God's vehicles for ministering to us.

Do you ever find yourself just wishing you had someone you could *really* talk to? God created you for such relationships and designed you this way on purpose. Consider the number of godly friendships in the Bible: Elijah and Elisha, David and Jonathan, Ruth and Naomi, Paul and Silas, Jesus and his inner circle of Peter, James and John. Unfortunately, many ministers neglect this form of intimacy using a variety of "reasonable" excuses. This is why 70 percent of ministers don't have even one close friend.

Scripture has much to say about the benefits of genuine friendships:

> A friend loves at all times, / and a brother is born for adversity. (Proverbs 17:17)

> There is a friend who sticks closer than a brother. (Proverbs 18:24)

> Wounds from a friend can be trusted / but an enemy multiplies kisses. (Proverbs 27:6)

> As iron sharpens iron, so a friend sharpens a friend. (Proverbs 27:17 NLT)

Intimacy with others is built on the foundation of intimacy with God. In our Christian friendships, we connect with the *imago Dei* (image of God) within them. This is one of the reasons Scripture has so much to say about our need for Christian community.

Of the thousands of broken ministers we've met, one of the common threads in their stories is a lack of genuinely intimate friendships. In general, why do you believe people have such difficulty with close friendships?

Same-gender friendships are also vital for accountability, especially when it's related to sexual integrity. Some might ask, "Why can't my spouse serve as my accountability partner? They know everything about me anyway." There are a few reasons this is generally a bad idea. First of all, a spouse can't necessarily fully understand the unique challenges inherent to your gender, including how to be the husband or wife you need to be for them. Healthy, intimate same-gender friendships are a unique source of feedback and support as we try to be godly men or women.

Second, our spouse is almost guaranteed not to be objective when it comes to helping us maintain our sexual integrity. As our sexual partner they will tend to take our sexual struggles personally. There's thus a tendency to not be gut-level honest with a spouse about sexual integrity due to a perceived risk of misunderstanding or abandonment. If we can't be honest, what's the point of accountability?

One of the fastest roads to moral failure in ministry is lack of accountability. Same-gender friendships help keep us on the right path morally and spiritually. Our spouse may not fully understand our unique gender struggles, but our same-gender friends likely struggle in similar ways. Most spouses don't want to hear about their partner's sexual struggles anyway; it's often uncomfortable for them. They frequently feel more secure knowing their spouses are accountable to a same-gender friend or group who takes their accountability seriously.

We highly discourage accountability on sexual matters with members of the opposite sex, not only due to the strong possibility of sexual temptation but also because of the perception it may create for the spouse (and others). Of course, outright physical infidelity needs to be disclosed and worked through with our spouse as quickly as possible. In such cases, there can be great benefit in seeking assistance from a mentor, pastor or Christian marriage counselor skilled at facilitating healing and reconciliation.

We all need accountability. This is the essence of what the writer of Hebrews emphasized: "Let us consider how we may spur one another on toward love and good deeds" (Hebrews 10:24). It's a two-way street, not a one-way street. As ministers, we need others who spur us on toward love and good deeds. We can risk allowing someone else to do that for us.

How difficult is it for you to allow someone else to minister in this way to you?

What circumstances in your past might have contributed to any hesitancy?

How might you challenge yourself to move past such hesitancy, allowing a select few men or women to minister to you in a more meaningful way?

BARRIERS TO INTIMACY AMONG OUR OWN GENDER

Some of the common barriers to intimacy for both men and women include

- being too busy with work or family
- not wanting to overcome the path of least resistance (reasoning, for example, that intimacy is "too much trouble")
- lack of modeling for how to cultivate "below the surface" relationships

Additional barriers for men include

- being taught from childhood not to be "dependent" on others
- not wanting others to know their problems
- fearing that others will think they're gay
- fear of rejection
- assuming (based on what they've observed) that talking about or playing sports equals intimacy

Additional barriers for women include

- female cliques
- comparing themselves with other women
- fear of being harmed by another woman's gossip

- fear of being misunderstood

- not being able to find emotionally "deep" women

Ministers have additional barriers including

- fear that being intimately known will make their leadership look weak

- misunderstanding that they shouldn't need things from those in their care

- suspicion of theological differences that biases them against those outside their faith tradition

- fear of ministerial politics that leads to distrust of other ministers within their own faith tradition

What are the unique factors about ministry that provide you with barriers to close friendships?

What added hurdles exist in your particular job and/or ministry placement that further complicate your pursuit of intimate same-gender friendships?

INTIMACY ACROSS GENDERS
(AND WHEN IT ISN'T WISE)

Because there are significant and legitimate differences between the genders, there is great need for each of us to have friends who can help us understand what is "normal" from the perspective of our gender and who can encourage us to live our lives to God's glory as men and as women.

There is, additionally, great benefit for ministers in opposite-gender friendships. Moses and Miriam, Esther and Mordecai, Jesus with both Mary and Martha—all are biblical examples of healthy opposite-gender friendships. In fact, most solid marriages develop from the healthy foundation of a close friendship with a member of the opposite gender. Furthermore, friendships across the genders are a place where single ministers can learn to relate effectively to the opposite gender.

Of course, the single minister pursuing a potential marital relationship will want to experience growth in intimacy and emotional interdependence. But given their position in ministry, it's still prudent to proceed with care due to the increased potential for harm to

Ministers looking for empathy they aren't getting from their spouse may find themselves moving toward an emotional affair every bit as deadly to their marriage and ministry as a physical affair.

both themselves and their ministry.

Opposite-gender friendships among married ministers can also be healthy—to the extent the minister's spouse is aware and involved. However, when such friendships become as intimate as we are suggesting here, they often spark emotional dependency or erotic attractions that threaten fidelity to the marital relationship. Ministers looking for empathy they aren't getting from their spouse may find themselves moving toward an emotional affair every bit as deadly to their marriage and ministry as a physical affair. Such risks are not wise; we ought to do our best to avoid slippery slopes that might lead toward moral compromise.

How satisfied are you with your present opposite-gender friendships?

How might you improve those relationships?

If you are married or engaged to be married, to what extent is your (future) spouse aware of and in agreement with the nature of your closer opposite-gender friendships?

5. Intimacy with Your Spouse (and What to Do if You're Single)

A well-matched, godly spouse is for many a gift second only to the gift of salvation itself. Such a spouse becomes not only a partner in life but often a partner in ministry as well. Yet like all significant relationships, our marriage will give back in direct proportion to our ongoing investment in it. Nurturing our spouse will likely reap tremendous rewards in excess of our investment. Neglecting our spouse for a time may see little consequence. But like a large oak tree in drought, the relationship will eventually show signs of stress, begin dropping leaves and then slowly but surely die.

It's important to keep our finger on the pulse of our marriage. We might invite feedback from our spouse about the health of our relationship and be willing to hear some difficult words, if necessary.

Ask your spouse the following:

1. *On a scale of 1 (ignored) to 10 (well cared for), how much are you feeling cared for by me?*

2. *What would it take to get it to a 10?*

Use the space below to process your conversations or to jot down important insights.

Intimacy with a spouse is best realized when we have a solid intimate relationship with God and a few deep, same-gender friendships in place. Both support us toward becoming the person we were designed to be—and the one our spouse needs us to be. Without our intimate relationship with God, we lack the power to love unconditionally. Without intimate same-gender friendships, we likely lack the affirmation, accountability and gender perspective needed to fulfill our role as a godly spouse.

I (Michael Todd) have a close (or what I thought was close) Christian brother and accountability buddy who appears to be headed for divorce. Too far into his deception to hear wise counsel to disclose and terminate his affair, he caused himself and his family untold grief. If he had prioritized intimacy in our relationship, I would have done all I could to help him avoid his infidelity, or at the very least rebuild his marriage and family in the wake of it. That's the power and benefit of a solid Christian friend in a time of need (Proverbs 17:17). Instead, my friend is on course for God giving him exactly what he's asking for—no little bit of hell, indeed (Romans 1:24).

We need to do whatever is necessary to build strong, intimate relationships with God and godly same-gender friends. They're that important. Only when these are in place can we be the helpmate our spouse desires and the helpmate God intended us to be. We will also have more reasonable expectations from our marriage partner because some of our general intimacy needs will have been satisfied through such close friendships.

In no way should what we're saying be interpreted as same-gender friendships being more important than a marital relationship. For the married minister, the biblical priorities in relationships are intimacy with God first, followed by marital intimacy, followed by intimacy with godly same-gender friendships. Said another way, our covenant relationship with our spouse is a higher priority than our other relational commitments—and our relationship with God is the highest priority of all.

INTIMACY EXPRESSED

Within marital relationships, genuine intimacy has many facets of expression. We suggest there are five major ways intimacy is expressed: spiritual, emotional, intellectual, social and physical.

Spiritual intimacy refers to those things done to participate in and encourage the building up of our personal love relationship with God. Prayer, corporate worship and spiritual readings or discussions together are all examples of such intimate relating spiritually.

Emotional intimacy grows in proportion to our ability to express our positive and negative feelings with each other. This requires practice and risking vulnerability with one another but is necessary to experience deeper intimacy of the soul.

Intellectual intimacy includes dreaming about and planning for the future, use of humor with one other, making deliberate choices as a couple and engaging in stimulating discussions on topics of mutual interest over a lifetime together.

Social intimacy might involve spending time with other couples, serving together on a community service project, taking a day trip together or going out without the children to dinner or a favorite activity.

Physical intimacy includes nonerotic hugs and kisses, gentle love pats, and back or foot massages after a long workday. It's more than just sexual intercourse.

Healthy marriages have a balance among the five expressions of intimacy.

How in or out of balance is your marital relationship?

What gets too much or too little attention these days? Why do you think this is the case?

Together with your spouse, brainstorm at least one way you might deepen your intimacy in each of the five expressions of intimacy:

Spiritual:

Emotional:

Intellectual:

Social:

Physical:

UNMARRIED MINISTERS

Biblically speaking, the marital relationship is the only one in which erotic sexual intimacy should be fully enjoyed (Hebrews 13:4). Unmarried ministers will want to pursue the entirety of their intimacy needs from the first two sources (God and close friendships), relating with Christ as the "heavenly Spouse" that he really is (Ephesians 5:21-33). Also, they should seek to either fully embrace their celibacy or actively pursue an earthly spouse in a way that honors the Lord.

As a never-married single adult until my late thirties, I (Michael Todd) don't say this from some lofty ivory tower. My wife (never married until her early thirties) and I know what waiting for God's best feels like. Many days were a faith-building exercise and, from a human viewpoint, downright tough.

Some of those days required leaning heavily on intimate Christian friends who could deeply encourage us and at times cry with us, friends with whom we could simply have fun as an alternative to bitterness. In many ways, our relationship with God was even more intimate than it is now because we were placing the majority of the weight of our waiting upon him. I took great comfort in the knowledge that Jesus, himself a single adult, understood my struggles (Hebrews 4:15). My wife gained even greater support than I did from her Christian girlfriends, married and single alike. Such same-gender relationships were invaluable for both of us, providing us a practical means for redirecting erotic desire and tension toward other healthier outlets. Journaling, exercise and prayer were also helpful tools that made our extended tenure in singleness a season of deep meaning and value.

And here's an interesting observation from our singleness: when our genuine soul intimacy needs were being met by God and close friendships, the desperation for erotic sexual intimacy was reduced because our real intimacy needs were being met the way God intended—through deep relationships of the soul.

6. Practical Steps Toward Deeper Human Relationships

No matter the condition of our marriage or Christian friendships, there's good news: at any time, we can move toward deeper human relationships. It will take work and will likely require risk, but the benefits are well worth the effort. Consider some of the rich rewards of such intimate relationships.

REASONS TO RISK GREATER INTIMACY

As we read earlier, having others intimately involved in our lives provides a more accurate mirror into our own behaviors and even a window into our motivation for doing things. None of us sees ourselves objectively. It often takes someone looking from the outside. Intimate others who are part of our lives over time can challenge us to "keep the main thing the main thing" even when we've lost perspective. "A friend," says Donna Roberts, "knows the song in my heart and sings it to me when my memory fails."

Having an intimate friend gives us a place where we don't have to be "on" all the time. In fact, intimate friends challenge us to take off our mask with them.

Remember a time when you lost your direction or heart for ministry. What was that time like for you?

Reflecting on that time in your life, was anyone there to "sing your song back to you"? If so, who was it and what impact did their concern have on you?

While we can reflect on God's complete acceptance of us because of what Christ has done on our behalf, the actions and touch of a fellow believer make God's love for us all the more real. Allowing for a few intimate relationships permits us to experience a similar type of acceptance from another human being.

Such deep acceptance requires disclosure of who we really are. Without it, others will only be accepting us for who they think we are. This is not to say that we should stand before our ministry team next week and confess our every imperfection. However, we would benefit from having a few select people in our lives who know us at this level.

Describe any experience of such open acceptance from another human being, whether from a spouse or a close Christian friend.

If you've never experienced this type of unconditional acceptance from another, describe how it might feel if you truly received it.

When someone knows us deeply and still accepts us as we are, we can rest assured that person is genuinely committed to us. "If one person falls, the other can reach out and help. But someone who falls alone is in real trouble. Likewise, two people lying close together can keep each other warm. But how can one be warm alone? A person standing alone can be attacked and defeated, but two can stand back-to-back and conquer. Three are even better, for a triple-braided cord is not easily broken" (Ecclesiastes 4:10-12 NLT). An intimate friend will do anything to help us become a better person than we act sometimes. They can also encourage us to become more conformed to the image of Christ.

What Christian friends can you think of who, with a little extra effort, might offer greater intimacy and unconditional acceptance to your life?

What would it take to get your relationship to that deeper level?

Having an intimate friend gives us a place where we don't have to be "on" all the time. They don't require us to wear any kind of mask, including our "ministerial mask." In fact, intimate friends challenge us to take off our mask with them. Getting used to this kind of friend might require some adjusting on our part. Yet this person is all right with our being imperfect, real, genuine—and above all, human. This is especially true during our times of deepest suffering and pain. As Henri Nouwen puts it:

> When we honestly ask ourselves which person in our lives means the most to us, we often find that it is those who, instead of giving much advice, solutions, or cures, have chosen rather to share our pain and touch our wounds with a gentle and tender hand. The friend who can be silent with us in a moment of

despair or confusion, who can stay with us in an hour of grief and bereavement, who can tolerate not knowing, not curing, not healing, and face with us the reality of our powerlessness, that is the friend who cares.[4]

If you've ever experienced a relationship like this before, describe that person. How did they create an atmosphere that allowed you to remove your mask and to be yourself in their presence?

As ministers, we're most often in a position where others are expecting something from us. We give and give and give. And when we feel we have nothing left, we're often asked to give some more. Intimate relationships allow us a place to recharge our batteries without draining from us like everyone else does. In fact, it's not a one-way relationship at all. It's a two-way deal. Sure, we give to them at times, but as a peer rather than a pastor or minister—and they give to us as much as we give to them. That's a big difference!

Think about those individuals who have most given to you. How did they give to you in ways that were meaningful?

Was it easy or difficult allowing them to meaningfully give to you? What did it take for you to allow them to do this?

Whether we are new at fostering such intimate relationships or simply desire to grow our current relationships to a deeper place, we can allow these benefits to be our motivation for change. Not only will our soul experience an oasis of refreshment but our ministry can take on a new depth of realness that those to whom we minister will find absolutely captivating.

PRIMING THE INTIMACY PUMP

Mark Laaser was a pastor who early in his ministry mistook his need for real intimacy as a need for sex. He was dismissed from his full-time counseling ministry and pastoral duties after multiple affairs with women he counseled. Now decades later, Mark writes and conducts seminars to help Christians find freedom from sexual addic-

---

[4]Henri Nouwen, *Out of Solitude* (Notre Dame: Ave Maria Press, 1974), p. 34.

tion. In his workbook *Faithful and True: Sexual Integrity in a Fallen World,* Mark discusses some of the major factors needed for genuine intimacy in relationships.[5] Some of his ideas are applied here to the context of close friendships. They may also be just as easily adapted to strengthen a marital relationship.

Take the Risk Toward Relationship

Intimacy involves a decision to more deeply relate with others. We can invite someone to breakfast or a movie, to watch or play sports, or to share prayer requests over coffee. The activity we share isn't as important as taking the initiative toward starting a new relationship or growing an existing one. We can also take the risk of letting the other person know we really care about and enjoy spending time with them.

Learn to Express Emotions

We may have been taught that our feelings can't be trusted, ignoring them altogether. This style of life divorces our decision-making faculties from our true heart, a disconnect that prevents us from being fully capable of following the deeper passions of our calling.

If you have trouble identifying your feelings, appendix A has a starter list of feeling words that can help you recognize your feelings. If you keep a prayer journal, consider writing down a few sentences daily, something like this: "Today I felt _____ because _____." This will give your feeling muscles a workout and increase your feelings awareness.

Fight Fair

We risk losing intimate relationships when we attempt to force our way. Intimacy doesn't work like that. Instead, we can choose to be vulnerable and risk sharing how we feel about a particular issue. Prioritizing time to discuss differences of opinion enhances intimacy and fosters understanding. The term "fighting fair" can be a reminder to allow the other person to express a differing point of view without taking it as a personal attack. When others disagree, the intimacy of our relationship relies on our ability to not take personally their differing opinion. Learning that others can hold different opinions from ours and still love us is a great lesson toward healthy peer relationships.

After serving one year at Crown College as dean of men, Charles Shepson (founder of Fairhaven Ministries) became the college's dean of students. With the new position came the added responsibil-

---

[5]Mark Laaser, *Faithful and True: Sexual Integrity in a Fallen World* (Grand Rapids: Zondervan, 1996).

ity of meeting regularly with the school's decision-making cabinet.
He recalls:

> My first meetings with them were frightening. I found them to
> be men who were bluntly and candidly frank. My inner
> thought was, *I am not going to risk suggesting anything! I can't han-*
> *dle their pointing out all the weaknesses in my proposal!* But I no-
> ticed that no matter how vehemently they had disagreed, when
> the vote was taken they all got behind it as if they'd all voted the
> same way. When they left the room, they were just as good of
> friends as they'd been when they walked in!
>
> Slowly I discerned they weren't rejecting the other person,
> they were only rejecting his idea! This concept of differentiat-
> ing between rejection of my idea and rejection of my person
> was liberating. It was a pivotal point in my development as a
> leader and enabled me to become more intimately associated
> with each of those wonderful men. It also empowered me to
> lead more effectively in subsequent years.

Express Anger Positively

We can openly express negative feelings such as anger, resentment
and disagreement. A simple but effective way to foster this type of intimacy is to share how something affects us rather than accusing the
other person. For example, saying, "I feel unimportant when our
lunch appointments get cancelled a half-hour before our meeting
times" is a healthy alternative to "I can't believe you are so irresponsible, always waiting till the last minute to cancel." The first statement
takes a risk in sharing how the other person's behavior impacts us.
By contrast, the second statement attacks the other person. This will
likely engage their defenses and spawn a fight, with each person
seeking to hurt the other in a war of words.

Venting anger only masks the real issue and seeks to punish the
other for having "hurt" us. It will not promote what's actually
needed: reconciliation. The first statement above lays the real issue
on the table to be dealt with; the second buries it and piles more garbage on top. Anger won't solve the problem: "Human anger does
not produce the righteousness God desires" (James 1:20 NLT).

Welcome Help

Some ministers have difficulty asking for help. For others, it's more
difficult to accept help when it's offered. Either way, pride may prevent us from wanting to appear needy or inadequate. A humble
"thank you" can be one small antidote for such pride. We must recognize we can't be "all things to all people" and at times need others'
help, both personally and in ways related to our ministry.

Offer Help

We can make suggestions without feeling rejected when they aren't taken. This one may go against the grain for an organizational leader, especially if we're used to our ideas being accepted and implemented most of time. But close friends won't last long in relationship with us where their values, ideas and input aren't given as much weight as our own. Speaking our mind as suggestions works much better with intimate relationships than dictating actions.

Physical Affirmation

Appropriate physical touch doesn't carry hidden sexual meaning. Handshakes, hugs, pats on the shoulder and strokes on the arm are all means for warmly communicating, "I care about you and I trust you." Reading sexual connotations into such gestures or giving such gestures as a way of trying to meet sexual needs may have potentially dire consequences.

Those who read sexual messages into all touch are often "touch deprived." Some grew up in families where affectionate touching was rarely given. They grow up believing sex is the only acceptable form of touch, eroticizing all touch as sexual. Rewiring this thought pattern may require help from a Christian counselor. Allowing appropriate touch without sexualized interpretation is critical. At the same time, clear physical boundaries are still important to assure healthy touching doesn't inadvertently lead to inappropriate sexual touching.

Taking ourselves too seriously is a sure path to burnout.

Laugh More

"A cheerful heart is good medicine" (Proverbs 17:22). Taking ourselves too seriously is a sure path to burnout. Seeing the lighter side of life is essential to mutually enjoyable relationships. What do we find funny, and what kinds of things are worthy of our best laugh? We can read the comics in the Sunday paper, order a joke book to read and integrate into our ministry, watch children at play, and learn to laugh at our mistakes instead of becoming angry.

Adventure with Others

Sometimes our seriousness about life leads us to a safe routine that may eventually result in boredom. We can change things up a bit in the simple areas of our lives to add some spice to life, such as trying our spouse's favorite dish or trying a buddy's favorite restaurant with cuisine from a different culture. We can consider trying one of their favorite hobbies or activities, such as camping, taking a guided tour, playing tennis or snorkeling. Or we might try cultural activities such as the theater or an art museum, attending concerts, taking guitar or piano lessons, getting together with a friend for coffee and talking about anything besides work-related chat (avoiding such topics as theology, ministry, the church and working with youth), having lunch regularly with a friend to talk about the latest movies or news topics, or simply sharing prayer requests and praying for one another.

Making greater investments in noncompetitive, nonwork-related activities rounds out our life in healthy ways. And rather than getting bent out of shape because we tried something we didn't like, we can tell ourselves that we're investing in the relationship.

Others sometimes assume that as ministers we're either "too busy for relationships" or "must have more friends than we can handle." Their first assumption might even be an excuse *we* sometimes use to avoid intimate relationships. If we're going to prioritize intimate friendships, we will at times have to initiate contact with others rather than waiting for them to contact us. For those who do pursue us, we can accept their offer regularly. However, we will want to make a distinction in our mind between visits where we are in the minister role versus time spent with someone who truly allows a two-way relationship as a fellow human being. We must limit our time with those we experience as draining. These will always require (and at times demand) something from us. These folks represent ministry, not intimate relationship. There is a time and place for both.

Play with Others

Some laypeople make negative comments if they hear about ministers not working 24/7, especially those within smaller traditional church settings. This may flow from the subconscious idea that ministers are little "gods" rather than people. Like everyone else, ministers need time for relaxation and restoration. We need time devoted to activities that allow us to unwind and play.

When we take life too seriously, we may lose sight of what's fun for us. If so, we can join someone else in an activity they consider fun. That's a double blessing: we will try something new and we will be investing in relationship with another. If we're still stuck as to what's fun, we can ask a kid—and do whatever they say! It might sound crazy, but if we simply loosen up a bit and experience life through the eyes of a child, we just might tap into the child inside us who never grew up and has been waiting for such a moment to arrive!

Look back over the above list of suggestions. Which ones have you tried and can attest to their effectiveness?

Which ones do you struggle with most?

What practical steps might you consider in the near future to address these areas?

7. Finding and Growing a Few Good Same-Gender Friendships

Of the three types of intimate relationships we discussed, ministers consistently have the most difficulty with close friendships. Consider the following as a guide rather than a formula or method—something to give direction for developing healthy relationships, especially if this is new territory.

STEP 1: BRAINSTORM A LIST OF POTENTIALS
On a sheet of paper, make a list of people you know on a personal basis. They can be laypeople in your church, ministry, seminary, neighborhood health club or wherever. They can be leaders of other ministries or even those who work within your organizational or denominational structure. Relationships in town will have more potential than those out of town. Anyone we know on a personal level (no matter how well) can be a part of this initial list. We shouldn't include those to whom we provide leadership unless we are willing to redefine the relationship to them as peers.

STEP 2: ASSIGN AN "INTIMACY VALUE" TO EACH RELATIONSHIP
Assess your current level of intimacy with each person according to Gary Smalley's five levels of intimacy.[6] While these were initially applied to marital relationships, they may be easily applied to intimate friendships.

Level One: Clichés
With some folks, we merely bounce off one another in ways that actually prevent us from knowing anything of importance about the

Genuine accountability takes place in sharing our real struggles with another human being, whether it's pride, sexual temptation, temper or the unedited realities of our life in ministry.

---

[6]Gary Smalley, *Secrets of Lasting Love* (New York: Free Press, 2001), pp. 29-31.

other. The only relationships we would likely put at this level would be those in our ministry who desire that "special" relationship with their minister but who would bleed us dry if we give them as much attention as they desire. Having a relationship at the level of clichés doesn't mean we avoid relating with someone; we can still minister to them effectively and care for them while not desiring a personal relationship with them. No one says we must have an intimate relationship with everyone. However, if we have more than a few relationships in our lives at this level, we might be suffering from burnout and need to seek help to address the issue.

Level Two: Facts

This is the most basic level of intimacy. We feel safe enough to allow the other person to know things about us on a factual level: name, spouse and children's names, where we grew up and went to school, what we do in ministry, etc. This level is the building block for all intimate relationships. All deeper relationships at some point began here.

The level of intimacy for any given relationship is only as deep as its least invested partner.

Level Three: Opinions

A relationship moves to the level of opinion when we feel free to share our beliefs about things without fear of being made fun of, ridiculed or rejected. Talking about sports, politics or personal views of theology is this level of intimacy. This level also requires having an active interest in the opinions of the other person, as well.

Level Four: Feelings

Sharing our feelings is deeper than just sharing facts and opinions because we run the risk of being hurt and misunderstood. We also run a greater risk of rejection. Feelings such as excitement, joy and appreciation are just as important to the relationship as loneliness, hurt and disappointment. Successes and failures are equally shared at this level. Again, this level of relationship requires as much comfort hearing the other person share such feelings as we are comfortable sharing them ourselves.

Level Five: Deepest Needs

Few relationships attain the deepest level of intimacy. In fact, we will likely only be able to prioritize a handful of these relationships because they require significant time and energy to sustain. Level five relationships are comfortable sharing hopes and dreams as well as being honest about the bitter heartaches and fears of life. This is where genuine accountability takes place in terms of sharing our real struggles with another human being, whether it's pride, sexual temptation, temper or the unedited realities of our life in ministry.

While accountability at earlier levels can be somewhat beneficial, such accountability would not likely facilitate the honesty required to truly be held accountable. Accountable relationships at the level of deepest need have the influence necessary to accomplish deep and lasting impact.

At this level we are truly known for who we are—warts and all— and are sure of the other person's desire to still be with us. There's no need for pretending to be something we're not. If we ever begin hiding our flaws from such a friend, we immediately feel the difference and cease to be at this level of intimacy. Without reconciliation, the relationship will quickly unravel.

When evaluating the level of intimacy for a particular relationship, it's important to remember that intimacy is a two-way street. If we relate with someone at a level two but he or she relates with us at level four, that relationship is only a level two relationship. In other words, the level of intimacy for any given relationship is only as deep as its least invested partner. This truism should prevent us from being fooled into thinking we have more intimate relationships than we really do. It should also help us differentiate between ministry to someone (relating at a 2/5, for example) and friendship (relating at a 3/3, 4/4, or 5/5).

STEP 3: RANK CURRENT RELATIONSHIPS BY INTIMACY VALUE

Once you've rated each of your relationships, transfer the results to page 64. Rank them by number, with level five relationships at the top of the chart, then level fours and so on. It's OK for now if there aren't currently any level fours or fives; the point of this exercise is to take an honest inventory of what we do have so we can make an intentional effort to improve them.

STEP 4: PRAY FOR THESE INDIVIDUALS REGULARLY

Looking over the list, we may discover ones with whom we'd be willing to deepen our relationship. Highlighting these relationships, no matter what level they are currently at, we can begin to pray regularly for each of these individuals. More specifically, we can pray that God would speak to their hearts and place within them a hunger for greater intimacy with us.

As we pray, we can look for opportunities to spend time with them in nonwork settings. If they invite us to spend time together, we should attempt to do anything reasonable to make it happen. Married ministers will want to share the list of names with their spouse. This allows our spouse not only to pray with us on the matter but also to be more understanding and supportive when opportunities arise to spend time nurturing such friendships.

STEP 5: TAKE INITIATIVE WITH BOLDNESS

When we're ready to pursue a particular relationship, we don't have to wait for that person to move toward us. Instead, we can take the initiative to move toward that person. Of course, we're taking the risk that he or she might not share the same desire for deeper relationship. While this will be disappointing, it is to be expected sometimes. Not every person we pursue will have the same desire for a closer relationship. The same reason we got butterflies in our stomach approaching a new friend in elementary or middle school will be the same reason it will happen here: the risk of rejection. This is normal. We must be willing to suffer the disappointment of intimacy rejected in order to find those who will have a mutual desire for deeper intimacy with us. The potential benefits are worth it.

STEP 6: ALLOW INTIMACY TO DEEPEN NATURALLY

Once we've found a friend who desires to spend time with us, we shouldn't feel compelled to immediately take it to level five. If it's currently a level two, we can take the relationship to level three over time by finding out each others' opinions about the world through good conversation. We can move it deeper still by periodically sharing our feelings about things, including our relationship. If they also desire a deeper relationship, they will reciprocate over time by sharing their feelings as well.

If we currently have a level four relationship, moving to level five will require disclosing the deeper desires and fears of our heart. Once we take the risk, we will have to wait to see what happens next. Are they responsive? Do they appear comfortable with our sharing that deeply? Do they eventually share in similar fashion? These would be signs of their desire to follow us to a level five relationship. Alternatively, we may decide to have a direct conversation with them to discuss our desire to deepen the relationship. If so, we might share this section of the book regarding the five levels of intimacy and our hopes for the friendship, allowing the Holy Spirit time to work in their heart.

How can we tell if they aren't interested? Asking directly is perhaps best; they can just say, "No thanks." However, there are also other ways to tell. We can watch nonverbal cues over time. When we invest time with them, do we find that we do most of the talking? Does the other person fail to reciprocate our level of sharing? Do we always seem to be the one calling to spend time together? Do we perceive the other person distancing from us? These could be signs the other person isn't invested at the same level we are.

As disappointing as this may be, we don't have to throw the relationship away; instead, we can enjoy it for what it is. We need relationships at all levels (other than level one, of course). Sometimes it's enjoyable to get together with a group of friends and relate only at level two or three. There's a time and place for that. Just know that when the need arises for more intimate connecting, we'll want to turn to someone with whom we can relate on a deeper level.

Wrap-Up:
Foundation Stone 1—Intimacy

The greatest benefit you can derive from this book is to begin developing your own ministerial self-care plan. The "wrap-up" section following each of the seven foundation stones is your opportunity to synthesize what you've learned. As such, each wrap-up becomes your own tailor-made self-care plan for long-term ministry health.

Reflecting on all you've learned in this discussion of intimacy, use the space below to journal your most important takeaways.

INTIMACY WITH GOD
How might God be challenging you to deepen or modify your relationship with him?

MARITAL INTIMACY
To what extent is anything or anyone else coming before your relationship with your spouse? It may be helpful to measure this especially with regard to competing areas of time and emotional investment.

If you are unmarried and not in progress toward a marital relationship at this time, how are you presently fulfilling your needs for human intimacy?

Never forget that "the ministry" is still a job. If you're married or moving toward marriage, your ministry job ought never cause you to neglect your intimate relationships with God and with your spouse. Ask your spouse if they feel neglected or if they feel your ministry (and those in it) get the better part of you most days. If so, consult the Lord and your spouse for insight on how to repair this situation. Use the space below to jot down notes from those conversations.

INTIMACY WITH SAME-GENDER FRIENDS

Write below the names you came up with from step three of the last section (page 61). What level of intimacy do you currently have with each one? What level do you desire? Highlight those with whom you desire a deeper relationship. Pray regularly for your relationship with them to grow deeper, keeping watch for opportunities to do so.

Name	Current Level	Desired Level	Notes

CALLING

The Power
for Effectiveness in Ministry

Once upon a time, there were four ministers. They became friends while attending seminary together in a city near their respective home towns. Upon graduation, one became a youth worker for a campus ministry, one worked finance for a nationwide nonprofit, one became a music minister, and one went into mission work. Their busy lives prevented them from maintaining contact all that often, and within a few years they lost contact with each other altogether.

Ten years after graduation, they were invited to return to the seminary for an alumni event. Only one of the four attended. Saddened to miss seeing his friends, he was motivated to find out what happened. He discovered that one of his buddies had been fired from his job due to an affair. A second had become disillusioned with ministry and, after multiple jobs since graduation, finally concluded that it simply "wasn't for him." The third became overwhelmed by the pressures of her position and eventually burned out. The one who returned to seminary was the only one who had remained in his call. His passion for ministry remained—an energy that had sustained him during many trying times and dark days.

1. Understanding Our Call
to Ministry

If experience is the consummate teacher, then our collective experience says that thriving in one's area of calling not only provides personal success but also great fulfillment. Yet many have been badly harmed in ministry, some by their own hand and some by the hands of others. By learning fundamental beliefs about calling and a

means for more objectively evaluating our own calling, we can be encouraged toward ministry success while being directed away from
ministry peril.

THE FAINT-HEARTED NEED NOT APPLY

Calling into the ministry is filled with challenges that can easily de-
rail those with less than genuine callings:

- Sixty-six (66) percent of ministers and their families feel pressure
  to model the ideal family to their congregations and communities.

- Forty-five (45) percent say that they've experienced depression or
  burnout to the extent they needed to take a leave of absence from
  ministry.

- Seventy (70) percent say they have lower self-esteem now than
  when they started out.[1]

Our calling must be evaluated and tested to ensure its authenticity. As Thomas Oden said, "Classical pastoral wisdom has thought it
to be testable, and dangerous if unexamined."[2]

What initially drew you toward the ministry?

What do you find most challenging about being a minister?

Without a personal invitation from God to serve as a minister, we
lack the distinguishing factor for sustained ministry effectiveness:
perseverance. When all else is in doubt, confidence in such an invitation is critical. We must know without question we've been called
to do exactly what we're doing. Sometimes this "knowing" will be the
only tangible anchor during the stormy seasons of ministry—and of
those, there will be plenty.

LESSONS FROM THE FRONTLINE

My (Brad) telephone rang to the voice of a lay leader in a neighboring church who wanted to discuss a troubling issue. They had
reached an impasse with their minister. Although the specifics of the

---

[1]H. B. London Jr. and Neil B. Wiseman, *Pastors at Greater Risk* (Ventura, Calif.: Regal,
2003), pp. 20, 86, 118, 148, 172.
[2]Thomas C. Oden, *Pastoral Theology: Essentials of Ministry* (San Francisco: HarperCol-
lins, 1983), p. 18.

next step were uncertain, they were united on one thing: their minister was to be removed from the church.

A short time later, I received a call from the minister. Jim[3] was hurting deeply and didn't know what to do. He and his wife hadn't been at the church long. It was their first pastorate. He believed he was doing everything possible to fulfill his calling. We prayed together over the phone and set a time to meet face-to-face.

When they walked into my office, Jim and Jan sat uncomfortable and frightened in adjacent chairs. Their faces were filled with the pain and exhaustion of the last few days, surviving the haze one day at a time. We discussed their relocation to our church's Antioch Affection ministry[4], a program providing "refuge churches" to ministers removed from ministry. At these churches the ministers and their families are able to seek rest, healing and (if appropriate) eventual restoration to the ministry.

We helped Jim and Jan negotiate a severance package and an exit strategy from their ministry placement. In the weeks that followed, they relocated to our church and began putting their lives back together. I assured them God would use this opportunity to redirect their ministry for his greater purposes and for their greater good. Jan felt as if she could never be in ministry again. I assured her that if they were truly called, a day would come when God would heal their pain and restore their passion for ministry.

I drove out to meet with the church leadership late on a Saturday afternoon to talk with them about Jim and his wife. They obviously cared about their minister and his family; their biggest concerns related to some of Jim's program ideas. The lay leadership had a significantly different vision for the church than Jim did. As we continued to dialogue, it became evident this mismatch had existed from the beginning. The church wanted a chaplain but had hired a pastor with the heart of an evangelist. The church preferred a more traditional approach to ministry and had little desire to accommodate their minister's passion for the lost—not to mention his methodologies for reaching them.

Jim was much more motivated toward evangelism than pastoral care. His block parties drew in a different ethnic group than the current membership at the church. Although many were coming to Christ and joining the fellowship, a jealousy erupted within some of the church's longstanding members. As Jim challenged them to live out the Great Commission, he wondered why the church didn't sup-

---

[3]Illustrations containing only a first name are taken from our work with ministers removed from ministry. Such names have been changed to protect their identity.

[4]For more information about Antioch Affection and other programs for ministers in need, go to <www.Shepherd-Care.org>.

port his ideas. And some in the church simply wondered why the pastor had never visited them.

LEARNING FROM ANOTHER'S BATTLE SCARS

Both sides missed their obvious incompatibility. Was Jim so eager to serve that he simply took the first opportunity offered? Was the church so eager for a pastor they merely called the first minister expressing interest? Each side failed to communicate their honest expectations to the other. Jim had accepted an invitation to a church that was incompatible with his calling.

While our program ultimately brought resolution and restoration for Jim and Jan, there were many trying days along their journey. While Jim envisioned future ministry, Jan could not. But with time, God worked as only God could. Jan experienced a breakthrough, bringing her to a place of forgiveness that freed her to move forward in ministry. At the same time, Jim began growing in areas he'd never grown before. In the months that followed, both were able to embrace a ministry opportunity more consistent with their calling.

Jim and Jan now serve as overseas missionaries. People are regularly coming to know Christ through their ministry. They are clear about their calling and more satisfied in ministry than ever.

In his book *Musical Pulpits,* author Rodney Crowell claims that 34 percent of forced terminations are mismatched in ministry either due to personality conflicts or (like Jim) miscommunication about the talents required for the position.[5]

Describe a situation in which you or someone you know served in a place of "ministry mismatch."

What do you believe led to the initial idea that this was a match?

In retrospect, what red flags might there have been to indicate this position might not have been a good fit?

---

[5]Rodney J. Crowell, *Musical Pulpits: Clergy and Laypersons Face the Issue of Forced Exits* (Grand Rapids: Baker, 1992), p. 58.

Sometimes we get in a hurry. Not happy where we are, we accept a new opportunity as a "way out" of another problematic situation. Hasty decisions often result in regrettable consequences. If we feel we're serving in an environment that isn't conducive to our calling, we should slow down and allow God to give us clarity about our situation rather than jump into another mistake. An internal sense of desperation for a quick decision is generally a sign that we need to wait. Important lessons can be learned even in the midst of the "severe gift" of difficult circumstances:

> Consider it a sheer gift, friends, when tests and challenges come at you from all sides. You know that under pressure, your faith-life is forced into the open and shows its true colors. So don't try to get out of anything prematurely. Let it do its work so you become mature and well-developed, not deficient in any way. (James 1:2-4 *The Message*)

We can make certain our next move will be to where we are supposed to be and to what we are supposed to be doing. Knowing our calling is the key.

If we are certain of our calling, we won't be distracted by others who say "It can't be done that way."

DISTINGUISHING BETWEEN DIFFERENT TYPES OF CALLINGS

A call to vocational ministry isn't possible unless two more basic callings already exist. The role and function of each is distinct, building on the foundation of the one before it. For some, the callings occur in stages; for others, they happen at a single moment in time.

The Call to Faith

Each of us, assuming we've responded to Jesus' invitation for relationship, has experienced a call to faith. Our call to faith was God-initiated and wasn't based on our great human insight or wisdom (1 Corinthians 1:26). God revealed our sin and our need for repentance. That was the beginning of our adventure with God.

The Call to Minister

All Christians are given a call to minister to others (2 Corinthians 5:20). We also receive one or more spiritual gifts to build up the body of Christ (Hebrews 2:3-4). The gifts of the Spirit leave no place for pride, as such ability to minister comes only by the equipping and empowering of the Holy Spirit. The duty of all believers is to minister through a local fellowship, putting to use our unique spiritual giftedness. Every local church is uniquely gifted for ministry through the people God brings to it (1 Corinthians 12:18).

The Call into the Ministry

Beyond the call to minister is the call to ministry. God appoints certain individuals to serve him in specific vocations of service. A call to ministry is God's invitation to be set apart by God for surrendered vocational service (see Paul's self-description in Romans 1:1). God's call to ministry is by his choosing, as is his equipping for such ministry. God will not call us unless he also equips us for such a calling. He will also provide for his chosen minister financially—some through those to whom they minister (like Michael Todd in his counseling practice), some through the support of others (like Brad through his church members or Michael Todd's father-in-law through supporters of his parachurch ministry) or through part-time/full-time employment outside of ministry (such as a bivocational minister).

We must be in intimate relationship with God and free from the pressure to conform to traditional models to rightly discern the specifics of our call. The fact that this megachurch or that global ministry is following a particular model may have nothing to do with what God is calling *us* to do. We serve an incredibly creative God who enjoys capturing the hearts and imaginations of his beloved. God will use the unique talents and passions he has placed in us for that very purpose. And if we are certain of our calling, we won't be distracted by others who say "It can't be done that way." Tomorrow's ministries need not be defined by yesterday's church culture.

In the space below, briefly describe the time when you first became aware of your callings. If you aren't certain about your callings, discuss this with a mentor or close Christian friend.

Call to Faith:

Call to Minister:

Call into the Ministry:

If you are currently in a traditional context, is it a good fit? To what extent might you have chosen a traditional context simply because it was safe or predictable?

What risks are involved in trying something innovative and new?

If you are currently in a nontraditional setting, is it a good fit? To what extent might you have chosen a nontraditional path simply because it was trendy or exciting?

WHAT IS CALLING?

With the colossal ministry challenges we sometimes face, it sometimes seems easier to give up. Though we may try to resign the call, the call never resigns us. Even if we walk away, God's calling will continue to pursue us.

A man or woman truly called of God into the ministry will never be at peace pursuing anything other than what God has called them to do. I (Brad) remember quitting my calling at age twenty-seven. Like a shadow, the call chased me for five years. Five years I lived without the peace of practicing my calling. Though I tried to escape, the call remained.

God beckons us to live out what we were meant to be, to live out our purpose and to live with passion. Frederick Buechner wrote, "The place God calls you to is the place where your deep gladness and the world's deep hunger meet."[6] We are sustained by the knowledge that God called us to the ministry for a specific purpose, one which becomes a driving passion to embrace each challenge set before us: "One does not choose the ministry! A pastor is chosen. He is chosen by God for God's purposes, in God's time and place, and serves Him in God's ways."[7] We must continually reference our calling for affirmation, strength and perseverance.

Four out of ten ministers have occasionally doubted their calling, roughly the same number who've considered leaving pastoral ministry altogether.[8] In light of this, a discussion on the validity of our calling is very important. Great men such as Charles Spurgeon actively discouraged men from entering the ministry. Spurgeon was emphatic that if a young man could take another vocation and be happy, he should do so. He believed the only ones belonging in the ministry were those certain they had no other viable alternative, that no other vocation would bring satisfaction to life. Martin Luther warned young men to flee from ministry unless they were certain of their calling: "If God needs thee, He will know how to call thee."[9]

---

[6]Frederick Buechner, quoted in Paul Cedar, Kent Hughes and Ben Patterson, *Mastering the Pastoral Role* (Portland, Ore.: Multnomah, 1991), p. 28.

[7]Henry Blackaby and Henry Brandt, *The Power of the Call* (Nashville: Broadman & Holman, 1997), pp. 26-27.

[8]Foster Letter, November 10, 2002, p. 3.

[9]Martin Luther, quoted in Erwin Lutzer, *Pastor to Pastor: Tackling the Problems of Ministry* (Grand Rapids: Kregel, 1998), p. 14.

Both of us received similar advice from separate godly mentors while we were prayerfully considering the ministry: "If you can do anything else and be fulfilled, do it. There are too many ministers out there who have no business in ministry because they were never called. They are miserable and often cause great damage to the kingdom. Yet, if you're truly called, pursuing other vocations will leave you completely unfulfilled. Then you'll know you can't be satisfied until you surrender to the Call."

Great advice. It was a critical component for both of us in our respective vocational choices—Brad into pastoring and Michael Todd into private Christian counseling.

WHAT CONSTITUTES A CALL INTO THE MINISTRY?

The call into the ministry is the possession of a "knowing" initiated and sustained by God and validated by Scripture. While God's call will be unique to us and specific to his plan for our lives, these elements are part of every calling.

All callings into the ministry are *initiated by God*. We weren't called by God according to our own merit but rather by the grace and sovereign choice of the One who called us. It is by his initiative, not ours. We can't call ourselves; we must be called by God. There comes a point where we realize there is absolutely nothing else we can do.

Paul possessed this knowing in his call into the ministry to the Gentiles. While Paul possessed many secular skills and could have fulfilled any number of professional roles, he was consumed by a passion and calling he didn't initiate. Yet many have found the hearing easier than the heeding. Jonah heard God's call to prophecy to the Ninevites but responded by running from it. God ultimately gained Jonah's attention through more drastic means. God patiently does whatever is necessary to bring us to the place of surrender to our call—however long it takes.

Such knowing about our calling into the ministry is not only initiated but also *sustained by God*—certainty of the knowing never really goes away. This does not mean there won't be times we might doubt the call. Troublesome times will cloud our vision, perhaps distracting us from our calling. But the Holy Spirit plants a seed deep inside, one from which we ultimately cannot hide—no matter how deeply we may bury it.

The call of God will also be confirmed by Scripture. God will speak through his Word and will not be silent. Through personal time in God's Word, the Holy Spirit will use the pages of Scripture to confirm not only our ministry calling but also his purpose in calling us. Certain passages will come alive with fresh meaning and application to our passions and unique area of calling in ministry. The Good Shepherd will gently lead those who listen intently for his voice (John 10:2-4).

Many callings into the ministry will also be recognized in some way by our faith community. However, faith traditions exhibit a wide variety of methods for confirming such a call, ranging from informal (one who claims an internal calling publicly proclaims such with the subsequent laying on of hands by elders) to more formal (an interview process, including approval by ministry leadership and public ceremony or announcement) to structured and "proven" (including inquiry, preparation through formalized study, followed by both written and oral examination, and finally public installation). In each case, such a process can be a meaningful time for introspection, learning, discovery and affirmation for the aspiring minister. It also serves as the ceremonial beginning of public ministry, whether such validation is before a group of elders, board members, denominational directors or the leaders of a Christian employer.

Before making a transition from my secular consulting role to a master's program in Christian counseling, I (Michael Todd) sought the counsel of mentors and mature Christian friends. I pursued such retraining only after the encouragement of such important relationships bore witness to the clear sense of "knowing" deep within my spirit and after God had used many Scriptures to reinforce my convictions about my new calling. Confirmation from the community of faith continued through my new mentors at my graduate training program, Psychological Studies Institute. Their verbal affirmations and eventual diploma represented both an informal and formal confirmation of my future ministry in the area of Christian counseling.

How did you sense God initiating your call into the ministry?

How has God sustained your sense of calling?

Where in Scripture have you sensed your calling validated?

How has your faith community supported the process of discerning and answering your call?

COMMON CHARACTERISTICS OF CALLING

While each minister's calling is in some way unique, callings from God have many other fundamental similarities.

God's Call Is God-Centric

Our call is ultimately not about us; it's about God's desire to use us in ministry to others. Though the call is personal in nature, there is a common compassion for the condition of others. He calls us not to pursue our own agenda but to fulfill his greater plan.

God's Call Is Awesome

In recent times, the word *awesome* has been so overused it has virtually lost its true meaning. But few words accurately describe the feeling of coming face-to-face with the transcendent ways of the Almighty and the humble realization that he has chosen us for a task.

God may refine our calling based on our unique experiences. Yet his calling of us is for a lifetime of service to him.

We must humbly and completely depend on the One who calls us, for the calling is always much bigger than we are. Moses sensed an enormous inadequacy for his calling. God chose him for the job both despite and because of his own human weaknesses: "Who makes a person's mouth? Who decides whether people speak or do not speak, hear or do not hear, see or do not see? Is it not I, the LORD?" (Exodus 4:11 NLT). God told Moses his weakness was designed to provide a greater display of God's strength.

What do the following passages suggest about the humility required in the pursuit of our calling?

2 Corinthians 4:7:

2 Corinthians 12:9:

God's Call Is Mysterious

God's call comes with an internal confidence so real it can almost be touched. Nothing else could lead us to be so decisive and sure. The call will represent our heart's greatest passion and desire. It's as if God, our intimate Lover, quietly and even seductively whispers to our hearts, "I have plans for you."

God's Call Is Unique

God uses where we've already walked in life to accomplish ministry that is unique to our journey. God's hand was on Moses as he grew up under the shadow of Pharaoh. Because such preparation allowed him to learn from a unique vantage point, Moses' royal Egyptian training was used uniquely by God as a catalyst for the exodus.

Like Moses, there has been a surge in the number of ministers entering ministry later in life with a passion for areas of ministry rooted in their unique life experiences. They are more frequently choosing nontraditional tracks in seminary and often start new parachurch organizations (like ShepherdCare) rather than pursuing traditional pastoring roles.

God's Call Is Lifelong

God's call lasts a lifetime. The geography of our calling may change (and often does with time). God may also refine our calling along the way based on our unique experiences. Yet his calling of us is for a lifetime of service to him in some sort of shepherding capacity.

Some ministers try to "shelve" themselves after being caught up in challenging circumstances, sensing God must be finished with them. But our call goes far beyond any momentary difficulties (2 Corinthians 4:17). Though God may permanently remove us from public ministry due to burnout or moral failure, he will again call us to humbly—perhaps even sacrificially—use our story for his kingdom purposes.

In what ways do you feel unprepared, overwhelmed or inadequate for your calling?

What practical measures might help you maintain a God-centered ministry?

How might the following contribute to keeping your ministry God-centered?
  accountability:

  memorizing Scripture:

  meaningful quotations prominently displayed:

  changing the standards by which you measure ministry success:

Sometimes the difference between getting off track in ministry and maintaining proper focus is simply a matter of surrounding ourselves with people and things that bring to mind the truth about our calling. While being called into the ministry is a wonderful thing, we must never forget we have an enemy who seeks to confuse us about our calling. Satan accomplishes this by convincing some to pursue the ministry from faulty motives and by overwhelming those legitimately called through questioning and doubt. To thrive in kingdom work we must acquire a certainty of our calling.

2. Being Sure of Our Calling

We don't have to be ashamed of ourselves or discount our worth if we discover that we've been operating under a false calling. It may be part of the painful process for discovering God's true calling for our lives.

Charles Bridges says ministerial failure can sometimes be traced "to the very threshold of the entrance to the work."[10] A false call results from misreading God's will—even if it was pursued with good intentions. Yet we don't have to be ashamed of ourselves or discount our worth if we discover that we've been operating under a false calling. If God in his sovereignty allows it to happen, it may be part of the painful process for discovering God's true calling for our lives. For those attempting to discern the validity of their call into the ministry, changes should be made slowly, deliberately and with much godly counsel and prayer. Decisions made during such a time of reevaluation will change everything.

WHAT *DOESN'T* POINT TO A FALSE CALLING

First, let's consider a few "signs" that should not necessarily be interpreted as a need for change in ministry.

Discouragement

Many, if not most, who are truly called into the ministry suffer at times from discouragement. This is a common experience, especially when ministry turns out different or more difficult than expected. During such times, it's important to remind ourselves of Jesus' own words to those first called to New Testament ministry: "In this world you will have trouble. But take heart! I have overcome the world" (John 16:33).

If our ministry is not "successful" based on worldly models (many of which are commonly used within Christian ministry), it is not a signal of false calling. Human measures or responses such as attendance, giving records, number of converts or praise within the Christian community don't necessarily validate calling. God calls some to

---

[10]Charles Bridges, quoted in Erwin Lutzer, *Pastor to Pastor: Tackling the Problems of Ministry* (Grand Rapids: Kregel, 1998), p. 11.

till the soil, some to sow the seed and some to reap the harvest (1 Corinthians 3:5-9). Jeremiah's ministry was successful not based on the number of "converts" but on his faithfulness to proclaim the message God gave him. Even though God told him the leaders of his own people would fight against his prophetic message, God nonetheless called him to be obedient to the task.

Struggle with Sin

We ought not be surprised that Satan would target ministers, enticing us to compromise our integrity because of the potential damage our moral failure can cause to the church at large. While not a sign of being falsely called, ministers who regularly struggle with a particular sin should take this very seriously and discuss it openly with a spiritual adviser, a Christian counselor or an intimate friend.

Removal from a Particular Ministry Location

Some of us enter the ministry only to "fail" at our first (or most recent) assignment. There are many reasons for ministry removal, some having nothing to do with a minister's calling. Forced exits sometimes result from mismatched talents or personality differences between minister and ministry organization. Even if our removal resulted from a moral failure and our public platform is never restored, in time God will eventually return us to some form of ministry on the other side of our repentance and restoration experience.

Remember Jim from earlier? Though he was genuinely called to ministry, he accepted a call to serve in a church that was inconsistent with his calling. He was in the wrong place. God ultimately used this misplacement to help Jim discover what he had genuinely called him to do.

WHAT *MIGHT* POINT TO A FALSE CALLING

We must look beyond the surface as we consider the origin of our call into the ministry. "I come from a long generation of preachers" or "My parents thought it was a good idea" or "Someone told me I would make a good minister" may be true, but none is evidence of a valid calling. If we came into the ministry by way of someone else's suggestion (whether formally or informally), but independent from any internal sense of vocation, there is certainly room to question our call.

Seeing Ministry as Simply a Job

Some denominations and Christian nonprofits engage in recruitment campaigns. The banners read, "Have you ever thought about a rewarding career in ministry?" If not handled with care, such an attempt at filling the ranks runs the risk of fostering false callings. If the ministry opportunity was "simply one of our options" for employment, we will most likely lack not only the passion but the power to be effective in long-term ministry.

Those genuinely called have a deep sense of knowing they belong in the ministry. If this has never been part of your experience, there is reason to doubt your call. If it once was there, however, other problems might be clouding your sense of call.

Lack of Passion

Some ministers exhibit what appears to be a passion for their ministry, but this turns out to be only a manifestation of a charismatic personality. True passion comes from a deep place within and continues to burn, even during tough times. We should be careful, however, not to jump to conclusions about our lack of calling if we no longer feel passion. An absence of passion, particularly where it's been there in the past, may be due to other problems, such as discouragement or burnout.

Self-Centered Desire

Do you desire a particular position or place of authority? Are your ministry plans designed according to your own personal goals? A genuine call places a priority on the benefit of others and not on ourselves. When God calls, he sends us to influence and serve. Simon observed the acts of the apostles and asked if he could purchase their ability (Acts 8:9-24). His desire was to become the center of attention, not to serve.

Satisfaction Doing Something Besides Full-Time Ministry

If we believe we might be just as satisfied in secular work or merely doing lay ministry, there is sufficient reason to question our call into the ministry. Many laypeople have a love for ministering alongside their careers. While these workers are vital to the church, laypeople are called to minister but not called *into the ministry*. Both secular and religious vocations are sacred endeavors before God and equally blessed and used by him. Yet the one called into the ministry feels a deep desire to integrate their work and their ministry into a primary vocation dedicated to kingdom work.

Scott and his family suffered the effects of two back-to-back forced exits from two different ministries. Church work was all Scott knew. Since his dad had been a pastor, Scott wrongly assumed God had called him too. Relationships in the ministry were always great at first, but each went sour within about a year. After an extended time of counseling, Scott realized that while both he and his wife enjoyed church work, neither possessed an inner confidence that God had called them. Scott and his wife were strong people of faith and both had an intimate relationship with Christ, but they had mistakenly based their calling on superficial, extraneous factors.

Where and when did the idea of ministry as a possible vocation first come to your mind?

Who invited you to enter the ministry? What else served as deciding factors?

Which, if any, of the potential signs of false calling listed above resonate with you?

What do you really want to do with your life? What are the deepest areas of passion for you?

OUR UNIQUE CAPACITY: HOW GOD MADE US FOR MINISTRY

An exciting thing happens when Christians discover how and why God has gifted them. It's equally exciting for ministers to discover their unique capacity to carry out the function of ministry:

> Just as each of us has one body with many members, and these members do not all have the same function, so in Christ we who are many form one body, and each member belongs to all the others. We have different gifts, according to the grace given us. (Romans 12:4-6)

Having counseled numerous ministers in crisis, we've observed many attempting to live out their ministry roles according to their expectations and assumptions rather than their true giftedness. Several comprehensive spiritual gifts assessments, some designed for general use and others crafted more narrowly for people within a particular faith tradition, have been designed to help determine our areas of giftedness and related issues of ministry compatibility.[11]

When our spiritual giftedness is in line with the responsibilities of our ministry role, it's amazing how much more enjoyable ministry becomes! As ministers, one of our challenges is to operate from reality rather than from perception or assumption. Finding our "best-fit" role and function in ministry requires us to discover how God has gifted us. Some ministers work in daily frustration because they serve in a capacity for which they possess little to no giftedness. We will find joy and freedom only by discovering how we have been designed by God for ministry.

OUR SPECIFIC OPPORTUNITY: GOD'S OPEN DOOR

Missionary Colleen Shepson felt a growing passion for reaching Muslims. When she graduated from Bible school and applied to the Christian and Missionary Alliance, they asked her to serve in Gabon, West Africa, because they were not sending single women to the Middle East at that time.

Colleen submitted to the authority of her organization and left for Africa, where she served faithfully for two terms. While there, she contracted a debilitating tropical disease that required her to return stateside. While recovering, she pursued her master's degree at Wheaton College, during which time her original passion to reach Middle Eastern Muslims resurfaced. When she brought this sense of call to Christian and Missionary Alliance officials, she was told, "That's interesting! We've just been informed by the missionary doctor that we are not to send you back to Gabon, lest you be further infected with this disease. Why don't you talk to the person who is over the Middle East."

Colleen did as instructed and rehearsed to him what she felt God was doing in reviving her passion. "That's interesting," he responded. "We've just made the decision to send single women into the Middle East, but they must have a master's degree!" God, who had earlier presented her with a closed door, now in his timing presented her with an open door—along with the newly acquired credentials to walk through it! She ultimately spent twelve years following her heart's passion by ministering to Muslims in the Middle East.

Being in ministry means depending on God to open and close opportunities. If God isn't opening a door, that's a pretty good sign we need to stay where we are. Beware of forced entries! But when a

---

[11]Many instruments have been created to measure spiritual giftedness, including the *Team Ministry Spiritual-Gift Based Ministry* (www.churchgrowth.org), *Spiritual Gifts Self-Assessment* (www.ELCA.org), *Spiritual Gifts Inventory* (www.PCUSA.org) and *Catholic Spiritual Gifts Inventory* (www.siena.org/spgifts.htm).

door begins to open, there's benefit in walking up to the threshold to see if God is waiting on the other side. While not all open doors are of God, we can be prayerfully discerning about specific opportunities.

Paul's missionary trips offer an example of God's open door (Acts 16). Paul and his associates were "kept by the Holy Spirit from preaching the word in the province of Asia" (v. 6). Paul was willing to go anywhere to influence people for Christ, but God was the holder of the map and had a specific opportunity in mind for Paul and his companions.

Incidentally, God's open door got them beaten, arrested and thrown into jail—a reminder that being in the center of God's plan doesn't ensure ministry will necessarily be easy.

OUR OVERRIDING PASSION: MINISTRY FROM THE HEART

The experiences of our lives, our spiritual journey, our special areas of interest and our level of intimacy with Christ will all have great impact on the yearnings of our heart. Paul felt compelled to preach (1 Corinthians 9:16). If we are consumed with Christ, he will plant the desires he wants for us in our heart (Psalm 37:4). We will be exponentially more effective than those who rely only on their own charisma to fulfill their ministry obligations.

What capacity of ministry might you serve in almost tirelessly if God were to open the door?

What evidence do you have that you are well-suited for your current ministry position?

What evidence do you have that you may be better suited for something else?

Don't be overly concerned if you aren't able to see things clearly just yet. Trust God to work things out in his way and timing.

3. Called Versus Not Called: The Negative Effects of Working Outside Our Calling

If we're called to do something, there are other things by definition we're not called to do. It's a simple concept, but many ministers have never seriously considered the implications of this reality.

THINGS TO WHICH I AM *NOT* CALLED

Well-meaning ministers sometimes misapply Paul's proclamation, "When I am with those who are weak, I share their weakness, for I want to bring the weak to Christ. Yes, I try to find common ground with everyone, doing everything I can to save some. *I do everything to spread the Good News* and share in its blessings" (1 Corinthians 9:22-23 NLT, emphasis added).

At first glance, Paul may seem to imply that he would do anything and everything in ministry for the sake of the gospel. But his challenge wasn't about working harder and longer; rather, he was trying to keep the gospel message relevant to unbelieving hearers. Paul's desire was to identify with the lost in any way possible in order to see their lives transformed by Christ.

Unless our ministry is a one-person show with *zero* volunteers, we are not responsible for every single task in our ministry. Scripture teaches that many make up the body of Christ; we are only a part of it! Every believer is bestowed with spiritual gifts to fulfill a ministering function because every believer is called to minister. Therefore, the professional minister's role isn't to do all the work of ministry but primarily to equip individual members to engage in such ministry. If we're trying to do it all, or if we're dictating up front what we will or will not do, our pride may be getting in the way.

Some say, "That sounds great for you, but you don't know the ministry I serve in." Contemporary ministries live in the shadow of megaministries (those with large followings, deep pockets or tremendous influence within the Christian community), a phenomenon that has created the concept of "specialized ministry" in narrowly defined areas. Smaller ministries can't usually operate this way. The average church, for example, has fewer than one hundred members and has one person on staff. Many Christian nonprofits are run by a single director on a shoestring budget. Yet regardless of the size of the organization, ministry wholeness balances the three main components of proclaiming God's Word, caring for God's people and leading God's people.

Someone might say, "I'm just called to _____. Somebody else

needs to do _____." As your ministry grows, this may be a natural temptation. The church I (Brad) serve is too large for me to visit everyone, but that doesn't keep me from doing some of the visiting. I realize that if I didn't spend time with my people, my preaching would cease to be relevant because I wouldn't really know well enough the people God called me to shepherd. We ought not try to get out of doing the things we don't like to do but rather fulfill the role and duty of our office.

FINDING OUR TRUE NORTH: CREATING A PERSONAL PURPOSE STATEMENT

Socrates said, "The unexamined life is not worth living." If we are unaware of the factors influencing our self-expectations, we will have no center from which to evaluate our own day-to-day ministry activities. A clear sense of calling is that center. One way to maintain the course of our calling is to create a personal purpose statement. A personal purpose statement becomes the "true north" guiding our entire life and ministry. No two individuals will have identical purpose statements; not only is each of us unique in our calling from God, but we also differ in our personalities and the way we express ourselves. For example, consider both the similarities in and the differences between Michael Todd and Brad's personal purpose statements:

> Relying on the foundation of my intimate relationships, I will apply God's wisdom to deeply impact others and to call Christian professionals to live intentionally from their true hearts. (Michael Todd)

> To love the Lord my God with all my heart, soul, mind and strength. To love my wife and my children and to influence as many people as possible for Kingdom purposes. (Brad)

Our statements are both externally focused on service to others. They also both place a high value on important primary relationships. However, notice the many differences. Michael Todd mentions the importance of his intimate relationships in general terms, while Brad mentions specific relationships. Michael Todd's statement is written as one long sentence, while Brad's is presented almost in bullet form. Michael Todd uses more psychological/heart language, and Brad more theological/head language.

Crafting a personal purpose statement is a very personal matter related to your unique personality, calling and giftedness for ministry. Don't worry about "getting it right." Consider it a "working definition" to be refined over time as God gives clarity. Minor modifications over time are normal as our life situation changes and we gain greater clarity about our life's purpose. Brad's statement, for example, would have been different before his wife and children came along; Michael Todd's statement changed from "Christians" to "Christian professionals" to reflect a narrowing of his ministry focus. Finally, we can take comfort that we are not creating our purpose but rather discovering the purpose God is patiently unfolding in us.

What key words or phrases might naturally fit within your personal purpose statement?

What passions have you identified so far in this study? How are they related to either your key relationships or to your calling in ministry?

Some of those we lead have been robbed of the opportunity of serving by our do-it-all drivenness.

Share this brainstorming exercise with your ministry coach, spiritual director, spouse or accountability partner, asking for their feedback. Write down any helpful comments or suggestions you receive.

MAINTAINING PEACE IN OUR CALLING: DEVELOPING THE CALLING OF OTHERS

If God has called us to the organization we serve, we can rest assured that he is surrounding us with others who have complementary gifts to ours. As the minister has an obligation to serve in their area of giftedness, so the congregation or volunteer staff has responsibility to serve in their areas of giftedness. Once we understand people's gifts, we can more effectively invite them to help us.

We ought to allow people who are better than us in specific areas to come alongside us. Some might think, "If I ask for help, people will know I'm weak." Often the people in our care already know we're weak in that area and are just waiting for us to admit it. Trusting God to work through our weakness (2 Corinthians 12:9-10), we can let pride and ego go before they ruin a perfectly good ministry.

As Christian leaders, we must help those within our ministry discover what God has for them to accomplish. When we empower our people to serve in their giftedness according to their passions, we reenergize our organization and give people a reason to stop "ministry hopping" and become more engaged. Andy Stanley says it this way: "Perhaps the two best-kept secrets of leadership are these: (1) The less you do, the more you accomplish. (2) The less you do, the more you enable others to accomplish."[12]

---

[12]Andy Stanley, *The Next Generation Leader* (Portland, Ore.: Multnomah, 2006), p. 15.

Pastor Dennis Siebert shares this story about a lesson he learned related to this "doing less and accomplishing more" principle:

> When I was a student in seminary, a pastor came to talk with us about the schedule he was keeping. Constantly on the go, making contacts, visiting people, and preaching preparation kept him busy an average of 12-16 hours daily. He proudly explained, "I have the agreement with the board that I run my own schedule. When I'm exhausted, I take as much time as I need to get rested and go full throttle again." Something didn't seem right about this, but as a seminary student I admired his commitment.
>
> Years later, I read an article by the same pastor where he commented on his previous hectic pace. Now, he was being led by the Lord to begin each morning in extended prayer, some days spending 2-3 hours entrusting his day to the Lord and then going about the tasks the Holy Spirit led him to do. His conclusion? Ministry was now much more effective and he felt more empowered—allowing the Lord to direct his ministry rather than his own human efforts.

The folks we lead don't need a people-pleasing minister. They need a minister with the backbone to follow God's calling no matter what.

Some of those we lead have been robbed of the opportunity of serving by our do-it-all drivenness. Such a ministry style can sometimes serve as a cover for our workaholism, perfectionism, fear of losing control or mistrust of others to do as good a job as we expect.

What do you think about Andy Stanley's quote on doing less and accomplishing more?

To what extent might you be allowing pride to get in the way of others serving out of their giftedness?

In what way might your ministry unintentionally encourage your average ministry member to be more "spectator" than active participant?

What ideas could encourage those on the sidelines in your ministry to take a more active role?

HANDLING OTHERS' EXPECTATIONS

Take a look at one minister's commentary regarding the sometimes impossible expectations placed upon ministers:

> If I wanted to drive a manager in the business community up the wall, I'd make him responsible for the success of an organization but give him no authority. I'd provide him with unclear goals, ones the organization didn't completely agree to. I'd ask him to provide a service of an ill-defined nature, apply a body of knowledge having few absolutes and staff his organization only with volunteers who donated just a few hours a week at the most. I'd expect him to work 10 to 12 hours per day and have his work evaluated by a committee of 300 to 500 amateurs. I'd call him a minister and make him accountable to God.[13]

Some ministries expect their minister to be a "hired hand"—someone who will do all the work (regardless of the task). They've "hired themselves a preacher." I (Brad) sat down recently with a discouraged minister, Craig, who shared his disillusionment with his current congregation. He'd been serving faithfully not as a minister of the gospel but as a hired hand. He was the preacher, janitor and gardener, bearing the full responsibility for the church yet not having any of the decision-making authority. Members and members' friends would call him at all hours of the night. When he attempted to delay something until the following morning, he was reminded he was hired to attend to their needs. Congregational leadership worked their hired hand according to unrealistic and unhealthy expectations while his children ate on the reduced-lunch program at school.

While some ministries exist to this extreme, the rest of us can likely pursue healthy changes to our present situation by educating those we serve about reasonable expectations. People often expect of their minister far more than what's actually spelled out in the job description. It's important to identify their expectations so we can discuss which are reasonable and unreasonable. We can negotiate reasonable alternatives and create priorities consistent with our personal purpose statement, altering them only in the case of a true emergency. And although we might assume people will be against such a conversation, that's not necessarily true.

Like every other minister, we want people to like us and to appreciate our ministry. The folks we lead, however, don't need a people-pleasing minister. They need a minister with the backbone to follow God's calling no matter what. Moses discovered this the hard way.

---

[13]James Hamilton, *The Pair in Your Parsonage* (Kansas City: Beacon Hill, 1982), p. 10.

When spies returned from the Promised Land with a negative report, Moses allowed the people to decide not to go into the land, angering God and resulting in forty years of wandering in the desert. Doing the right thing by our family, our ministry and our God is more important than trying to cater to the ever-changing expectations of others.

What do you think are some of your organization's unwritten expectations of you as its minister?

How do you typically handle these expectations? What ways might you better handle them?

"NOT CALLED" ACTIVITY HARMS EVERYBODY

Serving outside of our calling will have adverse effects on us, our family and everyone else within our ministry. One day, Moses received a visit from Jethro, his father-in-law. We don't really know, but maybe Moses' wife complained to her dad about how much time Moses spent doing "God stuff" and how little time he spent at home. Like many other busy ministry professionals, perhaps Moses was too exhausted when he arrived home to carry on an intelligent conversation with her. In any case, Jethro vocalized his concern about how exhausted Moses appeared:

> What you are doing is not good. You and these people who come to you will only wear yourselves out. The work is too heavy for you; you cannot handle it alone. . . . Select capable men from all the people—men who fear God, trustworthy men who hate dishonest gain—and appoint them as officials over thousands, hundreds, fifties and tens. Have them serve as judges for the people at all times, but have them bring every difficult case to you; the simple cases they can decide themselves. That will make your load lighter, because they will share it with you. If you do this and God so commands, you will be able to stand the strain, and all these people will go home satisfied. (Exodus 18:17-23)

Like Moses, we can't do it alone. We'll wear ourselves out, and our people will become exhausted too. Our ministry isn't receiving our best if we're spending time working in areas we aren't suited for. We can get others involved in the process by teaching them how to do things. We can then take on the duties only we are equipped to do and let others handle the rest.

Those serving in small ministry settings (especially the single-staffed variety) have to work as generalists and don't have the luxury of specialization. In such cases, lay leadership can and should be developed to fill roles and duties that don't line up with our areas of giftedness. If we're not good at numbers and accounting, we might find a volunteer to keep the books or hire a specialized person from a temp agency for a few hours per month. If the only mouse we're familiar with lives in a hole in the wall, we might search for a layperson to manage the ministry's website. It's not wise to try to do it all by ourselves. Instead, we can pray for God to bring others along to help us and stop feeling guilty for asking others for help.

Working too far outside our calling often leads to potential disaster—both for us and everyone else in our ministry. As emotional trials set in, we will begin resenting our work, our coworkers and our volunteers, eventually leading to frustration, exhaustion and burnout. We may even become self-absorbed and seek relief by entertaining any number of destructive behaviors. It's not worth it.

In what ways are you currently operating outside your capacity and giftedness?

What practical steps might you take to help alleviate this?

4. Staying Versus Leaving: Called to Remain or Move Toward a New Assignment?

Transience is a reality in ministry. While many ministers would like to take root and remain in one place for a lifetime, many ministers (and many ministries) don't equip for long-term partnership. On one hand, pastors who keep a two- or three-year set of sermon files set themselves up for a move by simply repeating old stuff while never challenging themselves on new material. Such decisions stunt real growth, both personally and corporately. On the other hand, some ministries find it easier to get rid of a minister than to embrace change and new ideas. The attitude of "we were here before him and we'll be here long after" permeates a culture of stagnancy. Parachurch organizations sometimes grow and change focus in ways that are inconsistent with our passion or calling. Whatever the reason, we must sometimes contemplate the difficult decision of staying versus moving on.

Over the years, we've witnessed an increasing number of forced exits by ministers. Cliff Tharp of the Southern Baptist Convention's Research Services Department cites the two most frequent reasons for forced exits in his denomination: a small but powerful minority of members (66 percent) and factions in the congregation (41 percent). Half of the ministers in the survey had been forced out within three years of their arrival, and 78 percent of the churches had terminated previous ministers. Additionally, nearly 60 percent of the ministers said they were unaware of the church's history of forced terminations when they arrived.[14]

One of the greatest stressors in Christian ministry is navigating conflict-infested waters. Many ministers today suffer from unresolved conflict. The reality that "we may only be one business or board meeting away from unemployment" encourages us to be watchful for signs. Sometimes, we'll be oblivious to the indicators that a problem is brewing. Ministers are often the last to find out strategic information. While the following isn't intended to be an exhaustive list of potential "warning signs" that conflict is stirring, at least it might serve as a good reference point.

WARNING SIGNS OF A COMING STORM

The best way to head off potential conflict is awareness and a willingness to attempt proactive resolution. Conflict doesn't resolve itself, and we shouldn't fool ourselves into thinking it can't happen to us. It doesn't just happen to the young and inexperienced; it can happen to anyone.

While ministries are never complaint-free, we should pay attention to frequent complaints. We're certainly never going to please everyone. Yet we should become keenly aware of both the content and source of the complaints. Are they valid? Are they pointless and baseless? Generic, unfounded complaints may foreshadow real, more fundamental conflicts looming on the horizon. Notice especially when differences begin to surface over direction or vision.

We can also be aware of when people unexpectedly withdraw from us—either a physical distancing or an emotional retreat. Are our friendships showing signs of strain? Are people less available to us? Are people behaving differently around us?

Monitor drops in regular giving, attendance or utilization of min-

---

[14]Clifford J. Tharp Jr., "A Study of the Forced-Termination of Southern Baptist Ministers," *Quarterly Review,* October-December 1985.

istry services. Beware of basing effectiveness on attendance or giving, since success in ministry can't always be measured by quantifiable statistics. However, if significant individuals or families are no longer participating, or if people are coming to some functions but skipping worship, such changes might merit further investigation. Is there a silent group "voting with their pocketbooks" by withholding contributions? While there may be numerous reasons for attendance and giving fluctuations, we would be wise to discern anything noticeable.

On reflection, have you noticed any of these warning signs in your present ministry location?

Are there other trends or patterns not mentioned here that cause you concern?

What might be the best way to respond at this time?

SHOULD I STAY OR SHOULD I GO?

That church leader knew better than to catch you just before you began service, but he was upset: he'd just heard from someone else moments earlier that Ms. Jenkins hadn't been visited last week. There simply wasn't enough time with two funerals, eight hospital calls, four counseling sessions, four committee meetings and three sermons. With all the phone calls and other interruptions of the week, you wanted to see her but you had other "squeakier wheels." The conversation single-handedly drained your excitement about the morning's sermon.

Then there was that phone call late Sunday night about something that happened in the nursery. Susie didn't show up to work and so Mrs. Johnson had to step out of the service to watch three children in the nursery. She was beside herself, feeling Susie didn't take her job seriously and should have been more considerate to call. But there was more. Mrs. Johnson went on about the condition of the nursery. She complained about dirty toys and some sheets that hadn't been changed. There was also garbage in the can that should have been taken out after the morning service. Evidently, Mrs. Johnson wanted you to resolve this "major" problem right then.

The reasons for a ministry change ought to be more than the

Monday morning blues. There are, in fact, times when God's move-ment in our lives necessitates that we reevaluate the geography and function of our ministry. Legitimate reasons for considering a move might include (but certainly aren't limited to) a lack of sustaining support by the organization; when our personal or spiritual health or that of our family is jeopardized by staying, vision incompatibility between leader and organization; an inability to fulfill our unique calling in our current ministry; and when organizational expecta-tions prevent us from authentically being who we are.

We should think twice if we're packing our bags just because of personality issues. We sometimes make the mistake of believing that another place with different people will make the difference in liv-ing out our ministry dreams. The truth is, there's a Mrs. Johnson at every church. Within every location we find a variety of personalities. Some will be easier to get along with than others. Our challenge is to learn to effectively minister to all kinds of personalities.

It's also not advisable to pack our bags when we're tired, mad, frustrated or overwhelmed. Ministers make poor decisions when they're in crisis, acting on the whims of emotion rather than the un-derstanding of facts. We should make decisions only when we're well-rested and after significant times of prayer. This allows for op-portunity to hear God's voice from our heart rather than merely the voice of frustration in our head.

Also, it's a bad idea to pack our bags just to get even or "punish" certain people. Doing so ensures that we'll just relocate our anger to another ministry placement, entering our new assignment with a heavy burden on our back. Better to constructively work out differ-ences where we are and attempt to negotiate positive change. We may also distinguish minor nuisances of our job from the major is-sues or complaints we have regarding our current ministry position.

How often do you experience the "Monday morning blues"? To what do you attribute such feelings?

What are some of the persistent "minor nuisances" disrupting your present ministry?

To what extent are they having undue influence on your sense of calling?

With what major issues are you currently struggling in your ministry?

What would you consider legitimate reasons for leaving one place of ministry in search of another?

HELP IN MOVING ON

It's one thing to question staying; it is an entirely more serious issue to make the decision to move on. Leaving or preparing to leave a ministry location is a significant step and should not be taken lightly. It requires honest reflection, including significant feedback from our intimate relationships.

I (Brad) will never forget the advice given by a friend years ago. I was told there are two types of ministers: builders and battlers. Builders are those called to carry an organization to the next level. Many people attend their conferences and buy their "How to Be Successful in Ministry" books, wanting to be just as successful and dynamic as they are. Battlers, on the other hand, are perhaps best viewed as those ministers who prepare a ministry organization for future change—and for a future leader (a builder) who will take them to the next level in ministry. While the builder may reap external growth, the battler will challenge the system and more often promote internal growth of character. Their reward is often only the scars of conflicts waged on behalf of the ministry.

God calls and uses both builders and battlers. But we might ask ourselves, do we sense that God has called us to be a builder or a battler—one who challenges the system or one who expands the territory?

The following questions can help us discover whether God is directing us toward our next place of service. If God is clear in answering these, it's a good sign he's preparing us and our family for a new place of ministry. If God is silent, we might want to delay or reconsider our decision.

Are We Spiritually Discontent?

God sometimes uses spiritual discontent to prepare ministers for change. We can be in the very center of God's geographical and occupational calling and yet experience an overwhelming sense of discontent. Such discontent is not to be taken as discouragement, but a present lack of fulfillment. God may be in the process of preparing us for a move. This doesn't necessarily make where we are a wrong place for us at that moment. It may only be a temporary stop along the journey. It has a purpose in God's greater plan.

Elijah's experience is a great example of spiritual discontent (1 Kings 17:1-9). He was right where God called him, yet God allowed the brook to dry up and the provisions to disappear. In his discontent, God was preparing him for the next place in his life. He would soon be directed to a widow, where he was to discover a unique provision God had for him—in addition to his next assignment.

During a season of spiritual discontent, God may place vision, expectations and relationships on hold, causing our heart to contemplate future potential. This isn't about dissatisfaction with God or his provision. God may be preparing our heart to embrace something new.

What Has God Been Speaking to Us About?

Scripture plays a prominent role in the discernment of God's calling. What themes have been prevalent in our personal study? We might listen intently when our personal time centers on a theme that seems to prepare us for transition. We're not advocating proof texting or pulling something out of Scripture that's not there. Keeping and reviewing a spiritual journal and paying attention to our circumstance as it relates to what God has been teaching us can also be greatly insightful.

Do We Possess a Consuming New Passion?

As God prepares us for a move, he might place an unusual and even unexplainable passion in our heart. This could be a burden for a new geographical area, people group or type of ministry. God may be creating new vision that cannot be accomplished where we currently serve. God won't likely release us from the vision until we've successfully made such a transition.

Is There an Open Door?

Has another door opened recently? This could be God's new opportunity. But just because a door opens doesn't mean God opened it. Either way, such an opening can be a matter for significant prayer and even fasting.

Can we live out our unique passion and capacity in this new opportunity? This is an important question. God made us and knows the passions within our heart. He will provide opportunity to express our capacity and to fulfill our overriding passion.

We can create honest dialogue with our intimate relationships about these opportunities as they present themselves. Mentors, ministry coaches, spiritual directors, supervisors, pastors, close friends and our spouse all may have beneficial insight on our situation. Not

only may they be spiritually insightful, they also care about us and often may have better objectivity about our lives. Each relationship can
provide a nugget of wisdom from that relationship's unique vantage
point, proving the wisdom of many counselors (Proverbs 11:14). If
the people closest to us are highly concerned about a door that's
opened to us, we just might have our answer! Nonetheless,we should
still keep watch, because new doors aren't always the openings we
would have sought on our own. Sometimes God opens doors we
wouldn't expect.

*Considering the questions above, describe anything that you recognize might
indicate God could be leading you in a new ministry direction.*

What are your intimate human relationships saying during this time?

Where else could you turn to more fully discern God's will?

MOVING FROM "BAD TO WORSE" OR FROM "GOOD TO BETTER"?

Without a clear sense of knowing, our wisest option is to remain
where we are until God clearly leads us elsewhere. A move takes a
tremendous emotional toll on a family. This is especially true for
children, who do best where relationships are relatively constant. If
you're plagued by symptoms of burnout (such as feeling tired, exhausted, stressed, overwhelmed, bored, depressed or conflicted), the
best answer may be to stay put for the short term.

Instead of leaving outright, consider taking a few extra days off or
even taking a sabbatical. If we're going to thrive in our current ministry position, we'll want to take time to communicate our calling to
our key leadership and those we lead by comparing our call and giftedness with our present performance expectations. This would be a
good time to address any unwritten people expectations we're aware
of, too. We can dialogue about our strengths and create ways to compensate for our weaknesses by bringing others with differing giftedness alongside to complement us. Most people in leadership are willing to do what's necessary to help their people be effective.

If after taking an honest inventory of ourselves we're confident
God is moving us elsewhere, we'll want to consider reasonable ex-

pectations for our future ministry placement. We might review our current position description: are our current performance expectations acceptable, given our experience since we agreed to them? If not, what modifications might we require for our next ministry placement?

It's always best to negotiate position descriptions and goals with a ministry who is considering us *before* accepting the new assignment. If a ministry organization is unwilling to negotiate healthy expectations, the position isn't a good fit. We can ensure every item is reasonable and attainable by talking though each point and asking for clarification when needed. If the duties expected are unreasonable (especially when compared with our personal purpose statement and goals), we can attempt to negotiate a more realistic set of expectations or politely decline the opportunity.

We might also consider expanding the position description we're exploring into a covenant agreement with the prospective organization. Rather than settling for a one-sided list of expectations, we could explore an agreement on the expectations each side has for the other—both what the ministry expects of us and what we expect from individuals within the ministry and from the larger, corporate body. A covenant creates a two-way street of expectations everyone can agree to and follow.

List the items you might include in a covenant with a future ministry in order for it to be considered a "good fit."

What's the biggest reason you might hesitate to negotiate more reasonable expectations with your current ministry organization? How might you overcome this?

"Could I spend a lifetime in ministry here?" It's a big question. Here are some things to ponder related to tenured ministry.

Sustainable growth takes time; it doesn't just happen overnight. Why have many of the "fastest growing churches" of the past now plateaued, declined or even ceased to exist? A pastor leaves and the charisma evaporates because the emphasis was placed on the caricature behind the pulpit rather than the character in the pew. By contrast, real growth is realized one transformation at a time, compounded over time.

There are no miracle cures for organizational effectiveness where imperfect people are involved. If what the ministry needs is stability and consistency, are we willing to stick around and help lead the organization through to greater health?

The ability for substantive influence is earned over time. The seasons of the year are a fitting metaphor for the seasons we go through in ministry, in our relationships and in our tenure with a particular organization. Each goes through cycles of birth, life, decline, death and rebirth. To know a person or organization fully requires the cycling of many "seasons" of ministry together. True influence takes more than a single season: "The plain truth is that the shorter the period of time a pastor has in which to operate, the less impact he is likely to have in that ministry."[15] Leadership experts have suggested that it may take anywhere from three to seven years to begin to have significant long-term impact.

What would it take for you to consider remaining in your present ministry location for the next few years?

How might your influence increase over the long term if you remained?

What are the indications that God might be leading you to remain for an extended tenure?

---

[15]Gary L. Pinion, *Crushed: The Perilous Journey Called Ministry* (Springfield, Mo.: 21st Century Press, 2006), p. 167.

Wrap-Up:
Foundation Stone 2—Calling

Use the space below to record your most important takeaways from the foundation stone of *calling*.

Look back on page 79 to the questions related to "what you really want" and "areas of passion." Briefly summarize your answers here.

Look back on page 84 to the "key words and phrases" you considered including in your personal purpose statement. Briefly summarize your answers here.

Based on your answers to the previous questions, take a separate sheet of paper and write out a few initial possibilities for your personal purpose statement. Remember, there are no rules—it can be long or short; simple or complex; a sentence, paragraph or even a list of bullet points. The only criteria is that it be a true reflection of who God created you to be—*your* passions, *your* gifts, *your* heart for ministry. Once you've created an initial personal purpose statement, share it with two or three of your most intimate relationships and get their feedback. Listen for the "kernel of truth" in their criticism, making adjustments to your statement based upon your own convictions. Use the space below for any feedback you consider particularly helpful.

Remember that no one can ultimately judge your purpose statement: "They are responsible to the Lord, so let him judge whether they are right or wrong" (Romans 14:4 NLT). Graciously accept both positive and negative feedback, but realize this is your *personal* purpose statement. Consider modifying your statement in light of the feedback you received. Write the revised version here.

Return to this page after the completion of each subsequent foundation stone. Ask the Holy Spirit to clarify or confirm the fit of your personal purpose statement in light of your maturing through this process.

MY REVISED PURPOSE STATEMENT

After Foundation Stone 3 (Stress Management):

After Foundation Stone 4 (Boundaries):

After Foundation Stone 5 (Re-creation):

After Foundation Stone 6 (People Skills):

After Foundation Stone 7 (Leadership Skills):

3

STRESS MANAGEMENT

Avoiding Ineffectiveness and Burnout

There isn't a place on earth we won't find stress. Regardless of our occupation, age, economic status or geographic location, it's an integral part of the human experience. Most people think of stress as a bad thing, but this is due to an unfortunate misunderstanding about its very nature. Stress isn't the real problem; rather, it's the mismanagement of stress that wreaks havoc on so many ministers.

1. Stress: The Energy to Accomplish Our Calling

Stress is actually a necessary component of life, a biological response to environmental pressures. When life becomes difficult, the body compensates with a variety of changes that are designed to help us meet the physical demands of a given crisis. Increased heart rate, dilated pupils and increased blood pressure are all examples of such physical responses. The body also steps up its production of adrenaline, the hormone responsible for our ability to react more quickly and efficiently to the pressures of our environment—sometimes called the "fight or flight" mechanism.

Perhaps God knew we would need such a mechanism to handle aspects of life after the Fall. From a young girl running late for the school bus to a minister preparing for a big budget meeting to a firefighter rescuing someone from a burning building, stress is the trigger that propels us toward the attainment of a goal. Our body's stress response is a blessing; without it, we would likely aspire to very little in life.

Interestingly enough, too little stress in our lives is just as big a problem as too much stress. When stress is harnessed and managed

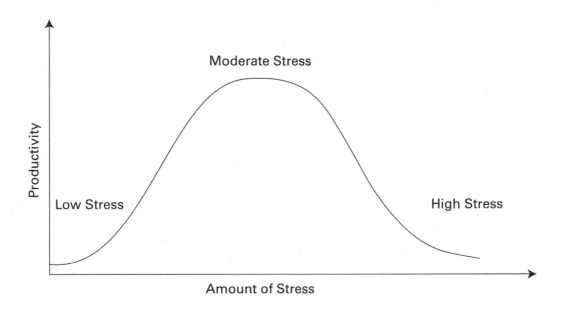

Figure 3.1. Stress versus productivity.

properly, it becomes the energy that allows us to focus singularly on accomplishing great things consistent with our calling. Figure 3.1 is helpful in understanding this principle.

Too *little* stress and we'll lack sufficient motivation to accomplish our calling; too *much* stress and we'll likely feel overwhelmed, leading to decreased effectiveness. That's why we need good stress-management skills. It's the lack of skills for managing stress that ultimately causes fatigue and burnout.

What circumstances are causing the most stress for you right now? Consider things from all areas of your life, including ministry, marriage, children, community, family, finances, health, friendships, etc.

Where would you place yourself on the bell curve based on your current stress level (circle one)?

Low   Low-Moderate   Moderate   Moderate-High   High

DISTRESS: TOO MUCH OF A GOOD THING

Lots of things in our lives contribute to increased stress: phone calls, e-mail, voicemails, environmental noise, children's schedules and a

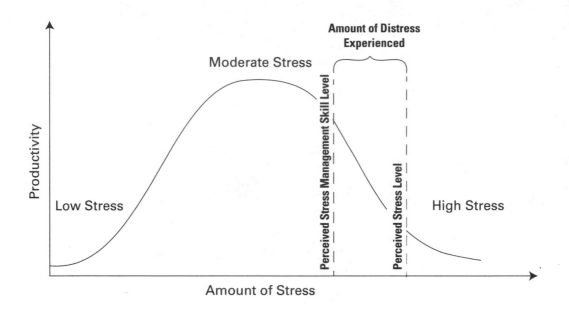

Figure 3.2. Distress.

seemingly endless array of choices in our daily routine. Add to this the unique stress ministers face: meetings with disgruntled people, emotional hospital visits or counseling sessions, weddings and funerals, staying under budget, managing staff (and volunteers!), casting vision and maintaining focus on our personal walk with God. These variables and many others are stressful for ministers. When our amount of stress exceeds our perceived skills to manage that stress, we experience *distress*—the emotional state of feeling unable to handle the load (see figure 3.2).

Our perception has a significant impact on our overall ability to handle stress. Not only do we need the skill to handle stress, we also must *perceive* our own ability to handle it. Lack of confidence in handling stress is just as problematic as not having the actual skills to manage it.

On the graph in figure 3.3 on the next page, draw a vertical line where you feel your current *stress level* is. Label this line "perceived stress." Draw another vertical line where you feel your current stress-management *skills* are. Label this line "perceived skills." The difference is a visual representation of the distress you may currently feel.

How does thinking about your feelings of distress impact your understanding of your current ministry environment?

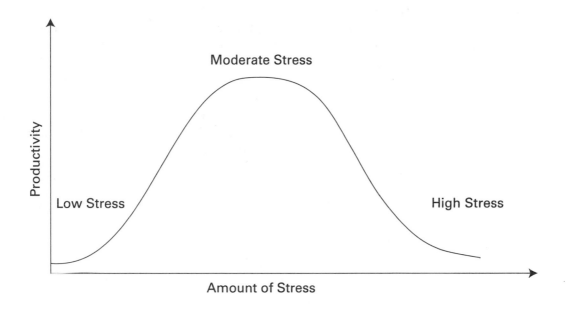

Figure 3.3. Your current stress level.

Most ministers are probably aware of many of the life circumstances that tend to add stress to their lives. However, underlying factors in our lifestyle or personality may also contribute significantly to our level of distress.

Unhealthy Need for Accomplishment

It's deeply satisfying to accomplish goals consistent with our sense of calling. Unfortunately, we sometimes allow the attainment of our goals to supersede our calling. We begin pursuing accomplishments as an end unto themselves rather than pursuing the One for whom such accomplishments were intended as an act of worship. Such idolatry requires greater and greater accomplishments to feel good about ourselves—a condition that will almost certainly lead to distress and eventual burnout.

Unhealthy Desire for Approval from Others

We all appreciate a good "attaboy" or "attagirl" every now and again. However, we may sometimes place so much focus on others' approval that we begin to define our goals by others' opinions rather than God's—even at the expense of following our unique calling. Trying to please everyone is not only impossible, it's also inconsistent with the life of faith (Galatians 1:10).

Perfectionism and Drivenness

The internal desire for personal accomplishment and the desire for others' approval frequently lead to perfectionism, a lifestyle pattern often established in childhood. Perfectionism is an internal standard of "rightness" we establish as a benchmark for everything we do. Perfectionistic thinking often leads to drivenness, the external compulsion of feeling that "enough is not enough" or of redoing a "good enough" project multiple times until we perceive it's done "right" by our internal plumb line. To the extent that we haven't done enough or gotten something right, we will experience anxiety and even fear.

Have any of your intimate relationships (God, spouse, close friends, colleagues, etc.) expressed concerns about your stress level or how you've been handling stress? What concerns have they brought to your attention?

To what extent do you feel their concerns are valid?

What changes could you make that might address their legitimate concerns?

A GLIMPSE AT THE GOAL

Drivenness is qualitatively different from the gentle leading of the Holy Spirit, which doesn't produce anxiety and distress (Matthew 6:32-33; Philippians 4:6-7). When we're led by the Spirit, we will rarely experience a difference between our perceived stress and stress-management skills. For certain, there are times we will labor under more stress than we can legitimately handle in our own strength. However, the Holy Spirit offers us strength and wisdom to make up for what is lacking in our time of need, empowering us to act accordingly by faith (see figure 3.4).

We don't have to be in denial about our amount of stress; instead we can echo Paul's heartfelt prison cry, "I can do everything through him who gives me strength" (Philippians 4:13). We can also surround ourselves with a healthy spiritual community that supports us, encourages us and reminds us of the Spirit's power in the midst of our own human weakness.

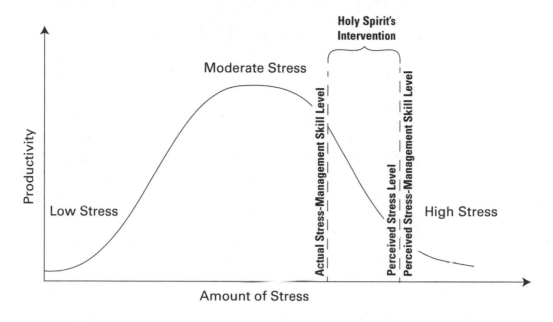

Figure 3.4. Stress and the Holy Spirit.

Which of the above personality traits explained above do you recognize in your own lifestyle? (Check all that apply.)

☐ *Unhealthy need for accomplishment*

☐ *Unhealthy desire for the approval of others*

☐ *Perfectionism*

☐ *Drivenness*

What areas of your life and/or ministry do you find most difficult to surrender to God?

What do you find difficult about surrendering these areas to God?

How might you more actively surrender to God in your present situation?

2. The Energy Drain of Stress Mismanagement

According to a survey taken by Focus on the Family's Parsonage website in April 2002, almost half of the ministers admitted experiencing depression or burnout to the extent that a leave of absence from ministry was required.[1] While most ministers are aware that spiritual deficiencies such as prayerlessness, unconfessed sin and pride lead to problems in ministry, many are not aware how physical and emotional deficiencies lead to similar problems. Consequently, we may sometimes assume we're struggling with personal sin or spiritual warfare when we're really just experiencing a sap of physical or emotional energy that's having a spillover effect spiritually. If clear spiritual roots aren't evident, it may well be traceable to problems of stress mismanagement.

Seventy-five to ninety percent of all visits to primary care physicians are for stress-related complaints or conditions.

HOW DISTRESS MAKES US SICK

In his book *Stress Management for Dummies,* Allen Elkin cites research estimating that 75 to 90 percent of all visits to primary care physicians are for stress-related complaints or conditions.[2] What would you suppose is the number one diagnosis of adults presenting with chest pains in America's emergency rooms? Heart attack? Hardly. The answer is stress-related anxiety. However, mismanagement of stress and untreated anxiety can eventually lead to a heart attack if they remain unaddressed.

Other documented consequences of stress mismanagement include muscular tension, muscle spasms, teeth grinding, tremors, headaches, chest pain, back pain, coronary heart disease, stroke, high blood pressure, high cholesterol, heart arrhythmia, constipation, diarrhea, gas, bloating, unwanted weight gain/loss, sleep disturbance, gastroesophageal reflux disease (GERD), irritable bowel syndrome, colitis, stomach ulcers, lack of sexual desire and sexual impotence. And this is only a partial list! Mismanaged stress may also play a role in the compromise of our immune system. While it might not play the primary role in such medical conditions, how well we manage stress may "tip the balance" in whether our body is able to fight the primary cause of these conditions. In some cases, prolonged stress mismanagement could actually be the primary catalyst.

Nonphysical symptoms that may also signal stress mismanage-

---

[1]H. B. London Jr. and Neil B. Wiseman, *Pastors at Greater Risk* (Ventura, Calif.: Regal, 2003), p. 172.

[2]Allen Elkin, *Stress Management for Dummies* (Forest City, Calif.: IDG Books Worldwide, 1999), p. 17.

ment include fatigue, feelings of helplessness or hopelessness, irritability, angry outbursts, nervousness, worrisome thoughts, impatience, sadness, forgetfulness, misplacing things, intrusive thoughts, feelings of restlessness, poor concentration, crying spells and even suicidal thoughts. These symptoms can also be related to a variety of mental health conditions, including clinical depression. Talking to a family physician or a competent Christian counselor could be the first step to alleviating the problem and getting back to a healthier place.

These lists are not exhaustive, but they do illustrate an important point: stress mismanagement affects every aspect of our life. Unless we choose to get it under control, it can have a devastating effect on our ministry.

Which of the following physical symptoms have impacted you at any time in the past? (Check all that apply.)

☐ Acid Reflux	☐ Headaches	☐ Sleep Disturbance
☐ Back Pain	☐ Heart Arrhythmia	☐ Stomach Ulcers
☐ Bloating	☐ High Blood Pressure	☐ Stroke
☐ Chest Pain	☐ High Cholesterol	☐ Teeth Grinding
☐ Colitis	☐ Irritable Bowels	☐ Tics (nervous twitching)
☐ Constipation	☐ Itching	☐ Tremors
☐ Coronary Artery Disease	☐ Lack of Sexual Desire	☐ Weight Gain (significant)
☐ Diarrhea	☐ Muscle Spasms	☐ Weight Loss (unintended)
☐ Erectile Dysfunction	☐ Muscular Tension	☐ _____
☐ Fidgeting	☐ Nail Biting	☐ _____
☐ Gas	☐ Rashes/Hives	

Which of the following nonphysical symptoms have impacted you at any time in the past? (Check all that apply.)

☐ Angry Outbursts	☐ Forgetfulness	☐ Poor Concentration
☐ Boredom	☐ Hopelessness/Helplessness	☐ Restlessness
☐ Change in Work Style	☐ Impatience	☐ Sadness/Depression
☐ Crying Spells	☐ Intrusive Thoughts	☐ Suicidal Thoughts
☐ Cynicism	☐ Irritability	☐ Worrisome Thoughts
☐ Detachment	☐ Misplacing Things	☐ _____
☐ Fatigue	☐ Nervousness	☐ _____

Now go back over each list and circle *any you've experienced in the past month.*

To what extent might mismanaged stress be a contributing factor for the above symptoms?

What could you do to improve your ability to manage these symptoms?

If you are hesitant to consider meeting with a physician or Christian counselor, describe your concerns here.

DRY MINISTRY FLOWS FROM A PARCHED HEART

If part of our responsibility is preaching or teaching, we might want to stop and listen to a recording of something we've done recently. "One of the signs [of a parched heart] is that we have started preaching about the Gospel and the truths of our faith instead of proclaiming them as a living message."[3] Without adequate renewal of body, mind and spirit, boredom will take up residence in our ministry. What once motivated and inspired us will interest us less and less with time. We'll lose the vision of our calling and become fixated on the monotony of the daily grind.

What did you find most motivating about your call when it began?

What things have chipped away at your excitement since that time?

FOR THOSE WHO "THRIVE ON CHAOS"

Over the years we've been working with ministers, a number of them would claim the opposite of what we're describing when it comes to stress. They are the "movers and shakers" of their field, ministers who love getting things done. They often rise to the top and may even lead the fastest growing ministries in America. Others look to them in amazement and desire to emulate their success.

These highly productive clergy are everywhere. They would say, "I love working under high stress because I'm more productive under such conditions. It's like I thrive on chaos." While this may be true to some degree, there may well be a dangerous monster lurking beneath the "type A" personality—namely, an addiction to adrenaline.

---

[3]James Taylor, *Pastors Under Pressure* (Surrey: Day One, 2001), p. 49.

"You mean I can become addicted to my body's own adrenaline?" Unfortunately, yes. Adrenaline is also known as epinephrine, the brain chemical after which the drug morphine was designed. Our natural epinephrine is many times more powerful than morphine. The rush of adrenaline temporarily numbs the body's sense of pain and produces a general sense of excitement most people find pleasurable. This rush of excitement is typically followed by a relaxed state.

There's no problem when this mechanism is triggered only during times of true emergency. Unfortunately, some find the numbing and pleasurable effects of their own brain chemistry so stimulating that they subconsciously create "emergencies" in order to experience the rush of excitement and subsequent relaxed state on demand. It becomes a drug ministers sometimes use for anything from self-medicating pain to creating an artificial zeal for life. And this "happy" drug is readily available in the pharmacy of our own brain.

Given this information on adrenaline addiction, how concerned are you that you may be vulnerable to it?

What evidence is there that you might create "emergencies" in your regular routine as an excuse for an adrenaline rush?

There may well be a dangerous monster lurking beneath the "type A" personality— namely, an addiction to adrenaline.

LIKE A RAT ON A WHEEL: THE ADDICTIVE-COMPULSIVE CYCLE

In addition to the excitement it brings, some use adrenaline to anesthetize emotional pain. They report a euphoric feeling that creates an almost godlike illusion of invincibility, helping them transcend their daily problems. For others, it simply provides an artificial and temporary sense of meaning to life. Frequent and prolonged abuse of adrenaline wears down our system and creates a state of "tolerance"; that is, it will take greater and greater amounts of adrenaline to produce similar results.

This is the very nature of compulsivity and addiction. This is why workaholics are compulsive about work. It's the same reason others may be compulsive about extreme sports, working out, shopping or any of a number of other behaviors. Such behaviors aren't necessarily bad in themselves. But when the primary reason for doing them is to either escape pain or produce pleasure for the purpose of dealing with stress or negative emotions, such behaviors have become compulsive or addictive, and potentially harmful.

Anything done as a means of coping with stress can turn into compulsive behavior. The main differences between healthy coping and a compulsive habit are frequency and intent: "As a dog returns to its vomit, / so fools repeat their folly" (Proverbs 26:11 TNIV). Take any of the items previously listed in this section, turn to it with some frequency to cope with stress, and make your intent to escape from reality and pain—there's likely a compulsion in the making.

The twelve-step community has an acronym—DDRUM—for compulsive/addictive behavior:

- *Destructive.* The behavior causes some level of problems, either for the person engaging in the behavior or for their loved ones.

- *Degenerative.* With time the behavior increases in severity of behavior or consequences.

- *Repetitive.* The behavior is repeated with greater frequency over time.

Anything done as a means of coping with stress can turn into compulsive behavior.

- *Unmanageable.* The person is increasingly unable to control or "manage" the behavior or its consequences.

- *Medicative.* The behavior is a means for medicating negative emotions or relief from stress.

What behaviors in your life most reflect some degree of compulsivity?

How might you see the DDRUM elements manifesting themselves in these behaviors?

Destructive:

Degenerative:

Repetitive:

Unmanageable:

Medicative:

The "medicative" point is frequently overlooked by many who are in denial about their problem. Yet it is the first symptom to manifest when compulsive behaviors begin. Other symptoms from DDRUM simply grow over time. As they do, the compulsive behavior naturally becomes more addictive.

I (Michael Todd) should know, because adrenaline has been my "drug of choice" for as long as I can remember. I used to boast about thriving on chaos, rarely slowing down to breathe. I've never used a street drug in my life, but adrenaline mismanagement has always been an issue for me. My mother used to accuse me of "failing to allow for the red lights on the road of life." I preferred to pack as much into a twenty-four-hour day as humanly possible. When I did slow down, I wouldn't be there long before I sensed the need to rev back up again. I didn't understand that I was detoxing from my addiction to adrenaline and craving a sort of "fix" until I returned to graduate school in the early 1990s and began reading literature about addiction, especially Archibald Hart's *Adrenaline and Stress*. He had a term for this condition: "hurry sickness."[4]

I still find myself at times fighting this old beast. But now there's a difference: I know I don't have to feed it. When I choose to starve the beast, it becomes weaker and is more easily defeated. The reason I know our methods for stress management work is because I've personally found many of them helpful in my own struggle to tame the adrenaline mismanagement monster.

What elements in Michael Todd's story do you recognize in your own life?

Even if you don't think your situation is as serious as what we've just described, consider speaking with a competent Christian counselor who can set you on the road to detox from adrenaline addiction and compulsive busyness (appendix B contains websites for reputable counseling resources as well as helpful related ministries). The first step to change in this area is to *admit a problem exists*. Prayerfully ask God to give you insight into your own behaviors, especially your motivation for doing them. Honestly consider the possibility of your own brand of "hurry sickness" or other forms of addiction to adrenaline.

3. Are You Distressed? Self-Evaluation Tools for the Weary

We don't have to be an adrenaline junkie to suffer from distress. Any minister who's sat at their desk on Monday morning with a glazed

---

[4]Archibald Hart, *Adrenaline and Stress*, rev. ed. (Dallas: Word, 1995), p. 31.

look knows the letdown from a physically, emotionally and spiritually draining weekend of ministry. This scenario (and many others similar to it) is all too common among ministers. As Gordon MacDonald points out in his book *Renewing Your Spiritual Passion,* many of us find ourselves "doing more and enjoying it less."[5] If we pay attention to the symptoms of distress, we can not only address them at their earliest onset but also begin to anticipate and head them off before they start.

KNOWING IS HALF THE BATTLE
Raising our awareness to times of distress is half the battle. The other half, of course, is doing something about it. We need to be honest with ourselves if we're to get a handle on our distress. Depending on our unique circumstances, we may also need to be willing to make some potentially radical choices.

Look back at the two checklists on page 107. How many symptoms (physical and nonphysical) did you circle as having experienced in the past month? Having a few symptoms might be explained by a variety of things. However, more than a few may evidence an overall syndrome of stress mismanagement.

THE HOLMES-RAHE SOCIAL READJUSTMENT RATING SCALE
Many life events are obviously stressful. Others (such as vacation and Christmas) we might not initially consider stressful in a negative sense. However, anything out of our daily routine has the potential for producing stress in our lives. The Holmes-Rahe Social Readjustment Rating Scale (appendix C) is a helpful tool that enables us to see the various life circumstances that produce stress. Each life event is given a numerical value based on its level of stress ranking. Researchers have determined the likelihood a person will contract a stress-related illness within the next two years, based on the total score over the past twelve-months.

Complete the "Life Stress Inventory" from appendix C. Enter your total score here: _____. Were you surprised at your overall score? Why or why not?

What significant life events from the list do you anticipate over the next few months?

---

[5]Gordon MacDonald, *Renewing Your Spiritual Passion,* rev. ed. (Nashville: Thomas Nelson, 1989), p. 22.

THE "LEVEL OF DISTRESS TEST": A CLOSER LOOK AT PERSONAL DISTRESS

Photocopy the test on pages 113-14. The test is taken in two parts. First, personally respond to each statement, using a scale of 0 to 3:

0 = Rarely/Never do I feel this way
1 = Occasionally/Sometimes I feel this way
2 = More often than not I feel this way
3 = Regularly/Frequently I feel this way

Next, give the photocopied version of the test to your spouse or a close friend (someone who will be *totally honest* with you). Have them rate you on the same items *based on their perception of you*. It doesn't matter if you agree or disagree with their perception. Just ask their honest opinion and accept it with humility (often, others who care for us deeply will see us more objectively than we do). Transfer their responses to the space adjacent to your own responses. Total each score at the bottom of its respective column. You can give this test to other close friends or relatives as well, if you feel you would benefit from a wider perspective of feedback.

The Level of Distress Test

Rating by:

Self   Other

_____ _____ I am exhausted and run down.

_____ _____ I become easily frustrated.

_____ _____ I have a tendency to be overly critical of others and/or myself.

_____ _____ The less time I can spend with people, the better.

_____ _____ If I could change my job, I would.

_____ _____ I am spiritually numb.

_____ _____ I am under constant pressure at work and/or home.

_____ _____ I wonder why I'm even in ministry.

_____ _____ I have no one I can share my problems with.

_____ _____ I find myself spending more time reading, watching TV, sleeping or on the Internet.

_____ _____ I have lost my interest for sex.

_____ _____ I no longer spend time in hobbies I previously enjoyed.

_____ _____ I use alcohol/prescription drugs/sleep aids to manage my moods and/or functioning.

_____ _____ I don't have a clear vision for what God has called me to do.

_____ _____ I feel unappreciated by my family and/or those to whom I minister.

Self   Other

_____   _____   I find myself working more and accomplishing less.

_____   _____   I am enjoying my ministry less with time.

_____   _____   I don't spend time alone with God.

_____   _____   I tend to harbor unresolved resentment or bitterness.

_____   _____   I have become more egotistical or cocky over time.

_____   _____   I feel sorry for myself.

_____   _____   My desk is messy or disorganized.

_____   _____   When I have a few moments to myself, I feel as if I have to be doing something.

_____   _____   When responsibilities demand more time, I cut pleasurable activities to get them done.

_____   _____   I need to feel in control of my surroundings.

_____   _____   I need to keep working on something until it is done right.

_____   _____   I expect things of myself that are far beyond anyone else's expectation of me.

_____   _____   I need to be seen by others as well put together.

_____   _____   My sense of humor is missing.

_____   _____   I am not very flexible.

_____   _____   I have a tendency to set unrealistic goals for myself and/or others.

_____   _____   I have difficulty relaxing.

_____   _____   I rarely take time off; when I do, it's often for being sick.

_____   _____   I tend to be an impulsive person and make decisions hastily.

_____   _____   I hesitate over decisions, not wanting to make a mistake.

_____   _____   I live in the extremes: it's all or nothing with me, with little room for middle ground.

_____   _____   I may appear confident on the outside, but inside I feel insecure.

_____   _____   Others have expressed a concern over my level of stress.

_____   _____   I have activities into which I retreat to avoid negative feelings.

_____   _____   I don't know how I feel.

_____   _____   **Total Score (0–120)**

Even relatively healthy ministers will have a small total, typically less than 40. Larger totals should be reason for concern. We don't want to create an arbitrary cutoff for "health" versus "concern," lest those who score just above or below the threshold ignore the meaning of their scores. Distress that remains unaddressed grows slowly over time. Therefore, the larger the total (no matter your overall score) the more you might want to be concerned about your general level of distress.

How do you believe your score compares with what it might have been twelve months ago? Five years ago? Ten years ago? When you graduated from seminary?

Do you notice any pattern of improvement or decline?

What was the difference between your self-rating and the rating given to you by your spouse or close friend? What do you suppose accounts for their difference in perception?

THE ANGER FACTOR: FUEL FOR THE FIRE

One added factor tends to fuel the fire of distress: unresolved anger. By itself, anger isn't the problem. Anger is an emotion common to the human experience. But unresolved anger—expressing our anger in unhealthy and harmful ways—will eat at us from the inside out.

In *The Anger Workbook*, Les Carter and Frank Minirth describe five types of anger: three effective, two ineffective.[6] Among the ineffective types are suppressive anger (denying angry feelings and stuffing them deep inside, acting as if they don't exist), open aggression (explosive, intimidating, blaming others directly and openly) and passive aggression (manipulative "through the back door" anger directed at others in more quiet or subtle ways). Each of these methods for dealing with anger not only damages relationships but does ongoing emotional damage to the one harboring the anger.

---

[6]Les Carter and Frank Minirth, *The Anger Workbook* (Nashville: Nelson, 1992), p. 24.

Which of the following types of anger are tendencies in your life? (Check all that apply.)

☐ *Suppressive anger*   ☐ *Open aggression*   ☐ *Passive aggression*

What consequences have you seen—both to others and to yourself—when you've chosen to indulge such expressions of anger?

Carter and Minirth identify two alternative methods for dealing with anger more effectively (see Matthew 18:15-22). Assertive anger is accomplished by proactively approaching others and dealing with them directly and honestly about the problem at hand. This method places all the issues on the table in plain view and encourages open dialogue leading to a mutually positive resolution. The second alternative is dropping anger; that is, overlooking the offense or simply letting it go. Pastor Dennis Siebert describes well what dropping anger practically looks like from his own experience and compares it with the mental exercise many confuse with forgiveness:

> One of the things I encountered in a time of personal bitterness was the difficulty of genuinely forgiving. I knew I was bitter and desired to forgive the individual, praying to forgive them many times. What I found happening was that as soon as something negative happened with the individual, I immediately began to re-experience all the old hurt feelings again.
>
> Then someone helped me see that I was only mentally forgiving the individual—merely a mental exercise without real forgiveness from my heart. What I found helpful in making the transition was to recall how I had been hurt, recalling the specific pain the individual had caused me. I then acknowledged and accepted the pain, choosing to release the individual from an expectation of "repaying" me for the injury. Only then did the bitterness begin to lose its hold on my heart.

Which of the alternative responses to angry feelings—assertive anger or overlooking the offense—do you find more difficult to put into practice? What makes this so?

What situations are you facing where one of these methods for resolving anger might be useful?

Resolving anger effectively—either by addressing it assertively or by overlooking the offense—will go a long way in helping us not accumulate additional stress on top of what we already have. Consider *The Anger Workbook* as a resource for practical help in the healthy resolution of anger. To develop other practical skills for resolving conflict directly, we might also suggest *The Peacemaker: A Biblical Guide to Resolving Personal Conflict* by Ken Sande.[7]

4. Practical Safeguards: Spiritual and Relational

Successfully dealing with stress requires both reparative and preventative measures applied over time. While quick fixes are sometimes needed, lifestyle change is more effective long-term. Practical safeguards will not only reduce but, more important, prevent distress.

At their root, all issues related to human suffering and brokenness have a spiritual component. Therefore, it's not surprising there are spiritual safeguards to resolving or preventing distress. While many spiritual safeguards could be discussed, we will consider two: (1) intimate connecting with God through practicing the spiritual disciplines, and (2) living with margin.

THE SPIRITUAL DISCIPLINES: INTIMATE CONNECTING WITH GOD

The first place we should turn in our distress is to God: "From my distress I called upon the Lord; / the Lord answered me and set me in a large place" (Psalm 118:5 NASB). God loves to come through for us, and when he does, he gets the glory (Psalm 50:15).

Two of the three types of spiritual disciplines laid out in Richard Foster's *Celebration of Discipline* are especially helpful for stress management: the inward disciplines (meditation, prayer, fasting, study) and the outward disciplines (simplicity, solitude, submission).[8] One of Foster's corporate disciplines, worship, is also a helpful spiritual safeguard for stress management.

Inward Disciplines
Meditation is simply creating time and mental space to reflect on spiritual truths, whether from Scripture, our prayer lives, nature or our daily circumstances. Being available for God to speak to us throughout

---

[7]Ken Sande, *The Peacemaker: A Biblical Guide to Resolving Personal Conflict*, 3rd ed. (Grand Rapids: Baker, 2004).

[8]Richard Foster, *Celebration of Discipline*, 25th anniv. ed. (San Francisco: HarperSanFrancisco, 1998). The outward discipline of service was left out intentionally.

the day opens our minds to spiritual lessons from God no matter where we are. Even the most seemingly mundane and unlikely time can be the very opportunity God may choose to speak (1 Samuel 3:1-14). I (Michael Todd) have found that frequently asking, "Lord, what are you trying to teach me through this?" has been a revolutionary tool for keeping my heart teachable in circumstances I'd rather not be in.

If during our time in God's Word a passage uses metaphorical language (deer panting, tree by the water, mustard seed, etc.), we can allow our mind to fully explore the metaphor and its application to our life. It can even be helpful to write questions about the passage that provide food for thought throughout the rest of our day, allowing opportunity for ongoing meditation.

Prayer is essential to our intimacy with God. While various faith traditions differ on its role and function, each agrees on its importance. First, prayer changes the one who is praying. The intimacy of prayer promotes the aligning of our heart with God's. In prayer we allow ourselves to become transparent and vulnerable with the One who knows us best. Second, prayer solicits a response from God. Our requests do not fall on deaf ears or to some unconcerned and uninvolved abstract being. God is personal, and he desires relationship with us.

Prayer is our opportunity to share our heart with our heavenly Father, who wants to hear anything and everything that matters to us. When we think of times we've seen a daddy intently listening to the random but heartfelt ramblings of his three-year-old, this is nothing compared with how intently our Daddy hangs on our every word! Through prayer, we have the privilege of sharing our delight in him, our praise to him, our confession with him and our requests from him. He not only patiently listens but also lovingly responds (Matthew 7:7-11).

It seems the program-driven nature of our religious culture has a bigger impact on our lives than we realize. Even our prayer lives can become "functional," with greater emphasis placed on confession and requests to the neglect of our praise and delight in the Lord. Whether we realize it or not, our distress sometimes comes from our own unconscious idolatry. When we place busyness over simple trust in God, we worship at the feet of accomplishment. When we place the demands of others over God's calling on our lives, we bow to the idol of people-pleasing. When we place baptisms, ministry participation, attendance or budgets over faithfully living out our calling no matter the result (even through apparent fruitlessness, like Jeremiah), we become slaves to the god of pride. When idolatry is at the root of our distress, it's only by the forsaking of our idols and resolving to rightly worship that we can lay down our distress before God through prayer.

If we find ourselves too distracted with ministry to spend quality time in prayer, we're simply too busy. By setting aside time for private worship, we allow our emotions to fully participate with our mind as we become lost in God's love for us. Nothing is more important for a Christian leader than sitting before our True Shepherd to receive instruction, direction and strength for the often draining work of ministry. Time with God is one of those items on our schedule we must protect, because no one else will.

Fasting takes on many forms but is primarily about voluntarily setting aside a need or desire for a specific period of time, filling the vacuum instead with meaningful connection with God. Things to consider fasting from include meals or specific foods, forms of entertainment, sex, personal spending and so on. Fasting may be prioritized on a regular basis (one colleague fasts every Wednesday to pray for those he serves), periodically to seek God's guidance on a particular matter (a job transition, for example) or merely as needed (perhaps to reestablish a closer relationship with God).

What has been your experience with fasting?

How might fasting serve you as a spiritual safeguard?

Whether we realize it or not, our distress sometimes comes from our own unconscious idolatry.

Study of Scripture sometimes gets crowded out by the "discipline" of having a "quiet time," which can become a sort of spiritualized busyness. Sometimes it's more beneficial for our soul to approach Scripture with no preconception of what we're looking for, with no agenda other than to hear the Word of God speak (Psalm 42:1). In times like these, we tend to approach Scripture differently and more intensely—much as a lover peers longingly into the eyes of the object of their affection. This is the heart God longs for.

The next time we study Scripture, we might pay close attention to one or two verses of a passage, asking the following:

- Who was this passage originally written to and why?

- How was the ancient reader expected to respond?

- What does this mean for my life, my family or my ministry?

Reflecting on the meaning of each word, we can ask for the Holy Spirit's illumination and application. Commentaries or other trusted resources can provide added insights.

Outward Disciplines

Simplicity is both an inward and an outward discipline. Internally, we focus more on the things God says are important. We do whatever is needed to allow our hearts to let go of desires for things that serve only to clutter our lives: pride, recognition, power, prestige, position, earthly security, money, an apology from a friend, more "toys," a bigger ministry, or whatever else distracts us from simple worship and devotion to God. Such internal simplicity motivates us toward external simplicity, selling or giving away things that are no longer needed or that clutter our lives. Each internal and external decision can be filtered by the knowledge of what's important to us in light of our calling and our intimate relationships.

What internal desires might God be quietly asking you to lay aside?

In what way could doing so lead to greater simplicity?

What external projects, unnecessary obligations or needless possessions might be worth letting go to cultivate a simpler life? What might you do with them?

Solitude is about experiencing God simply through silence. So often we spend our time surrounded by sound. We sometimes just need to "be still" and simply be. Getting away from the noise—both around us and within us—allows the chaos inside us to settle. Solitude is about being alone with God. This may take considerable time, especially as we first begin practicing this discipline. However, we will enter this time more readily and more easily with practice. As with Elijah, God may allow an extended period of silence before he chooses to speak (1 Kings 19:3-9).

Solitude has become a lost discipline for most American Christians:

> Few of us can fully appreciate the terrible conspiracy of noise there is about us, noise that denies us the silence and solitude we need for this cultivation of the inner garden. It would not be hard to believe that the archenemy of God has conspired to sur-

round us at every conceivable point in our lives with the interfering noises of civilization that, when left unmuffled, usually drown out the voice of God. He who walks with God will tell you plainly, God does not ordinarily shout to make Himself heard. As Elijah discovered, God tends to whisper in the garden.[9]

It's only been in the past few years that I (Michael Todd) have become reacquainted with such a wonderful spiritual reservoir of peace and fortitude. For me, there's nothing quite like sitting in my favorite chair in solitude, out on my screened patio early in the morning, coffee cup in hand. The stillness that once was difficult to conceive has now become a godsend.

Solitude isn't intended as a passive experience. In the silence, God sometimes speaks with greatest clarity—or maybe the silence simply gives our spiritual ears better acuity to hear him. We can find a quiet place where we won't be distracted (this may require some effort for ministers with small children) and turn off modern noisemakers such as cell phones and pagers. Our backyard, a local park bench or an empty church sanctuary are but a few possibilities. We may have to find a lonely place on our drive home from the church or office. Being outside in God's creation is a wonderful place to experience solitude with God, but anyplace that has few distractions can potentially be a place for reflection and introspection.

We shouldn't be tempted to fill the emptiness with words to God. Solitude is more about listening than speaking—even speaking to God. In a world full of useless noise, silence is golden. Sitting in the silence allows God to speak (or not speak) as he chooses. Having a journal and pencil handy to write down anything the Lord reveals is also helpful.

Submission "is the ability to lay down the terrible burden of always needing to get our own way."[10] Letting go the need to be right, to get our own way, to have the final word or to be in control offers freedom from worry. Whether it's submission to God, earthly authorities, our spouse, an accountability partner or a fellow believer whom God has provided for our rebuke or reproof, there is liberty in each. Sometimes submission will require letting go our own way to allow theirs; other times, submission will merely mean listening to and taking into account another's point of view before taking the action we think best. Submission is an attitude to cultivate in our hearts and, depending on the unique circumstance, a behavior to live out in our actions.

---

[9]Gordon MacDonald, *Ordering Your Private World*, 2nd ed. (Nashville: Nelson, 1995), p. 126.

[10]Foster, *Celebration of Discipline*, p. 111.

In what relationship(s) could God be leading you to exercise a greater atti-tude of submission?

What might such submission look like in both heart and deed?

The Corporate Discipline of Worship

Worship is a moment in time when we cease being influenced by any-one or anything but God. It's never about the worshiper but about the One being worshiped. Genuine worship invites freedom and in-timacy, and isn't dictated by traditions, rules or expectations—even when traditions are enjoyed within the context of worship. Rather, it's the enjoyment and celebration of the presence of God. The by-product of worship is a renewed spirit.

If our responsibilities include leading others in worship on a reg-ular basis, from time to time we may want to create opportunities to be led ourselves in public worship, either within our own congrega-tion (by allowing someone else to take the lead) or elsewhere (by at-tending another church's worship service). Doing so allows us the opportunity to focus purely on worship rather than being distracted by our own performance mode. It's also important to prioritize mo-ments for getting lost in private worship: "My soul thirsts for God, for the living God. / When can I go and meet with God?" (Psalm 42:2). As a spiritual leader, this must become our burning question. The quality of our public leadership in worship will reflect the quality of our own private worship when no one else is watching.

What are the circumstances and places, both individually and corporately, that most encourage your own worship of God?

MARGIN

None of these spiritual disciplines will amount to much unless we create space for them. This is the idea of *margin,* a term popular-ized by Richard Swenson in his book by the same name.[11] The con-

---

[11]Richard A. Swenson, *Margin: Restoring Emotional, Physical, Financial, and Time Re-serves to Overloaded Lives* (Colorado Springs: NavPress, 2004).

cept of margin is simple: it's the difference between our current level of functioning and full capacity—between how much is "on our plate" and how much we could theoretically handle at any given time.

The average American minister operates with little, if any, degree of margin. In many cases, ministers actually operate with negative margin, or in overload. It can be seen in many contexts: spending more than we earn, eating more than our metabolism can burn, pushing our body time and again beyond exhaustion.

To understand margin, think in terms of holding back a reserve—an extra amount kept back "just in case" it's needed. For example, someone needs money for a mission trip but we're already over budget; we have no "margin." The opportunity is missed. A visitor would like to meet with us during the week, but our schedule is so full we don't have time. The visitor decides to visit another church "where people care." A crisis happens with a relative requiring us to spend hours on the telephone with doctors and hospitals. Because we haven't maintained a "margin" of energy in reserve, we tax our body's immune system and become sick.

Financial margin is "saving for a rainy day." Building margin into our time might mean taking a day off during the week for rest or setting aside an hour a day to return phone calls or to catch up on miscellaneous tasks. Margin is also maintaining energy in reserve that can be tapped into at a moment's notice—at the time when it's most needed.

So why is margin considered a spiritual safeguard? Maintaining margin is really an application of biblical stewardship. What we value flows from our spirituality. Margin allows our spiritual values, rather than the urgencies and emergencies that clutter our lives, to guide the stewardship of our resources. Also, God often uses margin to perform "preventative maintenance" in our lives. If we're constantly running full throttle, it may be only a matter of time before our engine blows from lack of maintenance.

Those familiar with the long-term benefits of margin can attest to the improved quality of life and ministry we, our families and our ministries experience. But often, such margin has to be fought for. Building margin into our lives may require significant changes in lifestyle. Saying "yes" to margin will necessitate our saying "no" to the amount of work, time and money we have become accustomed to "spending."

Describe an experience you've had with adequate margin. How was the quality of life different from life without margin?

What do you perceive gets in the way of applying margin to important areas of your life right now?

What could you do to change this?

How well do you prioritize each of the following on a scale of 1 to 10 (1 = rarely, if ever, prioritized; 10 = most always prioritized):

_____   *Intimate connecting with God (any combination of spiritual disciplines)*

_____   *Margin*

Which of the individual spiritual safeguards mentioned would you most want to improve and why?

What one thing could you change about your lifestyle that might have the greatest impact in the area you just mentioned?

RELATIONAL SAFEGUARDS

In Mark 6, we find Jesus and the disciples engaged in a variety of ministry. Nestled in the midst of all this work, verse 31 might be easily overlooked if we weren't specifically looking for it: "Then, because so many people were coming and going that they did not even have a chance to eat, he said to them, 'Come with me by yourselves to a quiet place and get some rest.'" The three types of relational safeguards we'll discuss are all mentioned here in Mark 6:31.

Prioritizing Downtime

"Get some rest." If we took a mental inventory of our past week, how much of what we did would fit the category of rest? "Six days you shall labor and do all your work, but the seventh day is a Sabbath to the LORD your God. On it you shall not do any work" (Exodus 20:9-10). The principle of Sabbath rest applies to weekend ministers as with the rest of humanity. In a busy schedule, we must create space to ensure adequate rest because it's a restorative activity. We will only restore the energy we expend in the fulfillment of our calling to the extent we prioritize rest.

What does rest do for you personally?

How does the quality of "forced" rest (for example, stress-related sickness) differ from that of proactive rest?

Unplugging from Ministry

"By yourselves to a quiet place." In the midst of a strenuous day of ministry, Jesus encouraged his disciples not to neglect their own personal needs. But there was so much more ministry yet to be done and so many clamoring for their attention. Was Jesus encouraging his disciples to be selfish? "Each of you should look not only to your own interests, but also to the interests of others" (Philippians 2:4). Some ministers mistakenly interpret this verse (and others like it) to say Christians should be all about meeting the needs of others to the detriment of their own needs. Yet, the use of the phrase "not only" presumes the hearer already looks after their own needs. Scripture merely admonishes that the needs of others ought also form part of their concern: "The believer should not neglect the welfare of himself and his family (1 Timothy 5:8) in order to involve himself in the good of others. What Paul is calling for is a Christian concern that is wide enough to include others in its scope. When each member of the Christian community exercises this mutual concern, problems of disunity quickly disappear."[12]

Also, caring for ourselves is actually caring for the temple of the Holy Spirit within us (1 Corinthians 6:19). Self-care and rest are the very things God uses to prepare us for what he has next for us to accomplish.

Plugging into Nurturing Relationships

"Come with me." Jesus invited his disciples not only to get some rest and care for themselves; he invited them to spend time with him and with each other, away from the neediness of the crowd demanding their attention. Some may say, "But there's so much ministry work to be done!" That's true. But here, as in other places in the Gospels, Jesus encouraged relationship (Luke 10:1) and at times even redirected "viable ministry" in favor of connecting relationships (Luke 10:38-42).

---

[12]Homer A. Kent Jr., *The Expositors Bible Commentary,* ed. Frank Gaebelein (Grand Rapids: Zondervan, 1978), 11:122.

The creation story itself suggests the priority God placed on human relationships: "It is not good for the man to be alone" (Genesis 2:18). God designed humans to live in community with one another (Hebrews 10:25). Deep connecting relationships are encouraged (Proverbs 27:17) and accountability shared in such community further serves as an antidote to distress (Ecclesiastes 4:9-10).

As ministers, we are relational people. There are three basic types of relationships: those who primarily give to us, those who primarily take from us, and those who both give and take. The first group consists of *our* ministers; the second, our *ministry*. The third group is the only one we call *friends*. To be filled up ourselves, we must not neglect time with groups one and three. We also function best when we prioritize time to be alone and with God.

Rate yourself on how well you prioritize each of the following on a scale of 1 (rarely, if ever, prioritized) to 10 (most always prioritized):

_____ *Prioritizing Downtime*
_____ *Unplugging from Ministry*
_____ *Plugging into Nurturing Relationships*

Which of these would you want to improve most and why?

What one thing could you change about your lifestyle that might have the greatest impact on the area you just identified?

> *There are three basic types of relationships: those who primarily give to us, those who primarily take from us, and those who both give and take. The first group consists of* **our** *ministers; the second,* **our** ministry. *The third group is the only one we call* **friends.**

5. Practical Safeguards: Emotional and Physical

Ever just feel like you could use a vacation? We don't necessarily have to leave town to gain some of the benefits of a weekend getaway. Yet there's something about actually getting away for more than a long weekend that allows the body, mind and soul to fully let go the worries of day-to-day life. Some people in significant leadership positions report that it takes a *minimum* of one week's vacation before they actually feel relaxed (and that assumes they're not "checking in" with the office!). If this describes us, we may already be well on our way to burnout. We might consider talking with our colleagues or ministry leaders about taking an extended vacation or even a sabbatical from ministry to do some reparative self-care. Otherwise, our body might one day force us to take one through burnout.

EMOTIONAL SAFEGUARDS

There are many ways to build breaks into our lives. We can take frequent five- to ten-minute breaks throughout our workday to get out of our office and take in a breath of fresh air and enjoy the sun; call our spouse or kids and ask about their day or just tell them "I love you"; call a close friend just for a quick check-in; or simply kick back in our chair, prop our feet on the desk and daydream about the beach or a favorite vacation spot. The mind is a powerfully creative "muscle" that can create very real experiences, powerful enough for our body to respond by relaxing.

Another favorite minivacation for some is to turn up some favorite tunes in the office. Music is a language of the soul and is composed to elicit an emotional response from the listener. If classical, big band or inspirational music is your thing, try this experiment: stop what you're doing, close your eyes, turn on some of your favorite tunes, and allow yourself to completely take in the sounds along with any feelings that may accompany them. Allow the music to sink in and stir your emotions. If you enjoy Christian music, allow your mind to meditate on the lyrics, allowing God to touch your soul in a way only spiritual music can.

When was the last time you took
    (1) a sabbatical or vacation longer than one week?
    (2) a full week's vacation?
    (3) a long weekend getaway?
    (4) a day off?

How could you integrate "minivacations" into your work routine?

What role might music play in any future "minivacations"?

Paradigm Shifts: A New Point of View

Sometimes, distress is partly the result of our own "stuck" way of thinking about the challenges we face. No one is completely objective in that we see the world. Our difficulties often stem from our own points of view—our paradigm. It can be beneficial to invite others to help us gain fresh perspective on our situation. To accomplish this, we will want a community of others in whom we can confide (intimacy). We'll also want to be willing to listen to someone else's point of view, being secure enough in who God created us to be (our calling) that we can accept their feedback without feeling judged or becoming judgmental ourselves. "Plans fail for lack of counsel, / but with many advisers they succeed" (Proverbs 15:22). We may find the perspectives of godly friends, family and colleagues can create a shift in our viewpoint that helps us become unstuck and see an effective solution to a situation.

Another paradigm shift is godly self-talk. If distress inhibits our ability to think creatively, we can ask the Holy Spirit to bring Scriptures to mind that apply to our situation. When combined with a life of prayer, godly self-talk becomes a powerful tool for telling ourselves the truth.

For example, let's say I (Michael Todd) was struggling with reduced productivity and emotional anxiety over our ministry's lack of income. Having the confidence that God called me to this particular work and knowing God has historically provided in his timing (and often not a moment sooner!), I might engage in godly self-talk like this: "Right now I acknowledge I'm very stressed about our ministry's financial situation. It's causing me to be very distracted. Now Michael Todd, you know with certainty God called you to this work, so don't let yourself get too focused on the crashing waves around you when you're sure Christ is calling you to walk on top of them (Matthew 14:25-33). Have faith in the One who called you, for he is indeed faithful (2 Timothy 2:13). He's provided for the ministry's needs thus far under very similar circumstances. You have no reason to believe he won't continue because he's promised to care for his own (Psalm 37:25; Matthew 6:25-34). Just be obedient to the last thing God called you to do and trust him (2 Kings 5:10-14). It's his ministry, anyway (Matthew 25:14-30). He's able to provide for it much more than you ever could (Matthew 7:9-11)."

There's great benefit in regularly reminding ourselves of God's past faithfulness in our lives. Joshua and the priests of Israel created a monument to remind the people of God's miraculous provision for them (Joshua 4:4-7). Those big rocks from the bottom of the Jordan River would serve as proof of God's faithfulness, especially during times of hardship when they would be tempted to lose faith. We may need to create some "stones of remembrance" to remind us of God's provision in our own lives, encouraging us to remain faithful and not lose heart. A photo from a mission trip on our wall, a twelve-step chip in our pocket or a bracelet that belonged to our prayerful grandmother are a few simple examples of physical reminders of God's faithful provision for us in our times of need.

Who in your life would you trust to help you with a paradigm shift on your present situation?

What Scriptures have been personally helpful in getting yourself creatively unstuck?

What "stones of remembrance" do you currently have set up to remind you of God's past faithfulness? If you don't have any, what might serve as such a monument?

Organized Work Habits

No one wants to operate at less than their full potential. Unfortunately, many think the harder they work the more results they'll get. But there's a point where more time and greater effort suffer from the law of diminishing returns, where more investment produces *fewer* results. We become like a rat on a wheel, running and running but getting nowhere.

It can be helpful to periodically examine the efficiency of our work habits. Poor work habits can significantly add to our sense of frustration. Ministers have to juggle many responsibilities and frequently function in a variety of roles. CEO, CFO, secretary, janitor, counselor, funeral director, wedding coordinator, marketing specialist and "chief bottle washer" are only a few of the many "hats" ministers sometimes have to wear on any given day. Anything to help us keep straight the tasks needing attention can be worth its weight in gold.

Many helpful aids exist these days, such as a day planner or handheld organizer, to help us keep on task with what matters most to us and our ministry. A wall calendar enables a quick glance at what obligations we have in the coming weeks and months. A chat with the manager of the local office supply store could yield a high return in organizing our lives to work smarter or more efficiently. Talking with other ministers can alert us to effective methods for keeping a handle on ministry obligations. It's also a great way to create relationship with peers who could potentially become friends, paving the way for greater intimacy in our lives.

What organizational tools do you currently find helpful?

What other tools might you consider for improving your ministry's efficiency?

Rate yourself on how well you prioritize each of the following on a scale of 1 (rarely, if ever, prioritized) to 10 (most always prioritized):

_____ *Minivacations*
_____ *Paradigm Shifts*
_____ *Organized Work Habits*

Which of these would you want to improve most and why?

What one thing could you change about your lifestyle that might have the greatest impact in the area you just mentioned?

Lack of sleep is one of the more common problems leading to reduced productivity in the workplace.

PHYSICAL SAFEGUARDS

Sleep

The average American doesn't get nearly enough sleep for what their body requires to function at peak performance. Lack of sleep is one of the more common problems leading to reduced productivity in the workplace.[13] Studies indicate that even mild sleep deprivation may result in symptoms consistent with diabetes, hypertension, obesity, inattention, poor concentration, irritability, depression and memory loss.[14] Ongoing sleep deprivation may also hasten the onset of these symptoms as a long-term or even permanent condition.

Proper sleep is vital to our functioning as God designed it. Our cells reproduce and rebuild overnight as we sleep. During certain phases of sleep, our brain actually does a little housecleaning and re-organizing. Throughout the day, our brain accesses literally millions of pieces of information. While some of it will be thrown away, much of it will need to be "filed away" in the storage compartments of our brain. However, at the end of a grueling day of ministry, this information is strewn about the "office" of our brain: on the desk, on the floor, on little sticky notes everywhere!

[13]Microsoft Encarta Online Encyclopedia, 2007, s.v. "sleep."
[14]John Easton, "Lack of Sleep Alters Hormones, Metabolism, Stimulates Effects of Aging" <www.uchospitals.edu/news/1999/19991021-sleepdebt.php>, accessed on May 26, 2007. Alan Greene, "Sleep Deprivation and ADHD" <www.drgreene.com/21_621.html>, accessed on May 26, 2007.

Because we use our brain constantly during waking hours, it's only during sleep that our mind has uninterrupted opportunity to organize these bits of information into the shelves and files of our brain. Sleep deprivation reduces the time available for this important organizing function, making us less efficient in our mental office.

While it's not difficult to determine how much sleep a particular individual regularly needs, finding out may require a significant temporary adjustment to our routine. First, we'll need to allow our body to "catch up" on any current sleep deprivation. We put this in quotes because physiologically the body is unable to actually make up hours of lost sleep. However, if we're currently sleep deprived, our body will attempt to compensate for a few nights while it rebuilds our immune system and declutters our mental office. During this time, we should allow ourselves to wake up naturally (that is, without an alarm clock). We can keep a journal of the number of hours we sleep each night. Eventually, we will find our body settling into a routine, generally sleeping the same amount each night. This amount is the optimal amount of sleep our body requires nightly. We would then do well to arrange our available daytime hours around this optimal amount of sleep.

A more tolerable method for most busy professionals might simply be to systematically increase the amount we sleep in fifteen-minute increments until we no longer experience regular bouts of tiredness during the day. By the way, the body functions best when it operates on a set routine. Getting to bed and waking at roughly the same time each day (even on weekends) encourages peak performance.

A national clergy survey found that 76 percent of ministers surveyed were either overweight or obese.

Diet

Equally as important to a good night's sleep for efficient body function is a healthy diet. Unfortunately, it's not as convenient to eat healthy as it is to eat from the local burger joint or vending machine. It's also typically more expensive to eat healthy than it is to eat from the $1 value menu at our favorite fast-food spot. Even when we cook, it takes more time to prepare a healthy meal than it does to zap a frozen dinner in the microwave. All these are reflective of a central theme: lack of priority. Most people simply prioritize other things (short-term productivity, the path of least resistance, simplicity, time, etc.).

Such convenience appears to be taking its toll. A national clergy survey found that 76 percent of ministers surveyed were either overweight or obese.[15] Sadly, gluttony is one of the "acceptable sins" within Christian circles. It's also the one sin we can't hide. Some religious sarcasm features overweight, pious Christians as a stereotype.

---

[15]Bob Wells, "Which Way to Clergy Health?" *Divinity*, fall 2002.

But obesity need not compromise our testimony and influence. I (Brad) have to keep my body weight, physical activity and diet in constant check because I've struggled with obesity in the past and even now must work to keep the weight off.

When did you last feel you were within your ideal weight range?

Describe how different your life would be if you were closer to your ideal weight.

On a scale of 0 (impossible) to 10 (no problem), how difficult do you anticipate it would be to achieve your ideal weight over time and why?

While starting a healthy diet tomorrow may seem overwhelming, simple lifestyle choices can have a significant impact on our overall health. Here are a few achievable changes for consideration:

- Reduce portion size at all meals by 20 percent. When you've been successful for one month, reduce portions by another 20 percent.

- Limit fast-food intake to only twice weekly. When you've been successful for one month, reduce it to once weekly, then eliminate fast food altogether, saving it only for special occasions. Even then, order from the healthier choices on the menu, such as a salad instead of a burger, fruit cup or side-salad with fat-free dressing in lieu of fries, and grilled rather than fried menu options.

- Drink more water daily. At first, add one bottle of water daily. When successful for one month, add another. A good topside goal for maximum weight loss or weight maintenance is a daily intake of a half-ounce of water per pound of body weight daily. For a weight of 180 pounds, that would be 90 ounces of water daily. Coffee, tea, soda and juice don't count!

- Once per month, eliminate something unhealthy or problematic from your regular consumption. Some examples to consider are potato chips, ice cream, donuts, chocolate, candy bars, cookies, French fries, and extra portions of bread or rolls. Substitute a healthier alternative, such as a favorite fruit, almonds, grapes, yogurt, sunflower seeds or raw veggies. Only eliminate one type of item per month. Once it's gone, leave it gone except for special occasions.

- Limit eating after a certain time at night, such as three hours before bedtime.

Beyond these options, consider scheduling a consultation with a nutritionist or general physician to discuss options for personalized weight management.

Which of the above suggestions are possibilities for you?

What other healthy changes could you consider?

To increase our likelihood for success, we might try making *one change* for a month, attempting another only after we've successfully built the change into our routine. It is the slow, methodical lifestyle changes, not the so-called quick weight-loss methods, that will result in lasting change. Fad diets come and go, right along with the dieter's excitement and frustration. Lifestyle changes, on the other hand, are just that: changes in the way we choose to live. Nothing short of this will have much of a chance for having an impact over the long-haul.

One more practical consideration: we can be a voice concerning healthy nutrition in our ministry, our family and our community by exerting influence over options for meals, fellowships and receptions. So many religious functions are centered around food! We can do our part to ensure our ministry isn't promoting gluttony by offering unhealthy choices. Consider also offering support groups at church, allowing others to join in the journey. Many programs are available that focus on healthy living for the body, mind and spirit, offering both encouragement and accountability.

Exercise

Exercise is one of the easiest and most effective means for feeling better. Exercise (especially weight-lifting) encourages endorphin production, the body's own natural "feel good" chemicals. Even people with mild clinical depression have reported elevation of their mood by adding a regular exercise regimen to their weekly routine.[16] Yet with 76 percent of ministers overweight, there likely isn't much exercise going on.

---

[16]The natural release of endorphins into the body through regular exercise should not be confused with an addictive approach to working out, where exercise is merely used as a means for "getting high" on one's own brain chemistry. It's a matter of purpose and degree that makes them qualitatively different.

Compounding the problem for ministers is the sedentary nature of their work. Our days are filled with study, prayer, writing, visitation, e-mails, paperwork and meetings—things requiring very little (if any) physical exertion. Unless we purpose to fight inactivity, we're going to be one of the 76 percent.

Body stewardship is the practice of physical self-care: "Do you not know that your body is a temple of the Holy Spirit, who is in you, whom you have received from God? You are not your own; you were bought at a price. Therefore honor God with your body" (1 Corinthians 6:19-20). Body stewardship means taking seriously the honor of God through the care for our body. We can begin this practice by committing to a plan of regular exercise. A medical professional or personal trainer can help us create a routine and regime that is tailored to our unique situation and goals. Others who appear successful in their body stewardship may also have helpful advice.

Being in good physical condition doesn't mean we have to spend hours at the gym. We aren't likely to be the next champion bodybuilder. That's not a realistic goal:

The best exercise routine is the one we're most motivated to do.

A disciplined approach to our bodies will not involve, for most of us, running four miles before breakfast and for that we must be thankful! It will involve, however, a good balance between work, recreation, and sleep. It will certainly involve a decent measure of exercise. Some will jog on a regular basis, others will hill-walk, others will play golf (though that can cause severe anxiety symptoms!) and some will work out in a gym. If flabby bodies lead to jaded minds and arid spirits then who knows what the difference fit, well exercised and rested bodies will make.[17]

To become more physically active, we ought to be practical. The best exercise routine is the one we're most motivated to do. Here are just a few possibilities: racquetball, brisk walking, jogging, running, tennis, weight-lifting, gym workout, aerobics, swimming, rollerblading, spinning, bicycling. Anything is better than nothing. What's important is to get started and build it into a routine once weekly, then twice weekly—up to as frequently as five times a week. Remember, it's not about being the next bodybuilder or supermodel; it's about honoring God with our body.

If we're still having difficulty with exercise, we might try these suggestions: committing to exercise regularly with someone else (this will strengthen accountability *and* build the relationship); asking some of the leadership in our ministry what they do for exercise and joining them in their activities; finding a creative way to "hold ourself accountable" (for example, publicly pledging for a year to give

---

[17]James Taylor, *Pastors Under Pressure* (Surrey: Day One Publications, 2001), p. 53.

an extra $10 to missions for each day of planned exercise we neglect). The method isn't important. What's important is to keep trying until we find an approach that motivates us toward change that's consistent with our values.

Breathing

When we're under increased stress, we tend to breathe more shallowly than normal. This causes a problematic chain reaction: less oxygen gets deeply into the lungs, thereby allowing less oxygen into the brain, thereby making it more difficult to think clearly. Less oxygen in the body also increases the risk of hyperventilation and anxiety.

A simple antidote is to take a few long, deep breaths, holding your breath for a few seconds before exhaling. Exhale slowly, as if you were gradually releasing air from a balloon. Closing your eyes may increase the relaxing effect. Make sure to fully exhale, allowing all the carbon dioxide out of the lungs completely before taking another deep breath. Doing this five or six times will actually cause minor adjustments to the pH balance in our body, resulting in a more relaxed state. Appendix D offers a balanced breathing exercise for those who want a more extensive and well-researched technique.

Healthy Touch

It was once common practice for premature infants with medical complications to be left alone in hospital neonatal units. Consequently, many died due to "failure to thrive." Some of their deaths were unnecessary and untimely because all they needed was a bit of healthy touch. We now know that human touch results in the body's increases production of oxytocin, a chemical responsible for feelings of calm, relaxation and a general sense of well-being.

Babies and adults alike thrive best when they receive regular touch from others. Many Americans (especially men) are "touch deprived." Society often misinterprets much of the touching of adults by other adults. Unfortunately, some Christian communities shy away from appropriate touch for fear of being labeled a pervert, pedophile or homosexual.

In his book *The Five Love Languages,* Gary Chapman asserts that all people have a need for love in its various expressions: words of affirmation, quality time, gifts, acts of service *and physical touch.*[18] For many, physical touch is the primary way they perceive that others care about them. We're not talking erotic or sexual touch; just a simple hug, handshake or touch on the shoulder to let them know we genuinely care. And because ministers are people too, we also benefit from human touch.

---

[18]Gary Chapman, *The Five Love Languages* (Chicago: Northfield, 1992).

Another way touch can be helpful in reducing stress is through therapeutic massage. There are multiple options for healthy massage, including licensed massage therapists, couples classes and books. We can give ourselves care at work by massaging our own hands, arms, shoulders, neck, head, face, legs and feet—wherever we hold our tension. It's not as thorough as a massage from a licensed professional, but in a pinch (no pun intended), it may reduce a bit of the tension. In the proper context, mutual massage can increase intimacy between spouses. Christian sex therapist Doug Rosenau has a chapter devoted to couples massage in his helpful book *A Celebration of Sex*.[19]

Little Rewards

What would it be like if we regularly rewarded ourselves for little jobs done well? It's a principle of human nature: a child will repeat more often behaviors that are rewarded. This principle is no less true for adults. Whatever we draw attention to, we will see more frequently. Be careful however; this is true for bad behavior too!

Rewarding ourselves with a little treat when we do something consistent with our goals and values has at least two benefits. First, we reinforce good behavior and make it more likely we'll follow through next time with the same good behavior. A small piece of chocolate, a mid-afternoon nap, a thirty-minute TV break, a small vase of flowers, a brief walk in the warm sunshine or a latte at a favorite café are all examples of smaller rewards that might be used with some frequency. More substantial rewards, such as a day of golf or dinner at a fancy restaurant, might be used more sparingly for the attainment of larger goals.

Second, we reduce the likelihood of any addictive or compulsive behavior we may have a bent toward (as long as our little reward is healthy, of course). Those of us with addictive or compulsive histories sometimes have distorted thoughts: for example, "I've been working so hard all day and nobody appreciates me for what I do around here." If we don't do healthy care for ourselves, we may become resentful that others don't, either. We might be OK for a while without positive reinforcement, but if we fail to reward ourselves in good ways we can set ourselves up for unhealthy self-reward—compulsive behaviors such as alcohol, shopping, drugs, pornography, gambling or surfing chatrooms on the Internet. Healthy self-rewards for a job well done can be a means for giving ourselves encouragement to stay on the right track.

---

[19]Doug Rosenau, *A Celebration of Sex* (Nashville: Nelson, 2002).

Consultation with Health-Care Professionals

We become so used to setting aside our own discomfort to care for others that, over time, it may turn into a form of denial—denial that we hurt emotionally, denial that we need encouragement, even denial that we're physically sick. The very trait that makes us great at caring for the suffering of others will sometimes make us clouded to our own suffering. Slowing down our hectic pace is not only preventative care for our body, mind and spirit. The "quietness" during such times often reveals our own needs.

At times we need professional caregivers as much as anyone else. We can set an example for those we lead and serve by utilizing doctors, Christian counselors and ministers in our own lives. The lessons we live out before others will be more powerful than any newsletter or sermon we could ever create.

Rate yourself on how well you prioritize each of the following on a scale of 1 (rarely prioritized) to 10 (regularly prioritized):

_____ *Sleep*	_____ *Healthy Touch*
_____ *Diet*	_____ *Little Rewards*
_____ *Exercise*	_____ *Consultation with*
_____ *Breathing*	*Health-Care Professionals*

Which of these would you want to improve most and why?

What one thing could you change about your lifestyle that might have the greatest impact in the area you just mentioned?

Wrap-Up: Foundation Stone 3— Stress Management

Reflecting on all you've learned in this foundation stone, use the space below to write down your most important takeaways.

Prayerfully review the exercises in this foundation stone. Under each category below, write down specific changes you desire with regard to spiritual, relational, emotional and physical safeguards. Feel free to come back and add more action points over the coming months. Fill in the boxes to the right of each action point when you feel you have integrated a particular change into your regular routine.

Spiritual Safeguards

_____ ☐
_____ ☐
_____ ☐
_____ ☐
_____ ☐
_____ ☐

Relational Safeguards

_____ ☐
_____ ☐
_____ ☐
_____ ☐
_____ ☐
_____ ☐

Emotional Safeguards

_____ ☐
_____ ☐
_____ ☐
_____ ☐
_____ ☐
_____ ☐

Physical Safeguards

_____ ☐
_____ ☐
_____ ☐
_____ ☐
_____ ☐
_____ ☐

Return to the personal self-care plan on pages 98-99 to consider any modifications to your purpose statement. Change the statement in light of any insights the Holy Spirit has given you as you've reflected on stress management. If no change is needed, reinforce your statement by copying it as is into the space provided.

4

BOUNDARIES

Protecting What Matters Most

A boundary places a limit on something for a particular purpose. We can easily see boundaries everywhere in the physical world if we're looking for them.

Think about your home. On the lines in figure 4.1, list as many boundaries as you can think of. For instance, the exterior wall of your home is a boundary because it separates your family's living area from the rest of the outside world. Keep in mind that some boundaries might not be visible with the human eye. Boundaries may also be found on the property where your home is located.

The exterior wall

_____

_____

_____

_____

_____

_____

_____

_____

_____

_____

Figure 4.1. Boundaries in our homes.

Some boundaries are less obvious, such as the security system and the property line, because they aren't visible to the human eye. Some may not initially seem like boundaries at all, such as a toilet or chimney. However, these are vital boundaries for families.

Every boundary in and around our home serves an important function. The external walls differentiate where the inside of our home ends and the outside of our home begins; they keep the cold air out in the wintertime and cool the air during the summertime; they protect small children from both inclement weather and predators.

Boundaries define where one thing ends and another begins; differentiate what belongs to us from what belongs to someone else; distinguish our responsibility from someone else's responsibility; and filter bad things out while either permitting or keeping good things in. In short, boundaries help us prioritize and protect what matters to us.

To define boundaries properly, it's necessary to make value judgments. That is, boundaries are only important when they support our values. Because we value a comfortable climate for our family, we strengthen the boundaries of our walls by adding insulation to regulate ambient temperature. If we didn't value the climate inside our home, there would be no purpose for such insulation. The value of a boundary is limited to its function. For example, we install a backyard fence because we value privacy or the safety of our toddler or family pet.

In fact, our values inform the kind of boundaries we establish. If we value privacy from our nosy neighbors, we might install a high fence they can't see through. But if we value spontaneous conversation with our neighbors, we might install a lower, chain-link fence. Boundaries have meaning only when they are established against the backdrop of the things we value most.

1. Personal Boundaries

Personal and relational boundaries serve much the same purpose as physical boundaries. Personal boundaries help us prioritize our relationships (see foundation stone 1) and focus on things consistent with our calling (see foundation stone 2).

Personal boundaries define who we are (and who we are not), distinguish where we end and another person begins, determine what we should and should not expect from others, and allow good things into our lives while protecting us from things that might harm us. Some of the more common personal and relational boundaries involve geography, personal space, words, time, ideas and feelings.

GEOGRAPHY/LOCATION

The distance between us and another person may represent a boundary. Children who move out of the home use geography to help establish their independence, while an adult child who relocates back to the city of their elderly parents to better look after them

---

Personal boundaries help us prioritize our relationships (see foundation stone 1) and focus on things consistent with our calling (see foundation stone 2).

uses geography to demonstrate care. A congregant who relocates to another part of the country may desire to maintain a pastoral relationship with us, but their geographical distance would make such a relationship unrealistic for us and ultimately inadequate for them.

PERSONAL SPACE

A woman arguing with her husband and removing herself to another room of the house uses personal space as a boundary for either physical or emotional protection. However, a woman who snuggles close to her husband on the sofa uses personal space as an inclusive boundary to communicate love and a feeling of safety with her spouse.

WORDS

Some of the most powerful boundaries are established by two simple words: "yes" and "no" (Matthew 5:37; James 5:12). Children discover the world of boundaries around the age of two when they become acquainted with "No!" Saying "yes" to certain things that help accomplish our calling is critical to fulfilling God's purpose in our lives. But saying "yes" to one thing will necessitate a "no" to many other things. Saying "yes" to personal morning prayer, for example, might mean saying "no" to an extra hour of sleep or sermon preparation. Saying "yes" to our son's soccer game might mean saying "no" to a ministry meeting or being at the hospital during a parishioner's surgery. It's important that our boundary words be consistent with our calling and our most important intimate relationships.

TIME

When we schedule time for something, we set a boundary that effectively says, "This time is for this purpose only and nothing else." Allowing another activity to interrupt that time (such as telling our son we will help him with his homework but then running very late due to a ministry meeting) not only violates the "Let your 'Yes' be 'Yes' " of Scripture but also does significant damage to an important relationship, giving evidence of our true values. No matter what we say, our *demonstrated* values in this case are either (1) the rewards of the meeting outweigh the benefits of relating with our son or (2) the consequences of missing the meeting are more significant than those of neglecting a promise to our son. Honestly evaluating the consequences of our life choices can sometimes be quite sobering.

IDEAS

When others express an idea different from our own, they are establishing a boundary with us that is an extension of who they are. Even if we know their position is immature or even in direct opposition to

Scripture, we can respectfully disagree with them and lovingly show them what we believe to be truth.[1] We may minister to people living in unconfessed sin, but we don't agree with their belief that their sin is unimportant. We respect our non-Christian neighbors but don't downplay the doctrinal boundaries of our faith when we socialize with them.

FEELINGS

Human emotions serve many purposes. The ability to feel pleasure and enjoyment comes with the flip side of having to deal with agony and pain. Feelings are neither "good" nor "bad"; they simply tell us helpful information about ourselves at a given moment in time. A backache is helpful in a doctor's ability to diagnose and treat a physical ailment. Likewise, a person's "heartache," rightly understood, can be extremely helpful in "diagnosing and treating" emotional pain.

Sometimes we react to another's expression of negative emotions as though they were fighting words, especially if they express opposition or displeasure in us. Our attempt to remove or prevent such expression of feelings from another (including telling them "not to feel that way") can amount to our manipulation of them. In such a situation, we might choose to see their expression as an opportunity to listen more deeply to their concerns and achieve healing and reconciliation. We can feel a freedom to express our own feelings with others—even feelings of anger. But while we may use such feelings to condemn a behavior, we must be careful that we don't demean the person. Even those living in outright sin bear a broken image of God that deserves to be respected.

Which of these personal boundaries resonated the most for you? In what way will this be helpful to your personal and/or professional relationships?

---

[1]Denominations that practice formal church discipline are not necessarily violating a congregant's personal boundaries; by virtue of their membership each person has voluntarily submitted themselves to the church's authority. But churches still need to recognize the distinction between allowing an individual to choose their own response to formal discipline (either submission/restoration or rebellion/excommunication) and attempting to manipulate the individual into doing something. The first method allows the congregant to accept full responsibility for their sinful action; the second does not. Similar reasoning might also be helpfully applied to a rebellious son or daughter.

REPLACING COMMON MISUNDERSTANDING WITH BIBLICAL INSIGHT

For some, the term "godly boundaries" is an inherent contradiction along the lines of "jumbo shrimp." Such confusion results from faulty assumptions as to what boundaries are really all about. Boundaries for Christians are designed to protect Christlike values and help us to live a lifestyle consistent with Christian principles. In their bestselling book *Boundaries,* Henry Cloud and John Townsend lay out eight myths regarding boundaries.[2] Here are our thoughts on the ones we've heard most frequently in our work with ministers.

Boundaries Are Displeasing and Disobedient to God

Christians (and certainly ministers) are sometimes assumed to have a responsibility to be "all things to all people." This is a distortion of 1 Corinthians 9:22: "I try to find common ground with everyone, doing everything I can to save some" (NLT). To infer from this passage that all boundaries displease God is to take this verse out of context.

First of all, the passage should be read within the larger context of 1 Corinthians 9:19-23. Paul describes three groups of people he desires to reach with the gospel: the Jews (who are "under the law," or Jewish custom), the Gentiles (who are "not under the law") and the "weak" (those whose weak faith will not allow them to embrace certain freedoms we have in Christ). Paul respected Jewish customs when he was with the Jews so as not to offend them, even though he didn't have to because of his salvation by grace. He didn't practice the Jewish customs when he was with the Gentiles because of his salvation by grace and not works. Paul voluntarily abstained from certain freedoms he had in Christ, however, if they caused a weaker believer to stumble when he was with them (see also Romans 14:19-21).

To infer from this passage that all limit-setting is disobedient to God or displeasing to him is actually quite the opposite from what this passage teaches. Such critics are really saying, "Pleasing God means doing whatever someone asks you to do." But what if the Jews required him to sacrifice a burnt offering when he was with them? Would he have done so? Not at all. He would have helped them to see the old sacrificial system as merely a shadow of the ultimate sacrifice found in Jesus. And what if the Gentiles asked him to go with them into a pagan temple and perform sexually with a temple prostitute to please the gods? Would Paul have participated in order to gain their hearing? Of course not. Contrary to this common misunderstanding, appropriate boundaries are often necessary in the Christian life.

---

[2]Henry Cloud and John Townsend, *Boundaries*, rev. ed. (Grand Rapids: Zondervan, 2002), p. 103.

Boundaries Are Prideful and Selfish

Some ministers operate as if Christians should always be giving to others—even to the detriment of themselves. They quote the apostle Paul: "Do nothing out of selfish ambition or vain conceit, but in humility consider others better than yourselves" (Philippians 2:3-4).

Paul isn't teaching that we should only do what others want us to do. This would be ridiculous when taken to its logical conclusion. Some biblical scholars believe that the disciples wanted Jesus to establish a physical kingdom to drive the Romans out of Jerusalem. Shouldn't Jesus have been "unselfish" and done as they desired? Of course not. Jesus saw beyond what their human emotions were asking for into their true spiritual need for a Savior. Rather than being selfish, Jesus was living consistent with the long-term goal of the Father's plan.

Godly boundaries serve much the same purpose. When grounded in Christian values and principles, boundaries look beyond the perceived "needs" of the moment, seeking God's greater purpose in the world.

When grounded in Christian values and principles, boundaries look beyond the perceived "needs" of the moment, seeking God's greater purpose in the world.

Boundaries Will Hurt Me as Well as Others

Once a person understands that Scripture actually upholds the idea of godly boundaries, they may at times adhere to a more emotionally based objection: "Won't I (or they) get hurt if I set a boundary?" The root issue of what they're really saying is, "I don't want to suffer pain or be the cause of someone else's pain."

While no one would want to voluntarily cause another pain, doing the God-honoring thing may sometimes cause mild to severe discomfort to ourselves and others. The parent who carries her son to the doctor to set a broken bone will subject him to excruciating short-term pain for the long-term purpose of healing. Likewise, the parent who establishes tough consequences with a drug-abusing daughter may cause discomfort and hurt feelings but does so to serve a larger purpose.

By setting biblical boundaries we sometimes cause ourselves to suffer (feelings of guilt, for example), especially when our boundaries cause pain for others. In each of the above examples, the parent is doing what is ultimately in the long-term best interest of the child or allowing negative consequences to help the child take full responsibility for their unhealthy choices. While each parent might feel horribly about their child's suffering, they are doing what is best for the child. God himself does no less with his own children (Hebrews 12:5-11) and encourages us toward the same long-term perspective (1 Corinthians 9:24-27).

Which of the above misunderstandings has been a personal struggle for you?

If the struggle persists, what might help you to resolve it?

THE BENEFITS OF BIBLICAL BOUNDARIES

Now that we've dealt with a few common objections, let's explore some of the benefits for pursuing biblical boundaries.

Living Proactively

Boundaries facilitate our ability to live proactively from Christian principles and deeply held convictions. Sincere Christian faith requires us to live upon the foundation of biblical principles (Matthew 7:24-25). We must not only "listen to the word" but also "do what it says" (James 1:22). Otherwise, we will become like the Israelites who made decisions based on how they felt in the moment from their own limited human perspective (Judges 21:25).

> *Boundaries facilitate our ability to live proactively from Christian principles and deeply held convictions.*

God calls us to live out the gospel in our daily routine. If we desire an uncompromised life, we will have to put some clear boundaries into place because the world *will* try to squeeze us into its mold (Romans 12:2 Phillips). Only boundaried living will keep us from taking the path of least resistance when others tell us our unique calling in ministry "can't be done," or when Satan attempts to knock us off course through sexual temptation, or when the wooing of a larger benefits package tempts us to pursue a "career move" that doesn't align with our calling. Clear boundaries purposefully established ahead of time—not in the heat of the moment—may be the only thing that keeps us grounded during such times.

Encouraging Responsibility

Boundaries help us and others see that consequences (both positive and negative) follow choices. God requires us to accept responsibility for the choices we make (Hebrews 4:13). When we live by intentional boundaries established on scriptural principles, we will not only see the positive and negative consequences of our choices; we will also hold others responsible for how they respond to our boundaries.

For example, someone might try to get us to alter our planned family outing in order to help them do something they failed to do in a timely manner. Our commitment to our family, coupled with our refusal to be manipulated, will help us, our family and the one manipulating us to see more clearly the consequences on all sides. Our boundaries help us to say "no" to the manipulator and "yes" to our spouse and kids. It will allow others to learn from our healthy boundaries, as well—even though their actually learning from our example is never within our control.

Respecting Others

Boundaries help us distinguish "influence" from "control" of others, enabling us to respect their "no." God has given us significant influence for his purposes. When we seek to keep such influence in step with the Spirit, we will have the maturity to recognize the difference between using compelling words like Paul (2 Corinthians 5:20) and manipulative actions like the Sanhedrin (Acts 5:40-42). Our encouragement of others, coupled with a heartfelt prayer to the Holy Spirit, is able to produce more conviction in the hearts of others than any amount of nagging ever could. When someone responds to our request with a "no," we can share with them our reasoning and ask them to prayerfully reconsider the matter—then trust the Holy Spirit to work his will regardless of their final decision.[3]

Making Good Neighbors

As we establish strong boundaries around what matters most to us, many will come to greatly respect us and perhaps even model their lives after us. We likely will have less difficulty getting along with people because they will learn to predict our steady way of responding from deeply held principles. We may even find that they stop asking us to take responsibility for things they should do for themselves and instead ask us to do only things that are consistent with the way we live life anyway.

A healthy boundary also allows us to better assess whether someone is attempting to influence us or control us, based on their reaction to our boundary. Those merely wanting to influence us may still be disappointed, but they will accept our "no" and even respect us for it. Those attempting to control us will often become angry and irritable, perhaps to the point of spreading rumors about us as a form of passive-aggressive "punishment." Such trouble is sometimes one of the negative consequences we suffer for living a well-boundaried life. Yet with intentionally set boundaries, we'll no longer resent them for trying to manipulate us. Others will know they can rely on our "yes" being "yes" and our "no" being "no."

Eleanor Roosevelt supposedly once said, "Do what you feel in

---

[3]Of course, this does not apply to matters of blatantly inappropriate conduct, such as a church undertaking formal discipline for a man who refuses to stop his pornography use or a human resources department placing a woman on six-month probation for her violation of the organization's code of ethics.

your heart to be right, for you'll be criticized anyway." We simply can't please everyone. The earlier we recognize this, the sooner we'll have the confidence to make the difficult decisions necessary to live out of our unique calling.

Which of the above benefits makes the most sense to you and why?

What area of your life might benefit from becoming more boundaried? Describe what becoming well-boundaried in this area might look like.

2. Real-World Boundaries in Our Ministry Setting

The remainder of this foundation stone will be dedicated to generating ideas for applying new boundaries to the unique problems we face as ministers. In this section we'll examine ways to stay focused on what matters most in our particular ministry setting. Then we'll look at boundaries for prioritizing our values around family and friends. Finally, we'll explore their application to our relationship with God and ourselves.

ALLOWING OTHERS TO TAKE PERSONAL RESPONSIBILITY

Let's assume someone we supervise hasn't done some agreed-upon task. There are a number of reasons we might be inclined to take it over for them:

- We feel genuine pity for them.
- We don't want the project to fail.
- We don't want to see the person suffer.
- We feel pressured by others to "cover their load."

Like many things in the Christian life, the application of boundaries to this situation depends greatly on the unique situation, our attitude and what would ultimately bring God the most glory. When deciding what boundary is best, here are four considerations:

1. Is this person typically responsible or irresponsible? Does this person have a track record with us or are they someone we don't

know well? If they are typically responsible, the person may be under a genuine burden and would benefit from and appreciate our assistance. If they are typically irresponsible, this person may be waiting for a bailout to avoid taking responsibility.

2. Does the person own up to the problem or are they blaming others for their lack of follow-through? The person's admission of fault may indicate that our assistance will aid in their becoming more responsible. Their blaming, however, may indicate that our help will only be taken for granted (Matthew 7:6).

3. What is the attitude of our heart? This also plays a role in determining whether a particular boundary is best for a given situation. The mere presence of a need doesn't necessarily mean *we* are the ones called by God to meet it. Perhaps we've become accustomed to always being the one to "do the right thing." However, the fact that we quickly intervene to "rescue" might sometimes deprive someone else of the joy of giving to meet the need. Before deciding for or against helping, we might search our heart to discern our motives. Are we going to refuse because helping would take time from areas of our life that matter most (family time, other ministry obligations, etc.) or simply from a desire to not be inconvenienced? Would helping this person be motivated from a cheerful heart (2 Corinthians 9:7) or from a heart of resentment?

The mere presence of a need doesn't necessarily mean we *are the ones called by God to meet it.*

4. How might God be most glorified? Someone who approaches our benevolence ministry and appears to be milking the system for a handout will be more helped by learning the spiritual principle, "Those unwilling to work will not get to eat" (2 Thessalonians 3:10 NLT). But someone who is truly overburdened will receive our assistance as a genuine answer to prayer, resulting in their giving glory to God.

Think back to the most recent situation in which you either were asked directly or felt a strong pull to take on someone else's responsibility. How did you ultimately respond?

How might you have made the same or a different decision considering the insights presented here?

RIGHTLY PLACED PRIORITIES

Ministers living from crisis to crisis lead unfulfilled lives. Aligning our weekly and daily tasks to be consistent with the things we value most is critical for living out a Christ-centered calling. Some of the most "successful" ministers are so busy increasing the speed of life they haven't a clue whether their accomplishments are more driven by other people's priorities or their own. Ministers who manage by crisis merely complete tasks others press on them as urgent rather than the important things God calls them to do. Stephen Covey, author of *Seven Habits of Highly Effective People*,[4] defines "urgent" as a task requiring immediate attention but "important" as something that contributes to our mission, our values and our highly prioritized goals.

Covey created a four-quadrant grid (see figure 4.2 on page 150) to help people stay focused on what matters most to them. Quadrant 1 contains "important and urgent" issues. Crisis management takes place here, including pressing problems, deadline-driven projects, emergency meetings, unexpected funerals or hospital visits, misbehaving children, health crises, and heated arguments with our spouse. Quadrant 2 contains "important but not urgent" issues. This is where we plan and prepare for the future, and work on goals consistent with our values, including casting vision for our ministry, preparing for sermons or family vacation, having lunch with a friend, and taking extended time for personal prayer. Quadrant 3 contains "not important but urgent" matters, including interruptions, some meetings, some e-mails and phone calls, and so on—especially those matters that aren't consistent with our calling or that are in conflict with a higher priority. This quadrant is just as crisis-driven as quadrant 1 with one major exception: time in quadrant 3 is spent on other people's urgent priorities rather than matters consistent with our own calling. Quadrant 4 contains "not important and not urgent" matters, including trivial time wasters, irrelevant e-mails and phone calls, and things providing temporary escape from our daily routine (e.g., excessive TV or video games, surfing the Internet purposelessly, nonsensical busywork).

Covey says that highly effective people do whatever it takes to focus the bulk of their resources on quadrant 2 issues. Of course, quadrants 1 and 3 compete for our time the most on any given day. Quadrant 4 is generally a waste of time and should be eliminated from our routine by whatever means necessary.

Depending on their unique ministry setting, ministers sometimes have more autonomy in setting their schedules than the average per-

Ministers who manage by crisis merely complete tasks others press on them as urgent rather than the important things God calls them to do.

---

[4]Stephen R. Covey, *The Seven Habits of Highly Effective People* (New York: Free Press, 1989), p. 151.

son. Even if that's not true for us, it's our responsibility to ensure we spend adequate time on quadrant 2 activity. Reducing our quadrant 3 is a matter of either saying "no" to those time demands or appropriately delegating them to others. Reducing our quadrant 1 will require some initial "putting out" of fires. Once extinguished, however, most will likely become quadrant 2 priorities. We must then become proactive about prioritizing quadrant 2 tasks if we are to maximize our overall effectiveness in ministry.

Considering what's on your plate right now, use the following grid to prioritize each of your tasks into Covey's four quadrants.

Quadrant 1 "Important and Urgent"	Quadrant 2 "Important but Not Urgent"
Quadrant 3 "Not Important but Urgent"	Quadrant 4 "Not Important and Not Urgent"

Figure 4.2. Stephen Covey's four quadrants.

Which quadrant's contents were you most surprised by?

What actions might you take to become more quadrant 2 driven in your regular routine?

BOUNDARIED RELATIONSHIPS WITH MINISTRY PARTICIPANTS AND STAFF

There are two types of difficult people: those trying to get us to do something that for us is "urgent but not important" (quadrant 3) and those whose personality simply gets under our skin. We'll address the second scenario in foundation stone 6 (People Skills). Here, however, we'll focus on those who make urgent but unimportant demands on our time.

A request or demand from someone may be unimportant to us, but it's likely a quadrant 1 issue—both important and urgent—for the other person. It's not inherently wrong that someone has a different set of values from ours. While such individuals deserve to be handled with respect and politeness, we can still be lovingly firm in our response.

Let's say a woman believes strongly that our ministry should be helping the victims of an apartment-complex fire in a neighboring town. However, we know that our organization is presently at capacity helping with the fundraising drive to stock the local food pantry. We can be caring and polite to this woman (after all, she has a great heart!) but firm enough that she leaves with a clear understanding of our position. A variety of responses are possible: (1) thank her for her concern but let her know that the ministry's resources are being used elsewhere, (2) thank her for her concern and suggest that she approach another staff member or even a few other ministry members about starting such a ministry, or (3) thank her for her concern and tell her that we'll consider establishing such a ministry to address such tragedies in the future.

One person's sense of urgency does not change another person's sense of calling.

Notice there is no "right" answer. Helping fire victims is inherently no better or worse than stocking the food pantry. However, if the food drive is more consistent with the ministry's vision, it makes no sense to drop it in order to pursue something else. Suppose she doesn't take our answer; suppose she starts pleading or manipulating with reasons why we should reconsider: "They're our neighbors!" or "But they're in such need!" or "But my sister is one of the victims!" In such an instance, it's best to remember this truism: One person's sense of urgency does not change another person's sense of calling. We might simply restate what we said before, using the exact same words, if necessary. She may become upset that we don't see things her way and in fact may never agree with us, but she will eventually accept our answer.

Someone might say, "But she's going to be upset with me!" Should her being upset determine what ministry our organization engages in? If that's the case, we need to get ready for a bumpy ride: basing a ministry on who makes the loudest threats instead of God's calling is hardly the way to run a ministry. This kind of decision-making happens when ministers make decisions based upon their need to be liked by the people rather than a clear sense of calling for the ministry organization.

Think back on an interaction with someone that challenged your freedom to minister in a way consistent with who God called you to be. In what way did you respond?

How might you have responded differently to achieve a result more in line with your values and calling?

REASONABLE EXPECTATIONS FROM WORK

Even if we're certain of our calling into the ministry, it's important to maintain reasonable expectations of how satisfying our work is to us. We were created for intimate relationships; therefore, no amount of achievement in ministry will ever fully satisfy. With this in mind, we want to be careful not to subconsciously believe the lie, "If I can just _____ (get this ministry off the ground, accomplish this task, complete this project, see this person receive Christ, pull off this performance, etc.) I will be _____ (happy, fulfilled, satisfied, etc.)."

In their book *The Sacred Romance,* Brent Curtis and John Eldredge call this losing sight of the larger story for our own smaller dramas.[5] The smaller dramas are represented by our finite accomplishments. We get caught up in moving from one accomplishment to another, finding "meaning and happiness" when things go right and experiencing "depression and lack of vision" shortly after they're completed. The larger story represents the purposes God is carrying out around us all the time. These are often much grander in scope than we could possibly see at any given moment and involve not just what we do but also our significant relationships. We may sometimes find ourselves so focused on the pursuit of our calling that we've neglected our need for intimate relationships with God, close friendships and our spouse. Seeking a balance between intimacy and calling is the path to fulfillment.

Prioritizing time for our relationships requires creating time boundaries in our calendar. Relationships almost always fit into

---

[5]Brent Curtis and John Eldredge, *The Sacred Romance: Drawing Closer to the Heart of God* (Nashville: Thomas Nelson, 1997), p. 41.

quadrant 2 because they rarely demand attention as the "urgent" items in our lives—at least not until they've been neglected far too long. It's better to prioritize the *maintenance* of our important relationships, investing time into them and making them stronger in the process, than it is to wait until they enter a crisis mode and require serious repair.

To what extent have you tried to derive too much significance and fulfillment through your ministry work?

In what ways might you have neglected certain intimate relationships in the process?

What would you do to reverse any negative trends in this area?

REDIRECTING WORKPLACE DISCONTENTMENT

Maybe we've decided that lack of fulfillment in our work has nothing to do with lack of intimacy in our relationships. Carving out time in the calendar for prayer, fasting and personal reflection might prove beneficial. This kind of time won't happen by itself—and others may even balk at our need for such time (especially if supervisors or parishioners have a stack of quadrant 3 tasks lined up for us). Yet such time may be necessary to gain clear insight from God about our priorities. We may have to fight for such time, helping others see the long-term benefits of clarifying our ministry vision.

Journals, mentors or ministry coaches can help us see more clearly the passion and vision God has placed within us. God may appear to take his time revealing such things. We don't have to be in a hurry; answers of substance often take time—much like the roots of an oak tree, whose roots grow deep into the earth before the first sprouting of greenery can be seen. Be willing to sit with ambiguity, patiently enduring until his timing is made perfect.

If you sense a need for extended time with God to clarify your ministry vision, how might you go about doing so?

Who needs to be consulted to secure such time? How might be the most effective way to approach them?

REINING IN "OVERTIME"

According to statistics cited in 2001 by the research department at *Christianity Today,* fewer than two in ten ministers in traditional settings limit their work to only forty hours per week.[6] In fact, the average pastor works more than ten hours per day—six days a week. Burnout may be around the corner unless we intentionally place boundaries around our ministry time.

Overtime for some can be an attempt to gain fulfillment from calling alone, as if just one more task might deliver that elusive sense of inner peace. Other unconscious motives include justifying our salary, avoiding problems at home, responding to the "urgent" requests of others, confusing "sacrificial service" with burning ourselves out, attempting to "work off" our sins in service to God, trying to keep the power brokers in our ministry happy, believing "this is just how hard ministers have to work" or simply buying into the "busy is best" lie.

There are certainly times and circumstances in ministry where overtime is prudent and even necessary. However, the most successful and effective ministers we know are both passionate and intentional at evaluating their weekly and daily activities in light of their important intimate relationships and their unique personal calling.

Ministers who desire optimal effectiveness must learn to say "yes" to activities that result in strengthening their intimate relationships and accomplishing their calling and "no" to most everything else. At times, we'll have quadrant 1 tasks that aren't directly related to our intimate relationships and calling. However, these can be managed and minimized to ensure space for the things that are. Not everyone will be happy with the boundaries we set up. But such boundaries are the only way to true fulfillment and the best way to ensure the people who matter most in our lives—God, family and close friendships—aren't neglected.

TAKING VACATION (AND OTHER TIME AWAY)

If we have a day off, by all means we should take it! There's a reason we're given a regular day off. It's for the purpose of caring for personal matters—including time for our own regular refueling. Also,

---

[6]John C. LaRue Jr., "Pastors at Work: Where the Time Goes," *Your Church,* July/ August 1998, accessed March 3, 2007 <www.christianitytoday.com/yc/8y4/8y4080. html>.

all of us in theory have at least one week of vacation time. Some are fortunate to have two, three, even four or more weeks at their disposal. Like regular days off, vacation is also provided for a reason:

> I'm constantly amazed by the number of people who can't seem to control their own schedules. Over the years, I've had many executives come to me and say with pride: "Boy, last year I worked so hard that I didn't take any vacation." It's actually nothing to be proud of. I always feel like responding: "You dummy. You mean to tell me that you can take responsibility for an $80 million project and you can't plan two weeks out of the year to go off with your family and have some fun?"[7]

By the way, a "working vacation" is a complete contradiction in terms. If we're working, it's by definition not a vacation. Likewise, if we're truly on vacation, we won't be working. Most professionals require several days into a vacation simply to unwind from the stress and chaos of their working routine.

We should take *all* of the vacation available to us. There are organizations that provide free or reduced-cost getaways and retreat housing for ministers.[8] Even if we're unable to go somewhere or do something elaborate, however, we can still take a break at home by turning off our telephone, television and Internet—a true vacation from the world!

Some of us have days allowed in our schedule for professional conferences. Regularly taking advantage of conference time is an opportunity to hear what God is doing in other ministries. It's also a time to connect with like-minded ministry professionals, giving and receiving much needed encouragement and ideas.

Making time for regular days off, vacations, study days, conferences and retreats sharpens us and enables us to be more effective when we're back in our regular ministry routine.

How much vacation time are you allowed each year? On average, how much do you typically use in a year?

How might you plan to use all of the vacation time currently available to you as a practical step toward healthy self-care?

---

[7]Lee Iacocca and William Novak, *Iaccoca: An Autobiography* (New York: Bantam, 1986), p. 21.

[8]Some of these can be found on our website at <www.Shepherd-Care.org>.

What time and financial resources does your ministry make available to you for professional conferences or renewal? How might you take advantage of these resources in the near future?

LEAVING WORKPLACE STRESS OUTSIDE OF THE HOME

A corollary to working overtime is bringing the ministry home—physically or emotionally. We lull ourselves into believing we're not working overtime, yet our family knows better and may even communicate this to us in different ways.

In this digital age, most of us are far too easily accessible. Home phones, cell phones, pagers, text messaging, snail mail, e-mails and the Internet can keep us tethered to our job no matter where we are. To reclaim our sanity for the sake of long-term ministry effectiveness (not to mention our family's emotional well-being), we need to set a few boundaries around who has access to us and when. We can take the phone off the hook during family meals; not call into the office on vacations; instruct our receptionist to only call in real emergencies on our day off; only check e-mail at predetermined times; establish another minister or lay leader to be on-call for phone calls and hospital visitation when we need to be "unavailable."

We worked with one minister who actually was planning to leave his family vacation for an entire day and drive four hours one-way to conduct a funeral of someone who had *previously* been a member of his congregation—merely because they asked him to! To his family, the minister was unconsciously communicating, "Former church members are more important than my family." Fortunately, his accountability group helped him see the impact such a decision would have not only on his family but also on his own stated values related to his calling. This is a good example of accountability at work.

What feedback (verbal and nonverbal) have you received from your family or close friends related to your boundaries or lack of boundaries with work?

If this has been a recent problem for you, what adjustments might you consider to promote change?

If you're uncertain how to answer the last question, your loved ones and accountable relationships could likely give you a few ideas. Confess your recognition of the problem and your desire to improve them. Don't wait until you have possible solutions in mind. Take the risk to share from your heart that you don't have the answers yet, asking God to speak through their response.

3. Real-World Boundaries with Intimate Relationships

Relational problems in the home are bound to have a spillover effect on our ministry effectiveness. When problems exist with our spouse, children, extended family and close friendships, our minds and hearts will be mentally and emotionally preoccupied with such matters until they're resolved. Ministers sometimes create unnecessary burdens when a few common boundary problems are present.

SPOUSES: RESPECTING OUR HELPMATE

Earlier we discussed how skin is a personal boundary, defining where we end and another person begins. We are stewards of the body God has given us and we're responsible before God to care for it as his temple. Physically seeing ourselves in a mirror can become a daily reminder that God has specifically asked us not to join our "skin" sexually with someone other than our spouse (Genesis 17:10-11; 1 Corinthians 6:15-20; Hebrews 13:4). In addition, our spouse's skin is also the Holy Spirit's temple. To abuse them physically, sexually, emotionally or otherwise is to violate a very important boundary, not to mention the often severe relational consequences of such actions.

We are to care for ourselves and others in ways that honor God's image within: "Look not only to your own interests, but also to the interests of others" (Philippians 2:4). Applied to a spouse, this includes not merely respecting their physical body but also their time, space and ideas. Each partner benefits from having their own identity in the marital relationship. If one chooses to squelch the other's creativity and unique viewpoint, the couple loses much of the benefit of the partnership: a helpmate to encourage and comfort, to warn of dangers the other may not see, and to be an intimate companion along life's journey.

While our differences may be a great benefit, they also can become a great source for conflict. There's a human tendency to reject the perspective or advice of one whose viewpoint is different from our own. But our spouse's perspective is actually God's gift, because their point of view brings different input to the decision-making process. They just might have the missing insight we need.

"Don't Feel That Way, Honey"

Ministers sometimes squelch their spouses by preventing them from expressing their feelings—especially negative ones. Emotions are neither good nor bad but are simply a window into someone's heart. Taking personal offense at their feelings toward us may lead to shutting our spouse down by either criticizing the feeling (and the person) or attempting to remove the negative feeling with words such as, "you shouldn't feel that way." This effectively throws away opportunity for greater intimacy by allowing the negative expression to move us toward meaningful dialogue.

"I'll Just Have to Change Them"

A human temptation is to try to "change people" more to our liking by subtle or not-so-subtle manipulation. We can call it what we want—"training," "encouragement," the "velvet glove"—it's still manipulative. We might get the change we're fishing for, but we'll also get plenty of bitterness and resentment, and potentially more of the same type of problem in other areas. It will also only encourage our spouse to use similar manipulation with us.

Controlling others is ineffective in the long run. We are only able to control our own choices in life. Instead, our relationships mature when both parties dialogue openly about concerns, setting aside as much time as required to work through the issue effectively.

In what ways have you struggled with boundary issues with your spouse or significant other?

What actions might help to facilitate healing in your relationship?

Serious boundary problems that have gone unaddressed over the years may require help from a trained third party, such as a Christian marriage counselor. Getting such help now might be the best preventative step for avoiding future calamity, including divorce or ministry burnout.

CHILDREN: A BOUNDARIED PERSPECTIVE ON DISCIPLINE

Many of the topics addressed in the previous section on spouses also apply with children. However, there is one issue deserving special attention. As ministers, we are responsible to shepherd not only our own flock at home (Titus 1:6) but also the flock under our care in the ministry. As such, successes and challenges at home and at work are likely to have significant effect on one another.

The best method for disciplining a child is, of course, dependent on how the child responds to various types of parental intervention. Some youngsters require merely a certain look from a parent while others respond to nothing less than firm corporal methods. Some children also seem to be astute at knowing just the right button to push to get on their parents' last nerve. Regardless of what method we believe is best for child discipline at home, we strongly encourage a right understanding of the larger purpose of discipline.

Generally speaking, discipline is not a means for "getting kids under control," as if they were bucking broncos to be broken. Some parents use discipline primarily as a tool of convenience or for getting their kids to not be an "embarrassment." This is short-sighted and misses the long-range purpose: systematically instructing our kids in the teachable moments of childhood so they will mature into God-fearing, responsible adults (Proverbs 22:6). Ultimately, discipline is about preparing a dependent child for successful independence.

Discipline also isn't an opportunity for parents to displace their own anger. Discipline in this manner is not only ineffective but sends the wrong message to a child. We'll need to draw boundaries around our own negative feelings toward our children so we don't provoke them to anger by our own angry expression (Ephesians 6:4). Otherwise, our children will learn more from our anger than from their mistake, learning instead that it's the one with the power who can control others through anger.

If discipline without anger is difficult for us, we can remove ourselves from our kids until we've had time to cool down before administering discipline. Sending them to their room for a time to think about what they've done allows us a boundary of time to collect ourselves and to gain clarity of thought about discipline appropriately tailored to the context. We will then be better able to rightly understand their situation and empathize with their negative feelings without being emotionally triggered by them.

What role does anger play in how you discipline your kids? If you have different issues with different children, consider writing their names in parenthesis beside each issue.

How might you adapt your discipline techniques to better serve each of your children?

Sometimes problems with our children reach beyond the scope of our ability to know how to effectively parent them. At such times, it can be very beneficial to consider the help of a Christian counselor who specializes in working with children.

PRIORITIZING TIME WITH LOVED ONES

Complete the following sentence: "The biggest reason families of ministers are neglected is _____." Would it be the demands of the ministry, too many meetings to attend, ministry members who call at all hours of the night, not enough ministry volunteers? What prevents us from spending quantity and quality time with our family?

The most common answer seems to be lack of intentionality. Our desire may be sincere, but if we fail to block out sufficient time in our schedule to spend with our family, the time will get filled with quadrant 3 junk. Something "urgent" will come up and we'll feel responsible to deal with it.

If something urgent demands our attention during family time, we can legitimately say, "I'm sorry. I have an appointment I cannot break."

Ask your spouse and older children the following: "Who do you feel is more important to me, you or the church/ministry? How do I communicate that to you?" Use the space below to write their responses:

Either we'll be greatly encouraged by their answers or we'll have some very specific areas for improvement! Our family may not cry out for time with us until they're in excruciating pain. But by then, it's a crisis. We may need to sit down with our planner at the start of the week (or even at the start of the month) and block out time for both our spouse and our children, treating them as our most important appointments. We can use that time to minister to them as we would our most important client or church member. In reality, that's who they are. If something "urgent" demands our attention during family time, we can legitimately say, "I'm sorry. I have an appointment I cannot break." Our family will highly respect us for such a boundary.

But what do we do with the "urgent" matter? If it's urgent but not important (quadrant 3), we might refer the person to someone else. If the matter is urgent and important (quadrant 1), we might still refer the person to someone else. Alternately, we might attempt to schedule a later time to discuss and address it. A last resort might be to reschedule or modify our family time to accommodate the emergency. However, this option will wear thin if used too frequently. When possible, reschedule the revised family time *before* moving on to address the urgent matter. Charles Shepson, founder of Fairhaven Ministries, offers the following illustration of how family can be prioritized even in the midst of crises in ministry:

I had promised my sons I would take them fishing. They were so excited! As we were about to go out the door, the phone rang. One of my youth leaders had been in a serious car accident and was in the E.R. in critical condition. Ron was asking for me, they said, and that I should come immediately.

Knowing that disappointments like this can turn children against the ministry, I made a quick decision. "Boys, come sit down with me. That phone call was from Mercy Hospital. Ron has been in a terrible accident and I need to go to him. Before I go, there are two things I want to do. First, I want to promise you that we are going fishing. We will go later today if I get home in time; if not, we'll go tomorrow. Second, I want the three of us to take time right now and pray for Ron—he needs your prayers as well as mine."

I knew the time I spent with the boys explaining what had happened and the time we spent praying for Ron could have meant Ron might die before I arrived at the hospital. For the sake of my boys, it was a chance I chose to take. The boys' prayers with me for Ron made them a part of the ministry. Although disappointed, they weren't resentful of what had happened. I knew I'd made a healthy decision.

How could you plan ahead to protect important time with your family?

What practical adjustments in the way you use your planner might be helpful?

> *While we don't have the luxury of deciding who we minister to, we have every right to decide who we let in as friends.*

BOUNDARIES WITH SAME-GENDER FRIENDSHIPS

How is it we make ourselves available to some friendships and not others? While this often has to do with personality, it sometimes has to do with the level of intimacy in the relationship (see foundation stone 1). While we don't have the luxury of deciding who we minister to, we have every right to decide who we let in as friends.

It isn't necessary to feel guilty when others want to invest in a relationship with us at a different level than we do. Those who desire less intimacy than we do may be seeking to be ministered to by us, and therefore are not potential friends. Those who desire greater intimacy than we do may have ulterior motives of being the minister's "special friend," or we may simply not enjoy their company enough to justify pursuing a friendship with them. Defending our differing levels of friendship with people is a potentially sensitive area, especially if we're in a small, traditional church setting.

However, we don't have to make more of this theoretical problem than is necessary. If no one questions us directly on this, we shouldn't allow ourselves to be bothered with it. While some in our ministry may harbor private thoughts of jealousy, we most certainly aren't responsible for their negative feelings or the resolution of them. In the unlikely event someone approaches us directly on the matter, an honest answer respectfully given without elaboration is best: "Yes, they are a good friend" is often sufficient.

How do we tell the difference between good boundaries in close friendships and avoidance of accountability? If we have a few close friends and find ourselves backing away from them, this likely indicates a problem in the relationship. Sharing this concern with our spouse, our mentor or another close friend will provide an outside perspective on the situation, especially if they perceive that we may be at fault in some way.

BOUNDARIES RELATED TO SEXUAL TEMPTATION

Friendships with members of the opposite gender are important not only as friendships but also, for single ministers, as a means for locating a potential soul mate. However, we will want to be careful how our relationships appear to others, avoiding not only evil but also the perception of evil whenever possible. Single ministers ought to consider how some expressions of their significant-other relationship (such as going on vacation together, staying over for the night, more intimate displays of public affection) may appear, and count the cost ahead of time. Even if a relationship with someone of the opposite gender is purely ministry-related and platonic, married ministers should make sure their spouse (and if the other person is married, their spouse) is aware of their meetings. If either spouse is uncomfortable with such time together, it ought to be avoided—regardless of the meeting's benefits.

Each minister must decide how to apply Jesus' "whatever-it-takes" principle to their own quest for sexual integrity (Matthew 5:29-30). We must not be naive about the dark side of our hearts when it comes to sexuality. A crack left in the door often becomes a potential opportunity for Satan to exploit (Ephesians 4:27). If our adversary can take down our marriage, he will be successful at destroying our ministry for years to come. With a full 20 percent of American pastors admitting to having an affair while in the ministry,[9] 37 percent

---

[9]Save America Ministries, "The State of Ministry Marriage and Morals," <www.saveus.org/docs/factsheets/stateofministry2003.pdf>, accessed February 26, 2007.

admitting pornography as a current struggle[10] and countless more who struggle silently with such issues, broken sexuality appears to be one of Satan's favorite portals of entry for the destruction of ministers and ministries. To finish strong in ministry, we must address this issue head-on. We might consider meeting with one (or more) same-gender accountability partners on a regular basis to discuss how each can proactively address the issue in their own lives. This can keep us from having to reinvent the wheel when it comes to sexual boundaries—not to mention keep us from repeating someone else's painful consequences. Such transparency with a few trusted others will itself keep us from operating in secrecy about sexual temptation. As many long-time twelve-step participants would say, "you are only as sick as your secrets."

Spouses sometimes have more objective ideas of what practical boundaries might help protect our marital vows from sexual temptation than we may have. We would do well to heed their concern for the sake of our marriage. For example, a spouse's discomfort with a person's desire to meet with us privately for counseling may reflect an intuition about relationships that we don't possess. In some instances, our spouse could participate in a counseling session. If this isn't feasible or appropriate, during the session our spouse could work in an adjacent room with the office door ajar. Or we might simply decline or refer that particular ministry opportunity altogether.

There are no right or wrong answers regarding specific boundaries to establish (such as not going anywhere alone with a member of the opposite gender, keeping our door slightly open when meeting with a certain individual, making calls to our spouse from the hotel room when we are traveling). However, there are two major criteria to consider when determining good boundaries: (1) whatever we feel will help us maintain sexual integrity and (2) whatever will encourage our spouse to *perceive* our sexual integrity. Both are equally important and equally valuable to a healthy marriage.

Several helpful books offer good insights into sexual boundaries. See appendix G for recommendations.

What modifications might you consider in the way you interact with the opposite sex?

There are two major types of criteria to consider when determining good boundaries: (1) whatever we feel will help us maintain sexual integrity and (2) whatever will encourage our spouse to **perceive** *our sexual integrity.*

---

[10]Christianity Today Library, "The *Leadership* Survey on Pastors and Internet Pornography," <www.ctlibrary.com/le/2001/winter/12.89.html>, accessed February 26, 2007.

Schedule an honest conversation with your spouse, mentors, accountability partners or trusted friends for their insights. Use the space below to write down helpful insights you receive from such conversations.

4. Real-World Boundaries with Ourselves and with God

There's something inside us that doesn't like being restrained. Mastery of self is one of the most challenging facets of spiritual growth, requiring us to wrestle with our "inner demons." The apostle Paul struggled with the discipline of his own inner man (Romans 7; 1 Corinthians 9:24-27). Boundaries within ourselves result in a life not only pleasing to God but ultimately more successful in fulfilling our unique calling in ministry.

TIME

Most ministers have read at least one book or article on time management. Yet before time management can yield any real value, we must first prioritize *self-management*. Self-management is the practice of developing internal boundaries that enable us to say "no" to unimportant things because we are choosing to say "yes" to things consistent with what matters most in our life. As Stephen Covey says:

> You learn, basically, that all you have to do is to learn to say two words: "yes" and "no." The key is the sequence. You must have a burning "yes" inside your mind and heart around your most important priorities. Then, you will find your ability to say "no" is easy, it's effortless, it's guilt-free, it can be done pleasantly, cheerfully, even smilingly. But people that have not yet learned to focus on their highest priorities . . . and said "yes" to them cannot say "no" . . . without guilt. It is an amazing combination of two words: "yes" to the most important things—the main things—and "no" to that which may be urgent but is not important, is not central to your highest priorities. . . . The main thing is to keep the main thing the main thing.[11]

---

[11]Stephen R. Covey, *Focus: Achieving Your Highest Priorities,* audiobook (New York: Simon & Schuster, 2003).

We must do whatever it takes to spend time engaged in activities that fulfill these highest priorities in our life. To that end, here are just a few practical suggestions for consideration:

- Use some type of day planner or time organizer to help keep track of obligations.

- Place time obligations on the calendar at the beginning of the week (or month) before any other "urgent" matters have a chance to find their way into the schedule. Only genuine emergencies should take precedence over these prior commitments, and even then only rarely.

- Give a close friend permission to ask periodically how it's going keeping the calendar in line with our true priorities.

- Respond to requests about urgent but not important matters either with a polite "no" or by redirecting them to someone else.

- Have a secretary or administrative assistant screen "urgent" calls and unscheduled visits. Return calls at a time consistent with the day's priorities. If an assistant isn't an option, let calls go through to voicemail during important tasks.

- Place a sign and message pad outside the office inviting unannounced visitors to write a "Sorry I missed you" message.

- Schedule times to work offsite in private places such as a local bookstore, coffee shop or public library.

- At home, "unplug" from ministry by not accepting phone calls, pages and e-mails during family dinner, on date night, on vacation and on days off. If other "paid staff" aren't an option, recruit deacons, elders, board members, other ministry professionals or others to be "on call" during such times.

A little planning will allow time for psychological and emotional separation from ministry, enabling us to regenerate the energy needed to be fully present upon our return. Especially over short periods of time (such as over family dinner), the world isn't likely to fall apart if we're unable to return someone's call for an hour or two.

MONEY

Most ministers don't become independently wealthy working for faith-based organizations. Money can be one of our biggest stumbling blocks. God provides lots of encouragement in Scripture for managing money according to his economy.

It's essential that we live by some sort of budget. Some see a budget as a means for preventing fun. However, a budget is actually a very helpful tool to ensure we have money for the things that matter most to us. Basic budgeting information as well as a variety of tools are available from organizations such as Crown Financial Ministries (www.crown.org).

Credit cards have enslaved millions of American households. Some ministers have chosen to finance a ministry on debt rather than allowing God to supply their financial needs as they arise. If we have difficulty with discipline in using credit, we might set up an accountability plan for the use of credit cards or convert to a "cash only" system using checks, check cards and plain old cash.

We can also teach our kids a godly view of money, regardless of how well we're doing with it. This serves two purposes: (1) our children will learn early how to manage money and (2) they will hold us accountable for what we teach them. Whatever it takes to get debt under control is worth it in the long run.

CRITICISM

When boundaries are poorly established or guarded, our tongue has the power to create real problems (James 3:3-12). Each person has their own perception of reality. At times, their perception will be very different from our own, and we'll need to talk about it with them. Left unaddressed, anger that arises from such conflicts festers into resentment. This is the wisdom of not letting the sun go down while we are still angry (Ephesians 4:26). Instead of letting pride get the best of us when someone gives us critical feedback, we can consider it a valuable gift we were unable to give ourselves. God is using them to help us grow. If we overreact by becoming upset, we can confess our reaction as soon as we catch ourselves and thank them for having enough concern for us to risk such feedback. We can also

- ask the Holy Spirit for discernment regarding criticism.

- commit to memory passages from Scripture that address keeping the tongue under control.

- acknowledge wrongdoing right away.

- give intimate relationships permission to speak up when they feel hurt; commit to a balanced, respectful response to their concerns.

We can both approach others and allow others to approach us with the truth as they see it without becoming defensive, listening for their "kernel of truth" and being quick to admit when they are right or when we are wrong. We can also say in love what we feel needs to be spoken without disrespecting the other person through harsh words. Even if we don't agree with their point of view, we can choose to see their feedback as evidence they care enough about us to take such a risk. God may have a purpose in their bringing this to our attention. We can also ask ourselves how God might use this confrontation as an opportunity to strengthen the relationship.

Charles Shepson shares the following story from his Bible college days on learning that God wanted to teach him through criticism:

> I took a little black loose-leaf book and divided it into three sections. In the first section I recorded criticism I received from any source. I titled that first section "Criticisms." I named section 2 "True—Do Something About It!" I titled section 3 "False!" and divided that section into (A) criticism that I felt it best to simply ignore and (with God's enabling) to forget, and (B) malicious criticisms that could tarnish my reputation if they were not addressed. Under the heading on that page, I put the reference "Matthew 18:15-17" to remind myself of how God wanted me to deal with such false accusation. Through the years, God has taught me many valuable things about myself through both constructive criticism and criticisms leveled with intent to hurt. Of the latter, I can honestly agree with Joseph, "You intended them for evil, but God meant them for good!"

In what way has your reaction to criticism affected your important relationships recently?

How could you have handled the conversation differently?

How might you allow God to teach you through both the constructive and the malicious criticisms of others?

OUR RELATIONSHIP WITH GOD

Every believer knows what it's like to struggle in their relationship with God: lack of desire for reading Scripture, lack of motivation for corporate worship and the feeling that prayers are bouncing off the ceiling. When the struggle finally passes, we often realize that not only were we contending with our own weaknesses, but we were also struggling with an adversary who seeks to destroy any effectiveness we may have for God's kingdom. We must maintain strong boundaries around our inner life, for as soon as we relax them we may be attacked by an enemy who sees us as the gateway to hundreds if not thousands of souls.

What advice have you previously given struggling believers for maintaining a vibrant spiritual life (the more specific, the better)?

How might this advice apply to your own spiritual life at the moment?

What practical steps could you take this week to strengthen the boundaries in your relationship with God?

It may be helpful to have a routine location and time to cultivate our relationship with God. Some find a plan for regular "mini-sabbaticals" every week, month or quarter helpful. The frequency and amount of time aren't as important as prioritizing some time to periodically step back and allow God to show us our current ministry in the larger context of his overall activity in our lives.

In addition, we can enlist others to hold us accountable for our time with God. We can inform our family exactly where and when we will spend our study/prayer time and instruct them to interrupt us only in an emergency.

We might also commit to sharing daily with someone what the Lord has been teaching us. Not only can boundaries such as these help encourage the vibrancy of our relationship with God, they can also help us maintain a clear view of our calling in ministry.

Wrap-Up:
Foundation Stone 4—Boundaries

Reflecting on all you've learned in this foundation stone, use the space below to record your most important takeaways.

Consider the specific boundaries you'd like to work toward consistently applying in each of the following areas. Consider asking loved ones or accountability partners for feedback on boundaries that might be helpful for you, as they may be able to provide added insight.

New boundaries in my ministry setting:

New boundaries with my family:

New boundaries with my friends:

New boundaries with myself or God:

Return to the personal self-care plan on pages 98-99 to consider any modifications to your purpose statement. Change the statement in light of any insights the Holy Spirit has given you as you've reflected on boundaries. If no change is needed, reinforce your statement by copying it as is into the space provided.

RE-CREATION

The Fuel to
Re-energize Ministry

Tommy and Linda would do anything to help someone in need. While this might be a wonderful trait in many ways, some people (and even some ministries) took advantage of their giving nature. Tommy and Linda spent their ministry career giving to others but doing little reinvesting back into themselves. Their ministry was boundary-less and their phone rang often with requests. Slowly, their passion for ministry dissipated until one day Tommy crashed. He simply couldn't give anymore.

I (Brad) will never forget the first time we met. They entered my office with forced smiles, unsure of the future. There were so many questions without answers: How would they earn an income? What would they do with the rest of their lives? What about their kids? As we spoke, it became apparent both were deep into burnout and their tanks were empty. How did their lives get so out of balance? Weren't they pursuing a calling to invest in the people around them? How did they get to the point of wanting so desperately to abandon their ministry calling?

To be at our best physically, mentally, emotionally and spiritually, we must engage in re-creation—a necessary and God-intended part of the human experience that "re-creates" the physical, mental, emotional and spiritual resources we've expended in the pursuit of our calling. Without replenishing internal resources, we can't hope to carry out God's purpose in our lives long-term. Instead, we will prematurely flame out.

1. Slaves to the Schedule

A survey of 1,220 adults published in *USA Today* revealed that most people are looking for more rest in their lives. Nearly 70 percent of those surveyed cited a need for more fun.[1] For most busy ministry professionals, additional fun time won't happen without intentional planning. The survey further revealed that

- 67 percent said they need a long vacation.
- 66 percent said they often feel stressed.
- 60 percent feel their time is crunched.
- 51 percent say they want less work and more play.
- 49 percent feel pressure to succeed.
- 48 percent feel generally overwhelmed.[2]

When do you physically rest? How much "downtime" do you have planned into your regular routine?

What do you do for fun? *What are your hobbies (active or sedentary)?*

What activities do you participate in (either by yourself or with others) that are just *for you?*

At the dawn of the twenty-first century, time has become a god. The alarm wakes us, bells ring in cell phones and personal computers to notify us of appointments, and organizers dictate daily arrival and departure times at the office. Throughout the day our schedule determines how much time we give to a particular task or individual. Often it's the urgent instead of the important things that command our time. If we're not purposeful, even our time on weekends can become dictated.

As I (Brad) sit in my study writing, there are a variety of activities swirling around me. Some I am aware of, others I am not. On our ministry campus, a prayer meeting is taking place in the singles center. Steps away from my office, several hundred people are attending a wedding reception. Across the street in the Family Life Center, our students are participating in a weekend discipleship event. A few blocks away from our campus, my daughter is competing in a history

---

[1] Lori Joseph and Bob Laird, "Americans Working Too Hard," *USA Today Snapshots*, Hilton Generational Time Survey, January 2001.
[2] Ibid.

fair at the local college. As I left for lunch, I was met by a number of familiar faces. One individual commented on how busy she was—to the point of overload.

We live in an age of complexity and overcommitment. For most, time for personal refueling is dreadfully missing. While many people dream of having more money, just as many dream of having more time. Both are precious commodities. Time must be allocated for re-creating our vitality.

A THEOLOGY OF RE-CREATION

The need for re-creation finds its beginning in the creation story. Each day God created marvelous aspects of our world. At the conclusion of day six God rested. This is the pattern of God's creative activity in the world: "And God blessed the seventh day and made it holy, because on it he rested from all the work of creating that he had done" (Genesis 2:3). God designed the seventh day to be different from the other six. It wasn't that God needed rest; rather, he was illustrating to his creation *our* need for rest—for ceasing from labor. The Old Testament practice of six years sowing followed by a seventh year for allowing the land to rest also reflects the priority of renewal (Leviticus 25:1-7). God designed re-creation as a means for re-investing life and energy back into our lives.

What do you think of the concept of a "theology of re-creation"?

Re-creation as Sacred

The seventh day is *sacred*—set aside for a special purpose. Rest was a divinely ordained function, and routine labor was expected to be condensed into six-sevenths of our weekly schedule (Exodus 20:8-11). As humans rebelled against God's authority, our loss of intimate relationship with our Creator resulted. The chaos of sin entered the world, bringing with it the pain and suffering familiar to all of us. Now the concept of rest foreshadows the coming of our Savior who brought true spiritual rest through his death and resurrection and someday will bring an ultimate rest from all striving, even against sin and death. "Keeping the Sabbath" is a practical way for us to prioritize time for reflection on the Lord's provision for us—past, present and future.

Re-creation as Rhythm

Re-creation is like the rhythmic working of a clock, with a regular beginning and ending. "We can learn from this sequence of days in which God spoke energy and matter into existence. We can also learn from the repeated refrain, 'and there was evening and there was morning . . . and there was evening and there was morning'—on and on, six times."[3] Rhythm is a dynamic pattern. When functioning properly, our heart beats to a certain cadence. When that cadence is disrupted, our heart is at risk. A cardiologist might prescribe medication to regulate an arrhythmia or even a surgical implant to assure a more regular beat. Life itself was designed to function in similar fashion. Sabbath-keeping brings rhythm to life.

Re-creation as Obedience

Observing re-creation follows in obedience the plan God set for us and shows him honor. God instructed observance of the Sabbath as a way for us to regularly pause from our busyness to remember God's past provision for us (Deuteronomy 5:15), with the clear implication that the God who provided for our yesterday will most certainly care for our tomorrow as well (Hebrews 13:8).

Re-creation as Refreshment

The Sabbath is time God intended for us to spend with him for our renewal. The point isn't about keeping the times and dates of the Sabbath as much as keeping the spirit in which the Sabbath was given: "Some think one day is more holy than another day, while others think every day is alike. You should each be fully convinced that whichever day you choose is acceptable" (Romans 14:5 NLT). Many ministers work out of necessity on the day they celebrate as the Lord's Day. Even they, however, can set aside a day in their schedules for Sabbath. God created all human beings with such a need. To ignore this need is to neglect what is for our own good.

Which of the following concepts of Sabbath re-creation is most novel for you?

- *Recreation as Sacred*
- *Recreation as Rhythm*
- *Recreation as Obedience*
- *Recreation as Refreshment*

---

[3]H. B. London Jr., *Refresh, Renew, Revive: How to Encourage Your Spirit, Strengthen Your Family, and Energize Your Ministry* (Colorado Springs: Focus on the Family Publishing, 1996), p. 82.

How might these concepts challenge your current habits and behaviors regarding re-creation?

2. Common Excuses for Not Re-creating

The average minister works 10.5 hours a day, 6 days a week—a total of 63 hours per week.[4] Keep in mind, this means that half of all ministers are putting in *more than 63 hours per week*. The task of ministry can be overwhelming and ever-consuming. Every minute can be used for any number of urgent tasks: "If I just had more hours in my day or more days in my week, then I could accomplish everything that needs to be done." But the sad reality is, we wouldn't. The sooner we recognize this, the sooner we can break free from our denial about the real problem: what we often need isn't to do more but to do better. Prioritizing re-creation will help us do just that.

Figure 5.1 is intended to help us gain a better understanding of just how much time we really spend doing ministry by charting the number of hours we are involved in ministry during a typical week. We need to honestly consider *all* aspects of ministry, including

- *work at work.* All time spent on our ministry's worksite (including our home office) should be included in the total. Even if we don't consider what we're doing at any given time to be "work," our family likely does. Besides, anytime we're physically on-site at our ministry setting we're likely "on" for the ministry—that in itself constitutes work.

- *work off-site.* We shouldn't fool ourselves into thinking we're only working when we're "at work." Restaurants, coffee shops, our home, our car, other people's homes, traveling for work, conferences—all these are places we do ministry away from our regular work location. The following is only a partial list of activities that likely should be included in our time estimate: board meetings, breakfast/lunch meetings, casual conversation with others about ministry, e-mails, formal meetings, fundraising, impromptu ministry opportunities, Internet research, paperwork, phone calls, planning, praying, sermon preparation, visitation, vision-casting, worry. *Anything* connected to our role as a minister needs to be included here, regardless of where or what time of day or night it takes place.

---

[4]John C. LaRue Jr., "Pastors at Work: Where the Time Goes," LeadershipJournal.net, January 3, 2001.

	Hours Spent	Typical Activities Engaged
Sunday	_____	_____
		_____
Monday	_____	_____
		_____
Tuesday	_____	_____
		_____
Wednesday	_____	_____
		_____
Thursday	_____	_____
		_____
Friday	_____	_____
		_____
Saturday	_____	_____
		_____
Total	_____	

Figure 5.1. A typical week in my ministry.

Are you surprised by the results of the time exercise in figure 5.1? Why or why not?

Given your particular situation, what do you feel would be a reasonable number of hours in a typical week to dedicate to your work?

What specifically might you change about your routine to move toward this goal?

EXCUSES, EXCUSES, EXCUSES

So what's the big deal? Why is our typical schedule so important? The number one excuse ministers give for failure to prioritize time for re-creation is "I don't have time."

"I Just Don't Have Enough Time!" (A Problem with Stewardship)

Dale Carnegie once reportedly told the story of two men given the tiring job of clearing a field of trees. The contract called for them to be paid per tree cut. Bill wanted the day to be profitable, so he grunted and sweated, swinging his axe relentlessly. His buddy Ed, however, seemed to be working only half Bill's pace. He even took a break to sit down for a few minutes. Meanwhile, Bill kept chopping away until every muscle in his body was aching. At the end of the day, Bill was terribly sore but Ed was smiling and telling jokes. To Bill's amazement, Ed had actually cut down more trees! In disbelief, Bill asked, "But I saw you sitting around while I worked without a break. How'd you outwork me?" Ed smiled. "Did you notice I was sharpening my axe while I was sitting?"[5]

Good stewardship of our body and our time won't always mean exerting more energy. It may mean paying attention to our limitations and planning accordingly. Good stewardship recognizes our personal rhythm and establishes a schedule to optimize our resources—body, mind and spirit. This means including "axe-sharpening" re-creation into our routine.

"I Have Other More Important Things to Do!"
(A Problem with Prioritizing)

How many times have we told ourselves there are so many "more important" things to do than re-creation? Ministry obligations command our day. Phone calls, meetings, speaking engagements, pastoral care and the like are all very important. We will have to purposefully build time for re-creation into our planner at the beginning of each week (or month) to ensure the time is available when we need it.

While we might see more readily the importance for spiritual renewal in re-creation, we shouldn't neglect prioritizing other re-creative activities, too: adequate sleep and exercise re-creates our body; pleasure reading or vacation planning re-creates our mind; date nights with our loved ones and God-time re-create our spirit; play time and laughter re-create our emotional life. Body, mind and spirit are interconnected. When one is neglected over time, the others suffer. Re-creation replenishes what we need to be an effective minister. Practicing re-creation also models the importance of self-care to those we lead. That's leadership in action!

"I Have Too Many Responsibilities to Deal With!"
(A Problem with Delegating)

Ministers wear any number of hats on a daily basis. The solo pastor and nonprofit ministry entrepreneur have an especially challenging task in this respect. To prevent burnout, we must learn to delegate.

Some ministers are such micromanagers of their staff (paid and volunteer) that they effectively prevent others from reaching their

---

[5]*Stand Firm,* June 2000, p. 13. Author name and article title unavailable.

full potential in ministry. This is often an issue of mistrust. While we may not believe another person will do a good job, closer to the truth might be for us to admit that they won't do it the exact way we would do it. Our overcontrol may effectively inhibit their maturing in skills and confidence.

This struggle can often be traced to an issue with pride. There are probably only a limited number of tasks that only we can do. We need to ask God to help us let go of having to do things "our way" and allow others to help us in ministry. God will not only bless us personally but will cause others to rise to the occasion to improve our ministry's overall effectiveness.

What parts of your job are things only you can do?

What aspects of your ministry could be delegated to others?

What steps could you take in the near future to delegate some of those tasks?

"People Expect Me to Be Available!" (A Problem with Approval Seeking)
We've heard many ministers complain about the absurd expectations of those they serve. However, ministers often fuel this problem by their own lack of boundaries:

> Thinking how to remove unrealistic expectations is a stimulating exercise for an overburdened pastor. Amazingly, in the process he may discover that his expectations of his parishioners and his family may be as unrealistic as their expectations of him. Or even more amazing, he may discover that the expectations are in his head—that is, his expectations are mostly self-induced.[6]

This hits the nail on the head more often than not. If we're really honest, much of our striving to meet others' expectations is a distorted internal drive to avoid the disapproval of another. We want them to like us. This has nothing to do with ministry and everything to do with our own fragile self-esteem.

---

[6]H. B. London Jr. and Neil B. Wiseman, *Pastors at Greater Risk* (Ventura, Calif.: Regal, 2003), pp. 44-45.

Our agenda ought to reflect God's agenda for us, based on our calling: "I'm not trying to win the approval of people, but of God. If pleasing people were my goal, I would not be Christ's servant" (Galatians 1:10 NLT). The people we serve may need to adapt a bit and realize their minister can't personally hold the hand of every congregant every time. Another minister, an elder or a lay leader can do just as good a job as we can—and often they can do it better.

We all have a legitimate desire to minister to those under our care and we will most certainly try our best to do so. But sometimes saying "no" to the expectations of others is a healthy boundary that will communicate reasonable expectations to our clients and congregants.

"I Don't Feel Like I Need a Break!" (A Problem with Denial)

We can be workaholics and not even realize it sometimes. Unfortunately, there are many workaholics in ministry finding enjoyment in their work to the detriment of the rest of their lives. We've heard ministers say, "I don't need any downtime. Taking a break or wasting time with a hobby is just for those who can't handle the demands of ministry." This is not only bad theology but a potentially destructive practice. The blessing of the Sabbath was God's demonstration to us about our need for rest. Ceasing from labor one day in seven also provides needed opportunity for reflection on who we are, what we're doing and, perhaps most important, why we're doing it. Such time for rest and reflection encourages us to keep our focus on what's truly important, ensuring that our activities the other six days are consistent with God's calling on our lives and not activity for the mere sake of busy-ness.

Which of the above excuses have you used for not prioritizing re-creation?

What other excuses have you used that weren't discussed here?

If we believe we can't take time for re-creation, the long-term reality is that we can't afford not to. Re-creation is an investment in ourselves that will increase and renew our stamina—an energy regenerator in a schedule full of energy drainers. Believe it or not, our teaching will be better and our ability to handle crises more effective.

Others will notice we are more alive, more focused and more present when ministering to them.

Those who fail to engage in re-creation usually have only enough energy to cope with immediate demands. But effectiveness in ministry requires energy to not only function in the now but also in the future. Ministers who prioritize re-creation will find their ability to cast vision flowing more readily. Perhaps most importantly, re-creation will be a catalyst for re-creating and reconnecting us to our passion —the passion of our calling.

3. The Three *R*s of Re-creation: Rest, Recess, Renewal

To think of re-creation in more practical terms, consider its three significant facets: rest, recess and renewal.

REST

Rest refers to the physical repair and rebuilding of the body and mind. When we exert ourselves physically or mentally, we ache for the restoration of our energies. Even the emotional stress of sedentary work requires subsequent rest for the body and mind to recuperate.

Our first inclination for understanding rest might be to identify it with either physical inactivity or the ceasing of physical exertion. But the concept of rest is much more than merely not working. Remember Jesus' invitation to his disciples to "come with me by yourselves to a quiet place and get some rest" (Mark 6:31)? The disciples were so excited by all their ministry activity and the throngs of people seeking their attention that they hadn't even taken time to eat. Jesus led them to a place of quietness because he saw their fatigue and knew they needed downtime. Jesus knows our need for rest. He sees behind our masks and into the depths of our weariness. We can ask him to help us recognize the value of rest in our regular routine.

Take a few minutes to sit quietly with your heavenly Father. Tell him how you're really feeling. Feel free to express your heart.

Ministry can be a demanding and draining business. We won't survive long by spending twenty-four hours a day with people who are always taking from us. Those who subconsciously believe they are called into 24/7 ministry are often the ones who become disillusioned and angry when their expectations are shattered. Then they

Those who fail to engage in re-creation usually have only enough energy to cope with immediate demands.

wonder why God doesn't give them the ability to continue ministering. The reason is simple: they're not withdrawing into restorative activities and relationships that fill them up. Periodically, we must be willing to take time for rest away from people who need us. God didn't design us as maintenance-free beings. Like the Garden of Eden and everything else in the created order, we must be properly maintained.

What are some practical ways of resting? For starters, we can take an afternoon nap. It's amazing how much clearer our mind can think with as little as ten to fifteen minutes of nap time. Even if we're unable to fall asleep completely, stopping what we're doing to close our eyes for even a few minutes can alter our state of consciousness, causing us to relax and restoring a bit of physical energy. As prime minister of England, Winston Churchill took daily naps.

Like the Garden of Eden and everything else in the created order, we must be properly maintained.

Take a day off and don't fill it with work around the house: sleep an extra hour on a day off; go to a local coffee shop and read the paper; take a walk with a friend or loved one around the neighborhood and talk about anything but work or family obligations; read a good book for pleasure (rather than in preparation for a sermon or other ministry); sit in a favorite chair and listen to favorite music; go to dinner with intimate friends or family; write in a journal—there are as many ideas for rest as there are unique people in the world. The only way for us to find out what's restful to us is by trying something we think could be restful. If we feel more refreshed, invigorated or optimistic about life after doing it, we've found a restful activity.

Which of the ideas suggested above sound restful to you?

In an average week, how often do you pause for a bit of rest?

If you feel your regular amount of rest is insufficient, what practical step(s) can you take to add more rest to your weekly routine?

The actual implementation of rest into a busy schedule requires planning and perseverance. Most ministers' schedules aren't a nine-to-five operation. We don't have to feel guilty about scheduling additional rest time on a weekday morning when we will be working that evening. It's just wise planning and healthy self-care, taking the downtime necessary to be at our best. If unhealthy expectations exist concerning our "on call" or "office" hours, we might discuss them openly with our leadership team to help them understand our actions as making our ministry more effective over the long-term.

RECESS

In the middle of the daily routine of elementary school, we looked forward to *recess* as a time of running and playing. As children, we played with great abandon. Back then, our body needed to release all the energy it had built up from being cooped up in a classroom all day.

In reality, not much has changed since childhood. Adult bodies and emotions still require (and even yearn for) playful activity to release stress. While we believe that godliness has value for all things, we often overlook Paul's acknowledgment that physical training has value as well (1 Timothy 4:8). Exercise affords opportunity to physically care for our body; play allows us to mentally and emotionally connect to our childlike side. Whereas rest is characterized by relaxation and downtime, recess involves focused activity and enjoyable "uptime."

Special outings, sports, cultural events and weekend getaways offer a diversion from the rut of our everyday routine. There is great value in taking up a personal hobby or activity, allowing our mind and body to disengage from the responsibility of ministry and to ponder things a bit more entertaining. Playful exercise provides a great benefit not only to our physical state but also to our emotional and spiritual state. The American Heart Association reports:

> There are numerous benefits of daily physical activity: reduces the risk of heart disease by improving blood circulation throughout the body; keeps weight under control; improves blood cholesterol levels; prevents and reduces high blood pressure; prevents bone loss; boosts energy levels; helps manage stress; releases tension; improves the ability to fall asleep quickly and sleep well; improves self-image; counters anxiety and depression and increases enthusiasm and optimism; increases muscle strength; gives greater capacity for other physical activities; provides a way to share an activity with family and friends; establishes good heart-healthy habits in children and counters the conditions (obesity, high blood pressure, high cholesterol levels, poor lifestyle habits, etc.) that lead to heart attack and stroke in later life; and in older people, helps delay or prevent chronic illnesses and diseases associated with aging and maintains quality of life and independence longer.[7]

If you ask us, that's quite a list of benefits for exercise!

---

[7] American Heart Association report <www.americanheart.org/presenter.jhtml ?identifier=764>, accessed June 1, 2007.

RENEWAL

Renewal re-energizes our spiritual vitality. Activities that renew produce deep growth of inner strength and character, conforming us to Christ's likeness. Practice of the spiritual disciplines and intentional times of spiritual refreshment are examples of renewal activities.

Jesus often found places of solitude for prayer and contemplation (Luke 5:16). The Bible stresses the importance of renewal and transformation that comes through the continual renewing of our minds on God's Word (Romans 12:2). Our personal vitality, creativity and perseverance are direct results of our own spiritual renewal.

Which of the "Rs" are presently deficient in your life? Which do you feel might be difficult to integrate into a weekly routine? (Check all that apply.)

	Deficient	*Potentially Difficult to Integrate*
Rest	☐	☐
Recess	☐	☐
Renewal	☐	☐

What accounts for any difficulty you perceive you may have?

If we don't replenish our spent energy through re-creation, our body may eventually respond with physical ailment or burnout, or our congregation or board may respond in the form of ministry removal, or the demons crouching at our door will respond with temptations toward moral failure (Genesis 4:7). If we fail to prioritize time for rest, recess and renewal, we may not be as physically resilient, mentally sharp, emotionally stable or spiritually recharged as we need to be. If we take time for these things in the midst of our busy schedule, we'll smile more and probably even get more done.

4. Creating Our Own Re-creation Plan

My wife and I (Michael Todd) recently enjoyed eight nights on a beach in the Dominican Republic. There's nothing like sitting on the beach without a care in the world. But the trip required work on the front end to make it a reality: the destination had to be selected, a travel agent consulted, the flight arranged, money saved and a general itinerary planned. Even though our purpose for the trip was primarily to lie under an umbrella on the beach and do as little as possible, we still needed a plan.

Personal growth most often occurs through intentionality and planned strategy. Five questions can help create an effective personal re-creation plan: (1) What kind of journey do we want to take? (2) What is our specific destination? (3) How will we get there? (4) What's our first step? and (5) What would we do differently next time?

Regardless whether our method for planning is highly or lightly structured, everyone's style can successfully develop and implement an effective plan for personal growth and improvement.

WHAT KIND OF JOURNEY DO WE WANT TO TAKE?

Before we begin the journey of renewal, we must first determine what our goal is. Like planning a vacation, we don't just jump into the family car the first day of our vacation and ask, "Where should we go this year on vacation?" We determine where we want to go well ahead of time. What about the beach? Maybe the mountains? Perhaps overseas? Are we going somewhere to relax, to learn, to have fun or for some other reason? Each of these purposes will strongly influence the family's ultimate selection of a destination.

Likewise, before embarking on a journey of renewal, discovering "where we want to go" is key to creating a successful plan. Throughout this section, we will follow two examples of personal re-creation renewal. Janet desires growth physically through intentional exercise. Randall wants growth mentally through a planned sabbatical.

The process of discovery is much like a brainstorming session. Prayer and time with significant others can help us gain a sense of what changes are needed related to re-creation.

Brainstorm how you might like to experience renewal in the following four areas of your life. Spend time with God and with significant others who have insight into what might be healthy re-creational pursuits for you. Try to think in terms of an end result you would like to experience or achieve. Don't worry about how to get there just yet, only the goal.

- *Physically* (e.g., increase your stamina or simply feel better)

- *Mentally* (e.g., learn about a new area of ministry or simply get some mental "downtime")

- *Emotionally* (e.g., get in touch with some sadness or anger you've been feeling lately)

- *Spiritually* (e.g., increase your connectedness with God or gain a more *personal* sense of God's forgiveness in your life)

Resist feeling overwhelmed by all the areas you might want to pursue renewal in. Once you build re-creation into your life, your schedule will allow space for future changes. It's best to take it slowly, one change at a time.

WHAT IS OUR SPECIFIC DESTINATION?

Once we've decided what kind of re-creation we want to pursue, we will want to be more specific by defining our plan—clearly articulating what we intend to accomplish. If we've decided on going to the beach, to which beach will we go? If the trip will be educational related to American history, which city and which historical sites within that city will we visit?

Once we have a more clearly defined vision for personal renewal, we can write a *destination declaration*—a concise phrase of what we want to accomplish. This statement will serve as our guide along the journey, keeping us from becoming distracted and abandoning the plan when the going gets tough. A helpful destination declaration can be written in terms consistent with the acrostic "S-A-M": specific, achievable and measurable.

Specific means avoiding language that is vague. For example, while "I want to get into shape" is too vague, "I will lose ten pounds" or "I will do circuit training at the gym three days a week" is much more specific.

Achievable means avoiding a goal that is too advanced for what we're likely to accomplish. For example, "I want to learn to play the piano like Jerry Lee Lewis over the next six months" is not very realistic. More realistic might be something like, "I will devote three hours each week for the next six months to learning to play the piano." Another reason this second declaration is more achievable is that it focuses on the investment (something within our control) rather than the result (something not completely within our control).

A *measurable* declaration is quantifiable and can be proven to have succeeded or failed. Look back at the declarations we've given as examples thus far. Because "I want to get into shape" has no quantifiable measurements, we'd never really know if we achieved our goal or not. While a timetable is mentioned in the declaration "I want to learn to play the piano like Jerry Lee Lewis over the next six months," how would we know if we "learned to play"?

On the other hand, both "I will do circuit training at the gym three days a week" and "I will devote three hours each week for the next six months to learning to play the piano" are not only quantifiable but can be proven to have been accomplished. Each uses language of the will rather than the language of desire. Saying "I want to" is a wish, suggesting there are forces outside ourselves that may prevent us from achieving our goal. While this is factually true, using such language subconsciously gives us an "out" to blame our circumstances or others if our goals aren't realized. Saying "I will" is a choice we make in recognition that we alone are responsible for the outcome. Using such language lessens the likelihood of shifting blame for our failure to achieve the goal.

Consider a possible destination declaration for our two ministers:

JANET: "I will grow in my physical health through regular exercise consisting of weight training three days per week and two miles of speed-walking another two days per week."

RANDALL: "I will take a one-month sabbatical from ministry by the end of this year to recharge physically, emotionally and spiritually."

Looking back at your brainstorming exercise, create no more than one destination declaration for each of the following categories using "language of the will." Make sure your declaration meets the "S.A.M." test—specific, achievable and measurable.

- *Physically*

- *Mentally*

- *Emotionally*

- *Spiritually*

HOW WILL WE GET THERE?

It's now time to actually map out the details of our growth journey. Our family going on vacation has many options that will take them by various routes to their vacation destination. They might fly out of two different airports or they might drive a couple of major freeway routes by car. For a long drive, a family might decide to stay in a hotel a couple of nights along the way. There might even be "mini-destinations" along the way—a visit to extended family or a day's stop to tour a historic landmark.

To develop a path along which our plan can be achieved, we'll want to break down our destination declaration into a series of steps—action points that can take us step-by-step from where we are toward our intended destination. It will be helpful if each step is bite-sized and self-contained. Consider the following possible plans for our two ministers:

- To achieve physical renewal through a new exercise regimen, Janet might (1) consult a physician or personal trainer about program options; (2) select the most motivating option; (3) learn how to "work up to" that form of exercise safely and enjoyably (for example, two weeks at once weekly, then two weeks at twice weekly, then three weeks at three times weekly, etc.); and (4) add the established regimen to her weekly calendar.

- Randall might work toward a one-month sabbatical by (1) preparing a memo or scheduling a conversation with his supervisor or board of directors; (2) reviewing the ministry calendar with key leaders to determine the best time for the sabbatical; (3) researching options for what to do or where to go during the month off; (4) seeking input from ministers who've taken a similar sabbatical; (5) creating boundaries for staying disconnected from his ministry while away; (6) taking the sabbatical, keeping a journal detailing what God teaches him during his time away; and (7) debriefing the experience with key leadership, implementing any new ideas he gains from the experience.

Personal growth plans involving others in the process of our growth tend to be more successful (Proverbs 27:17). Others who are already engaged in the re-creative activity we desire can help inform our own experience. It's often best to speak with two or three such people when possible, since there's wisdom in many counselors (Proverbs 11:14). No two people will have done it exactly the same, nor do we have to do it the same as any one of them. However, hearing their perspectives can be quite beneficial.

In addition to personal interactions with those who've been successful, significant resources may also be available from public libraries, church libraries, university libraries, used bookstores, online book vendors and other trusted websites.

Just as marathon runners pace themselves for the goal of winning a marathon, we may also need to pace ourselves in the pursuit of our re-creation goal. Chances are, we're not yet "in shape" for the task and need training over time to become more disciplined—whether it's in setting boundaries or developing the discipline to actually carry it out. Whatever the plan, we should be realistic in choosing what will work. Beginning slowly and increasing over time will provide a sense of accomplishment rather than a sense of defeat. We can always make adjustments later, if needed.

Look back at your destination declarations from the previous exercise. Write what steps might be helpful to get from where you are to your goal. Remember to be as specific, achievable and measurable as possible.

- *Physically*

- *Mentally*

- *Emotionally*

- *Spiritually*

WHAT'S OUR FIRST STEP?

In implementing our new re-creation plan, it's not as important to do it "right" as it is to simply get started. There will be sufficient opportunity to reevaluate, tweak or completely overhaul the plan in time. We might try it for at least a couple of weeks before evaluating its effectiveness, especially before writing it off as "ineffective." Regardless of our initial experience, this is an opportunity for learning. God often ordains failure as a catalyst for future success. We might also consider keeping a journal to document our progress and to chronicle what we learn along the way.

WHAT WOULD WE DO DIFFERENTLY NEXT TIME?

An effective personal growth plan is always created with reevaluation in mind. Most of the time, we start a growth journey only to realize down the road the need for some adjustment. As we go, we can keep a record of what we'd do differently next time. Such evaluation time can be beneficial for our current re-creation plan as well as when we create new ones.

While it's important to succeed, there will always be room for improvement. We will never arrive at perfection this side of heaven. The most important thing is to start the journey by taking one small step, then another, then another. We don't have to be in a hurry; change takes time. That's why it's called a journey.

Wrap-Up:
Foundation Stone 5—
Re-creation

Reflecting on all you've learned in this foundation stone, use the space below to record your most important takeaways.

Make a list of "restful" activities you either currently practice or have interest in practicing. These activities should be energy-replenishing, not energy-depleting. Calculate the frequency or amount of time you actually participate in each. Then consider the amount of time you want to engage in each:

Activity I Consider Restful   *Actual Time Spent*   *Desired Time Spent*

Look back at the "destination declarations" you created for our four major categories (physical, mental, emotional and spiritual) and the action steps you subsequently developed. Copy them here, making any changes you deem appropriate. Don't forget to use "language of the will" and keep your declarations "S.A.M." (specific, achievable and measurable).

Physically
Destination declaration:

Action steps to attain your goal:
1.
2.
3.
4.
5.
6.
7.
8.

Mentally
Destination declaration:

Action steps to attain your goal:
1.
2.
3.
4.
5.
6.
7.
8.

Emotionally

Destination declaration:

Action steps to attain your goal:
1.
2.
3.
4.
5.
6.
7.
8.

Spiritually

Destination declaration:

Action steps to attain your goal:
1.
2.
3.
4.
5.
6.
7.
8.

Return to the personal self-care plan on pages 98-99 to consider any modifications to your purpose statement. Change the statement in light of any insights the Holy Spirit has given you as you've reflected on re-creation. If no change is needed, reinforce your statement by copying it as is into the space provided.

PEOPLE SKILLS

Managing Our Most
Valuable Resource

Our heavenly Father exhibited loving creativity in everything he made. He was so creative that not even two snowflakes are exactly alike. This uniqueness extends to God's crowning creation. We've long known that no two people have the same fingerprint. But with the advent of modern medicine, we now understand our uniqueness goes much deeper. From our voiceprint to our retinal pattern—even down to our very DNA—each of us is a unique design, a one-of-a-kind work of art. Ephesians 2:10 speaks of each person being God's workmanship, but an accurate alternate translation could be "masterpiece." Each of us is an original creation of inestimable value.

1. Personality and Personality Theory

Yet our Creator designed us with significant similarities, as well. The first person to systematize a theory of personality was Hippocrates, the ancient physician who created the Hippocratic oath. Centuries before the birth of Christ, Hippocrates speculated four basic types of personality—sanguine, choleric, melancholic and phlegmatic—each related to the four basic types of body fluids (blood, yellow bile, black bile and phlegm, respectively). Each personality was considered to create a particular "temperament," or emotional state, in people.

Throughout the centuries that followed, others created their own personality theories. Though they no longer referred to Hippocrates' four body fluid types, most retained the idea of basic types of personality. While Hippocrates may not have been accurate in tying them to body fluids, his observations about human personality appear as accurate then as in the modern theories today.

Because these temperament names are a bit cumbersome, we will be using a modern, easier-to-understand version of the temperaments called *MinistryStyles*.[1] Each personality style is considered a "tool" in the personality toolbox (hammer, Swiss Army knife, tape measure and duct tape), having its own unique set of positive and negative traits. Our goal in this foundation stone is to gain a general appreciation for the basic types of personality we'll encounter in ministry. This simple insight into God's design of people can transform our ability to get along with and minister to those God has placed within our sphere of influence.

Understanding how each person within God's family is tooled can also have beneficial application within our own families. Pastor Dennis Siebert recounts a time he and his wife first became aware of their differing personality styles:

> Before understanding our God-given differences in personality, I couldn't understand why my wife would become upset when I would do something that seemed natural and right to me. However, the personality inventory we took had us pegged and explained how we were naturally different from each other. It helped me give my wife permission to be who she was. Being different from me didn't make her wrong! My wife also realized I wasn't purposely trying to cause her trouble. Gaining appreciation for our differences led to our seeing one another more as complements than competitors. It has also contributed to good laughs and much more grace in our relationship.

What follows is a very basic personality inventory to determine our own "tool" preferences. We strongly encourage taking the test before moving through the remainder of this section.

WHAT'S MY TOOL?

Complete the test on page 192 in two steps. Place a check beside each trait you feel describes you more often than not, calculating a total score for each tool type. At the same time, have someone who knows you well also score it for you. Others sometimes see us differently than we see ourselves. If you both agree to your primary tool, it's likely you've obtained an accurate result. If, instead, your spouse or friend obtains a different result, consider having a second and even a third person score the test on your behalf—perhaps people who know you in a different capacity (family versus colleague versus

---

[1]Dennis L. Howard, *MinistryStyles Toolbox Analysis*, ProApse Software, 1st ed.(Fort Wayne, Ind.: HWSS, 2004), graphics and programming by Donald Ashley.

long-time friend). You may find that your differing social circles generate slightly different scores.[2]

Powerful Hammer	Versatile Swiss Army Knife	Adaptable Duct Tape	Precision Tape Measure
___Leader	___Confident, charming	✓Sensitive	___Reads all instructions, deliberate
___Takes charge	___Open-minded	___Loyal	✓Accurate, cautious
___Eager	___Persuasive	___Calm, even-keeled	___Consistent
___Assertive, confident	✓Enthusiastic	✓Avoids confrontation	___Controlled
___Firm	___Takes risks	✓Enjoys routine	✓Reserved
___Enterprising	✓Visionary	✓Warm and relational	___Predictable
✓Competitive	✓Motivator	___Moderate	✓Practical
___Daring, enjoys challenges	___Energetic	✓Generous	___Factual
___Problem solver	___Very verbal	___Cheerful	___Conscientious
✓Vigorous, productive	___Promoter	___Accommodating	✓Well-disciplined, orderly
___Bold	✓Friendly, mixes easily	✓Cautious humor, considerate	___Discerning
✓Purposeful, goal-driven	___Enjoys popularity	___Adaptable	✓Detailed
___Decision maker	___Fun-loving	✓Sympathetic	___Analytical
___Adventurous spirit	✓Likes variety	✓Thoughtful	___Inquisitive
___Force of character, strong-willed	___Spontaneous	✓Nurturing	___Precise
✓Independent, self-reliant	___Enjoys change	___Patient	___Persistent
___Unconquerable	✓Creative, goes for new ideas	___Tolerant	✓Scheduled
___Persistent	✓Group-oriented	___Good listener	✓Sensitive
✓Action-oriented	✓Optimistic	___Peacemaker	___Introspective
✓Determined	___Initiator		___Receptive
	✓Infectious laughter		
	✓Inspirational		
10 Total	10 Total	9 Total	7 Total

Figure 6.1. Dennis L. Howard, Family Care Center, Fort Wayne, Indiana. Used with permission.

---

[2]To obtain an individualized *MinistryStyles* report—as well as a license to use the *MinistryStyles Toolbox Analysis* software within your ministry organization—go to www.ministrytba.com. A secular version of this instrument, *Workstyles Toolbox Analysis*, is also available for Christian business owners at www.worktba.com.

Considering the positive traits for each personality style, check all that apply to you most of the time. Total each column and record your score for each tool at the bottom. Then, rank your tool styles below:

My **strongest** tool is _____ versatile swiss army knife

My next strongest tool is _____ adaptable duct-tape

My next strongest tool is _____ Precision tape measure

My **weakest** tool is _____ powerful hammer

THE FOUR BASIC TOOLS

Each personality style can be described by the positive descriptors in its respective column. (A list including both positive and corresponding negative traits for each personality style can be found in appendix E.) Don't be concerned if the description for your strongest type isn't a perfect match for you. Few people match perfectly. The *MinistryStyles Toolbox Analysis* distinguishes the four personality styles as follows.[3]

Powerful Hammer

Themes. "Let's do it my way!" "Let's move, shake and make it happen!" "Let's get it done *now!*"

Key strengths. Ability to take charge of most anything instantly; usually "results-oriented"; can see the "big picture"; ability to apply the pressure that will get results.

Tendencies when strengths are overexercised. Too bossy; insensitive; impatient; domineering; reluctant to delegate or give credit to others.

Emotional needs. Desires to be appreciated for and receive credit for personal accomplishments; wants his/her wishes obeyed.

Likes those people who do things their way; cooperate quickly; will be supportive and submissive.

Are reliable in work for their new and innovative ideas; ability to overcome obstacles.

Influences others by finding innovative solutions to a given problem; demonstrating a personal sense of power and confidence; empowering others; possessing a quick sense of what will work.

Could improve by using more patience, empathy, participation and collaboration with others; allowing others to make decisions; "nailing down" the details; not expecting everyone to produce as they do.

Can be "spotted in a crowd" by their restlessness; quick grab for control; fast-moving and high-energy approach.

Think about your closest relationships, both personally and professionally. Who might this tool describe?

---

[3]Howard, *MinistryStyles Toolbox Analysis.*

Versatile Swiss Army Knife

Theme. "Let's do it the fun way"; "Lighten up, don't take things so hard!"; "Don't worry, we can just wing it!"

Key strengths. Networks well with others; can talk about anything, anytime, anyplace, with anyone, with or without information; has an effervescent and bubbling personality; good sense of humor; likes to tell stories; naturally enjoys people; seems to know everyone even if they can't seem to remember names.

Tendencies when strengths are overexercised. Disorganized; difficulty managing details; rarely forgets a face but can't seem to remember names; embellishes and exaggerates; trusts others to do the work; lacks seriousness at times when being serious is necessary; poor on follow-through.

Emotional needs. Approval; acceptance; attention; possibly needs affection.

Likes those people who laugh; listen; approve; enjoy their funny stories.

Are reliable in work for their persuasiveness and ability to inspire others; ability for being natural promoters (can sell a dead horse to a cowboy); love for entertaining; colorfulness; creativity; optimism; tendency to cheer up others.

Influences others with praise and doing favors for them.

Could improve by getting organized; focusing on follow-through; keeping promises and completing tasks; not talking so much; learning to tell time.

Can be "spotted in a crowd" by constant chatter; animated and colorful expressions; enthusiasm; ability to mix easily; networking with others.

Who might this tool describe?

Adaptable Duct Tape

Themes. "Let's do it the easy way!"; "Don't make waves!"; "Let's take the path of least resistance!"; "Excuse me, can I say something now?"; "I don't know, what do you want to do?"

Key strengths. Usually "wears well" with others; "pleasing" personality; balanced/even disposition; dry sense of humor.

Tendencies when strengths are overexercised. May lack enthusiasm and energy; struggles with indecision; uncomfortable with change; no obvious flaws but may have a "hidden will of iron."

Emotional needs. "Keep the peace" and have no conflict; be understood; emotional support; a sense of being respected; feel worthwhile.

Likes those people who "like them"; will respect and appreciate their contributions; will make decisions for them; will not ignore them.

Are reliable in work for their steady, consistent and predictable pace; ability to be a peacemaker and to mediate between contentious people; cooperative and calming influence.

Influences others with accommodation; being "pleasing"; consistency in personal work performance.

Could improve by "standing up" for themselves; learning to cope with a reasonable level of conflict; expressing ideas; working faster than expected; setting goals and becoming self-motivated.

Can be "spotted in a crowd" by their calm, modest and accommodating posture; maintaining a low profile by "blending" into the social situation.

Who might this tool describe?

Precision Tape Measure

Themes. "Let's do it the right way!"; "But what about _____?"; "The job isn't complete until the paperwork is done!"

Key strengths. Ability to organize, manage details, analyze, set high standards and set long-range goals.

Tendencies when strengths are overexercised. Over-focused on details; may micromanage situations; remembers negatives; spends too much time on preparation.

Emotional needs. Having a sense of stability and order; need for silence, sensitivity, support and space.

Likes those people who appreciate their attention to details; are serious; are sensible; want to "play by the rules."

Are reliable in work for their high standards of performance; love of analysis; follow-through; detail orientation; compassion for others who may be hurting.

Influences others with organization; sensitivity to others' feelings; desire for quality performance; creative problem-solving.

Could improve by not having to get things done perfectly; not insisting others hold to their standards; not taking life so seriously.

Can be "spotted in a crowd" by their sensitive nature; serious conversations; well-mannered approach to others; well-groomed appearance (with some exceptions).

Who might this tool describe?

Notice that each type has both positive and negative characteristics. This is an important fact: there are no "good" or "bad" personalities. We each have strong and weak points.

Which of the four tool types do you find easiest to understand or get along with and why?

Which of the four tool types do you find most difficult to understand or get along with and why?

CROSS-TOOLING: TWELVE MAJOR BLENDS OF PERSONALITY

In reality, each of us is a unique blend of the four personality tool types. Some are strongly bent toward one tool as dominant, having only a small sampling of the other three. Others are more balanced among all four tools. For the sake of understanding common personality types, it may be helpful to categorize them into twelve common "blends" of personality. The first tool listed in each blend below represents the highest score in the profile; the second represents the second highest score.

Swiss Army Knife/Hammer	Hammer/Swiss Army Knife
Swiss Army Knife/Tape Measure	Tape Measure/Swiss Army Knife
Swiss Army Knife/Duct Tape	Duct Tape/Swiss Army Knife
Hammer/Tape Measure	Tape Measure/Hammer
Hammer/Duct Tape	Duct Tape/Hammer
Tape Measure/Duct Tape	Duct Tape/Tape Measure

WORKING WITH OTHER TOOL TYPES IN THE KINGDOM WORKSHOP

As ministry leaders, it's important to simply be aware that personality differences exist. Each type requires that we deliver our ministry a bit differently. We must realize that we, too, are a particular blend of tool types in God's workshop. The type of "toolbox" we live in will most certainly color our view of others. If we aren't aware of our own bias toward or against other personality types, we'll be tempted to call some "right" or "better" than others when in reality, they are simply different.

To what extent might your personality blend complicate your ability to minister effectively with other blends?

Considering the personalities of all the people in your life currently (friends, coworkers, congregants, ministry partners, etc.), list below the people with whom you have the most difficulty getting along. Looking back over the previous section, what would you guess each of their personality blends might be?

Individual	Personality blend (best guess)
1. _____	_____
2. _____	_____
3. _____	_____
4. _____	_____
5. _____	_____
6. _____	_____

Given their personality blends, how might you change your way of thinking about or relating to these individuals to improve your working relationship?

Individual	Possible improvement in approach or thinking toward them
1. _____	_____
	_____
2. _____	_____
	_____
3. _____	_____
	_____
4. _____	_____
	_____
5. _____	_____
	_____
6. _____	_____
	_____

PEOPLE AREN'T THE ENEMY

When we experience conflict with others, it's a part of our fallen nature to blame them without first looking inside ourselves to determine the source of conflict. Even individuals transformed by the Holy Spirit experience rocky relationships. Much of this may be attributed simply to differences in personality.

In such cases, we can resist the urge to blame others, and instead consider the role that personality differences might be playing. While this won't always be true, we could save much grief by considering this possibility sooner rather than later. Satan will attempt to use our own personality style against us, prompting us to spar with another whose blend is different than—or even identical to—our own.

God is the Master Craftsman not only of his global Workshop but also of each ministry context. In that specific locale, we as ministers function as a Master's apprentice in caring for our unique area of the workshop. To do this effectively, we must understand the variety of tool types around us, remembering that each of God's hand-crafted tools has a distinctive function.

Most ministries require a wide variety of people to function smoothly and effectively. Certain ministry positions may lend themselves to certain tool blends. For example, a person with some amount of tape measure will generally work better in a caregiving role than someone with no tape measure at all. A social coordinator with high duct tape may generally not work as well as someone with lots of Swiss Army knife. A board of directors often benefits from a broad representation of blends and at least one representative of the four basic tool types so as to have insight into the effect new ministry policies or programs will likely have on each tool type.

List the various positions or major functions within your ministry. (Use the margins if you need more space.) What tool types might be a best and worst fit for each vacancy?

Position/Function: _____
*Beneficial traits for the job:*_____
Possible "best fit" blends: _____
Possible "worst fit" blends: _____

Position/Function: _____
Beneficial traits for the job: _____
Possible "best fit" blends: _____
Possible "worst fit" blends: _____

Position/Function: _____
Beneficial traits for the job: _____
Possible "best fit" blends: _____
Possible "worst fit" blends: _____

PERSONALITY BLENDS THROUGH THE LENS OF SCRIPTURE

Scripture speaks to the importance of diversity within the kingdom Workshop. While someone's personality blend isn't the same as their spiritual giftedness, there is frequent correlation between the two, and our all-wise God gives gifts as he chooses. Consider the following passages that speak about God's design in diversity among the members of his body:

Romans 12:4-5. The physical body is a picture of how the body of Christ was intended to carry out different functions within God's plan for his church.

1 Corinthians 12:14-18, 21. Believers are discouraged from looking down upon others within the body simply because they're different. There isn't a single person in any ministry placed by accident. The phrase, "every one of them, just as he wanted them to be," leaves little room for misunderstanding. The most difficult person for us in a given ministry setting has a divine purpose for being there. Rather than complaining or grumbling, we can seek God in understanding his purpose. "Difficult people" will often serve as God's sandpaper to smooth out the rough edges of our own personality!

Ephesians 4:11-13. The diversity within our ministry is God-given so that it may be built into exactly what God needs it to be for its unique location and time in history. Unity of the body isn't simply a byproduct of learning to get along with other personalities—it's a primary vehicle through which God grants maturity of faith. It's also the means by which we attain the "whole measure of the fullness of Christ." And if that weren't enough, our unity is also one of the greatest evangelistic tools for a lost world to see the power of God actively working within us (John 13:34-35).

What additional applications do you see in the following passages?

Romans 12:4-5:

1 Corinthians 12:14-18, 21:

Ephesians 4:11-13:

KNOWING IS HALF THE BATTLE

Why is an awareness of personalities important in ministry? First of all, knowledge is the first step toward wisdom. If we have an appreciation for how our own personality blend interacts with others, we're halfway to solving many of the interpersonal conflicts within our ministry.

Like it or not, certain individuals within our ministry will feel motivated to be our antagonist "for our own good." Given that 40 percent of ministers report a serious personality conflict with someone in their ministry every month,[4] a basic understanding of how different personalities impact such misunderstandings is critical for effective conflict resolution. One of two methods is effective for most conflicts:

> *Overlook the offense.* Forgiveness is a major theme in Scripture, not the least of which is God's own forgiveness of our own wrongdoings against him. God asks us to forgive as we have been forgiven (Matthew 6:14-15; 18:21-35; Mark 11:25; Luke 17:4).

> *Dialogue.* If we're unable to overlook an offense for whatever reason (either because of personal inability or because it's inappropriate to do so), we are encouraged by Scripture to go to our fellow believer in prayerful and loving confrontation to seek reconciliation (Matthew 18:15).

Understanding our own personality bias prevents us from being blinded by the "eye-plank" of our own personality, allowing us more clarity to remove the speck from someone else's eye (Matthew 7:1-5). When dialogue is required to resolve conflict, we need good people skills to achieve effective resolution. We dedicate the remainder of this foundation stone for the practical development of such skills.

What personality conflicts in your life and ministry have become clearer as a result of this study of personality types? Which offenses might be best to overlook and which might be best to prayerfully pursue healthy dialogue?

Person I'm in Conflict With   *Overlook or Dialogue Needed*

---

[4]Fuller Theological Seminary, 1991 Survey of Pastors, Pasadena, California.

2. Active Listening:
Tailored Shepherding for
Our Unique Flock

Of all the things people want, acceptance and a sense of worth are among the most basic. Something deep within us longs for validation as people created in the image of God. Our people need to be reminded that their existence makes a difference in this world. We validate their worth by spending time with them, encouraging them and serving them. Authentically listening to them is critically important to all three and represents a staple dietary need for the flock under our care.

There's a big difference between truly listening and merely hearing. Hearing is a function of the ear; listening is a function of the soul. While all of us hear loud and clear those with whom we're in conflict, we often fail to prioritize true listening—giving attention not only to their words but to the concerns of their heart. If the unjust judge took time to listen to the concerns of the poor widow (Luke 18:1-7), how much more important is it that we listen to the cries of those we shepherd?

There's a big difference between truly listening and merely hearing. Hearing is a function of the ear; listening is a function of the soul.

Everything discussed thus far throughout the foundation stone has provided building material for the skill of active listening. "Who takes time to listen to the cries of *my* heart?" The intimate relationships we are building (foundation stone 1). "Why should I take time from my busy schedule to sit and listen to others?" Because it's part of our calling from God (foundation stone 2). "But I'm exhausted from all the listening people ask me to do!" We must learn not only stress-management skills (foundation stone 3) and healthy boundaries (foundation stone 4), but also purposeful re-creation to keep us energized for this task of listening (foundation stone 5).

Some ministers might say, "I already know what my people want and need." But do we? Listening to what people say (and sometimes even to what they're not saying)—listening long enough to get beyond their sometimes hollow words to tune into their hearts—is the only way to accurately understand and then meet their true underlying needs. The words people say are often imprecise and may not convey what they really mean. Not only is their communication going through the filter of what their words mean to them, once it hits our ears it also travels through our own interpretive filter. This represents a huge gap for potential human miscommunication.

Consider a parishioner who shares after morning worship that she didn't appreciate the sermon because "you don't understand the pain some people have been through." If we're not intent on understanding her heart, we'll hear only her discontent. We may become defensive about the sermon and the words we so carefully chose. We might find ourselves thinking of how we'll respond to her critique.

But what if the sermon brought back shameful memories of her teenage rape? She won't likely come right out and share this with us; we will earn the right for her to share that by the way we handle the situation. A defensive response would likely cause us to miss a great opportunity for deep spiritual ministry.

Authentic listening is not a passive but active process. Everyone has a story about an experience when they felt another person simply wasn't listening to them. The other person appeared distracted or preoccupied (perhaps repeatedly looking at their watch), or gave a simple platitude for a complex problem.

How often do you find yourself merely hearing others instead of actively listening?

The words people say

are often imprecise

and may not convey

what they really

mean.

Which category of people gets the worst "hearing" treatment from you (those you lead in ministry, coworkers, spouse, kids, friends)? Why do you think this is so?

Those receiving our worst treatment are, unfortunately, most often those we love most. Perhaps it's because we take them for granted. We might "get away with it" because we trample on the grace they so freely and regularly extend to us. We ought to keep these folks especially in mind as we continue our journey through active listening, asking God to teach us to apply these skills to our most important relationships. A few simple actions can transform our hearing into deeper listening: (1) preparing our context, (2) preparing ourselves, (3) attending, (4) remembering our reason for listening, (5) suspending judgment and (6) listening for themes in their story.[5]

PREPARING OUR CONTEXT

The first step toward active listening is to prepare the context of our conversation for optimal listening. Examples might include ensuring that our meeting place has a comfortable temperature, adequate lighting and minimal distractions. We might turn off the TV or radio,

---

[5]These suggestions are based on material from Robert Carkhuff, *Helping Skills* (Amherst, Mass.: Human Resource Development, 1993).

have someone screen our calls or turn off our cell phone. We might establish connection by placing two chairs facing each other without obstruction rather than having a large desk as a barrier. We can create a mood of confidentiality by closing the door. While such steps aren't always possible, such actions can help communicate that what the other person has to share is important and that they will have our focused attention.

How might you make your office or usual meeting place more conducive to heartfelt conversation?

PREPARING OURSELVES

A second preparation for active listening is to prepare ourselves. Whereas preparing the context seeks to minimize external distractions, preparing ourselves seeks to minimize internal distractions. Setting aside adequate time in our planner for the conversation is one of the most important means of self-preparation. What message does it send when we haven't thought enough of their concern to set aside adequate time for them? Other examples of self-preparation include researching their issue ahead of time, being fully rested and not falling asleep during a conversation. (We may laugh, but it happens!)

If we're the type of person whose mind is always going, we might not be able to prevent extraneous thoughts from popping into our head during a conversation. Having a pad of paper nearby offers an efficient way to jot down a thought without becoming overly distracted by it. Even if a dozen of them surface during the conversation, no worries—they're all written down!

What other struggles do you sometimes experience in being fully present?

How might you better prepare yourself for conversations with others?

ATTENDING

Attending is a nonverbal way of saying, "I'm paying attention to you!" The most obvious way another person knows we're paying attention is by our eye contact. Others will see right through us if we're staring out the window as they pour out their soul to us. Do we frequently glance at our watch? Is our body turned away from the other person? Are our arms folded tightly at our chest? These communicate a lack of desire for listening whether or not it's intentional on our part. But having our body facing the other person, arms uncrossed, good eye contact (occasionally glancing away to keep them from feeling stared at), smiling and nodding at appropriate times all communicate a desire to engage in the conversation and will encourage the other person to share their heart with more confidence.

Visualize a recent conversation you had while ministering to another. If you could freeze-frame any point in the conversation, would you see yourself attending to the person or failing to attend? What leads you to that conclusion?

REMEMBERING OUR REASON FOR LISTENING

Ministers sometimes lose sight of why they do what they're doing. Ministry is about giving our life for the cause of Christ and to those for whom he died. In our unique setting, these individuals are represented by the men and women under our care. Part of our calling is ministering to them in the ways God has uniquely equipped us.

Recall a conversation where you know you listened well. What role did remembering your reason for listening play in ministering to that person?

SUSPENDING JUDGMENT

Suspending judgment isn't about calling something "right" or "wrong." It simply means not jumping to conclusions about another's situation before having understood their problem from *their* point of view. Once we're able to demonstrate true understanding of someone else's perspective, we're more likely to be given the right to speak into the person's life the wisdom God has given us for them. From their vantage point, we will have earned the "right to be understood."

What makes suspending judgment difficult for you?

How might you improve your ability to do so?

LISTENING FOR THEMES IN THEIR STORY

People often share their problems with ministers before having a full sense of what their deeper issues really are. Our active listening helps them to hear the deeper feelings within their own heart as they share with us. However, if we listen carelessly, we'll miss the opportunity for deep impact. One practical way to help someone get in touch with their heart is to listen for major themes in their story. As we're listening to a person, we might ask ourselves a few questions until the themes are clear: "Who is this story about?" "What is this person's greatest concern?" "When did this problem first begin?" "Where did these events take place?" "Why is this person so concerned about this problem?" "How have they attempted to solve their problem thus far?" If we remain unable to discern the major themes of their story, this may be a sign we need to continue listening and asking ourselves clarifying questions.

What clarifying questions have you found particularly helpful in your experiences with active listening?

What are some practical ways you can guard against listening carelessly?

3. Reflective Listening

Reflective listening is merely active listening with one additional component: using our own words to reflect back to the other person what we've heard them share. There are many reasons this is helpful in ministry. First, it gives the other person "proof" that we're actually paying attention and that we really do care. Second, it enables us to "test" our understanding of their story to ensure we truly understand what they intended to communicate. Our reflecting back gives them opportunity to correct any misunderstanding. Third, it further holds us accountable for paying attention in the first place. It's more difficult for our mind to wander if we make it a habit to periodically summarize what another is saying.

Three sample stories will help give us practical insights with regard to reflective listening:

Jenny: "I'm having trouble getting my parents to appreciate the predicament I'm in. In the past, I've always spent Christmas with them and with my extended family. It's tradition. However, because I got married earlier this year, I now have another family to spend time with during the holidays. And unlike my parents who live here locally, my husband's parents live in California. We feel it's important to go out west to visit them this Christmas because we see them so infrequently. We see my parents all the time, but they just don't get it."

Tom: "I just don't know what to do. I've been sending out resumés and meeting with people almost every day for the past three months, and I can't seem to find an engineering job anywhere within an hour's drive of here! We've used up our savings, and I'm not sure what we're going to do about our mortgage payment when it comes due next month. I guess I'll have to take a night job cleaning office buildings to make ends meet. I don't want to do that, but I guess I'm willing to do what it takes to keep us from bankruptcy."

Brandon: "Yeah, it's been really tough trying to care for my wife since the birth of our son last month. I mean, I knew I'd have to step up to the plate and help out more around the house and with the baby. But I never dreamed she would suffer such bad depression. The doctor called it 'postpartum depression' and said it's fairly common among women after their first pregnancy. I'm just not sure if I really know how to be there for her like she needs me to be."

With these stories in mind, let's consider three basic types of reflective listening skills: reflecting (1) what they say, (2) how they say it and (3) why they said it.

THEIR UNIQUE STORY: RESPONDING TO WHAT THEY SAY

Reflecting the *content* of a story is the most basic method for reflective listening. Here's how reflecting content might look in each of our examples:

Jenny: "So you're saying your family isn't happy with your intentions for spending Christmas this year with your husband's family out in California."

Tom: "Wow! You've really been having financial difficulty since you lost your job three months ago. You might even have to take a night job to provide for your family since there aren't any engineering jobs locally."

Brandon: "It sounds like your wife's really having a battle with depression since the birth of your son last month and you're questioning if you have what it takes to be there for her."

The above examples represent a one-sentence summary for each story. Notice we didn't "parrot" back the same words used by the speaker but converted them into our own words. Periodically reflecting the "what" being shared allows the other person to know we understand them. It will also encourage further sharing.

Ministers who've never been taught such listening skills will sometimes ask, "That's all you want me to do? It doesn't seem like it would be very helpful to just say back what they've just said." We realize this might be difficult to believe. Our culture has taught us that, as ministerial "experts," we must have an answer for everyone who comes to us. This is in error for two reasons: (1) sometimes we *won't* have an answer for them and, even if we do, (2) often they won't be ready to hear the answer anyway.

Some types of human pain (such as the death of a child) are extremely difficult to discuss with those who've experienced such loss. The only legitimate answer lies in the sovereign will of our heavenly Father. But in moments of intense suffering, theological truths might be received as mere platitudes falling on them like lead balloons unless we have first empathized with them in their place of pain.

Reflective listening is a method for conveying such empathy. It can sometimes be a means for healing in its own right, or it can be used as a way for first understanding their pain so we might eventually be given the right to later speak theological truths with greater receptivity. The unique circumstances and the strength of our relationship with them will determine which is best. Either way, we will communicate the same message: "I care about your pain and I'm here for you."

In moments of intense suffering, theological truths might be received as mere platitudes.

How might you feel if another person reflected back to you an accurate understanding of some pain you've experienced?

Recall a time someone used reflective listening skillfully with you. How did you feel after your conversation with them?

THEIR STORY'S FEELINGS: RESPONDING TO HOW THEY SAY IT

The second method for reflective listening is to reflect back the *feelings* others share in their story. Sometimes this will be easy to determine, especially if they actually use feeling words. Other times, we'll have to infer how they feel based on their language and their manner of expression. If they haven't directly stated how they feel, asking ourselves *If I were in this person's shoes, how might I feel?* can give a better idea for how the other person might be feeling about their situation.

Feelings have different categories and different levels of intensity. Categories of feelings include happy, loving, strong, angry, confused, hurt and sad. Any feeling category might range in intensity from mild (inconvenienced) to moderate (upset or irritated) to severe (enraged or irate). Here are examples of reflecting feelings based on the stories given earlier:

Jenny: "You feel disappointed and misunderstood."

Tom: "You feel overwhelmed."

Brandon: "You feel helpless."

In each story, the speaker never directly stated how they felt. Yet we can infer a fairly accurate feeling response from their stories and from using the *How might I feel?* question. While we might not find the perfect words to reflect how the other person is feeling, perfection isn't tremendously important. In trying, we'll often find the person either correcting us or sharing more to help us gain a more accurate picture of where they are emotionally. Either way, we will be giving them something to react to and will encourage them to share more deeply as the conversation continues.

What might you look for in a conversation to assess a person's feelings?

A list of feeling words arranged by category can be found in appendix A.

THEIR STORY'S MEANING: RESPONDING TO WHY THEY SAID IT

The last method for reflective listening combines the previous two. People naturally pursue meaning in their lives. This is especially true during difficult times. When people find a "why" for their pain, it gives them a greater ability to endure and to see beyond their suffering. When put together, the content of their story gives *meaning* to the feelings they experience. As ministers, we will eventually help them to transition their meaning from the human dimension to the divine dimension. But to win the right to explore the divine meaning to their story, we must be willing to understand the meaning they may have already assigned it. Here are three sample statements reflecting meaning in each of our three stories:

> *Jenny:* "You feel disappointed and misunderstood because your family doesn't respect your intentions for spending Christmas this year with your husband's family in California."

> *Tom:* "You feel overwhelmed because you might have to take a night job to provide for your family and avoid possible bankruptcy."

> *Brandon:* "You feel helpless because you're questioning if you have what it takes to be there for your wife."

Reflective listening isn't rocket science but rather a simple means for helping people explore their situation, how they feel about it and the meaning they've assigned to it. Using these skills not only helps us understand people but will also help them to get to the root of their issues. Once someone genuinely feels understood, we can begin speaking a divine perspective into their lives with greater confidence in their willingness to embrace it. We will have earned the right because we first took the time to care.

What responses might you have given if you were ministering to Jenny, Tom and Brandon?

Jenny

- *Content response:*

- *Feeling response:*

- *Meaning response:*

Tom

- *Content response:*

- *Feeling response:*

- *Meaning response:*

Brandon

- *Content response:*

- *Feeling response:*

- *Meaning response:*

OPEN VERSUS CLOSED QUESTIONS

Important details are sometimes left out when stories are first shared. While one method for exploring the missing elements would be to continue using reflective listening skills, another option might be to employ the art of questioning. There are two basic types of questions: open and closed. Each has its benefits.

Closed questions are helpful when we need a direct answer. By definition, closed questions don't lend themselves to elaboration but are instead short and to the point. Examples of such questions include "How long will you be gone to California?" "What kind of engineer are you?" "Who is your wife's doctor?" These questions can be answered in a few words, and there is only one correct answer. Such questions are useful for eliciting specific information rather than helping the other person explore to a deeper level.

Open questions, on the other hand, are useful not only for gathering additional information but also for encouraging the other person to more fully explore their situation. Examples include "Why do you think your mom is having such a difficult time with your not being home for the holidays?" "How do you feel about moving to another city?" "What are your biggest concerns for your wife?" Not only may these questions not have simple answers, they also will likely encourage the person to dig deeper inside themselves toward discovering a new level of understanding about their situation.

Both open and closed questions have their place. The key is learning when and how to use each type at the best moment. Such skill comes from intentional practice over time, as will be true for all active and reflective listening skills. They are like muscles, becoming stronger and more useful with greater use.

Looking back at our three stories, write one closed and one open question you might ask.

Jenny

- *Closed:*

- *Open:*

Tom

- *Closed:*

- *Open:*

Brandon

- *Closed:*

- *Open:*

WHEN *NOT* TO USE REFLECTIVE LISTENING

The more we put these skills into practice, the more people will be drawn to us by our empathy. This brings up an important point. We should use these skills only when we have time to truly listen with full attentiveness. We will send mixed signals to others if we say with our words, "I'm listening," but our body language says, "Hurry up, I'm late for a meeting." Using these skills when we don't have time to talk will only serve to make people feel unimportant. At the same time, we'll only frustrate ourselves because we aren't setting healthy boundaries around what's most important in that moment.

If we're unable to give the other person our undivided attention, we might consider setting a healthy boundary: "I really don't mind talking with you, but I'm running late for a meeting. Can we get together tomorrow around 2 p.m. for coffee? I could be much more attentive to you then." We will avoid feeling trapped and they will appreciate our honesty and integrity.

Write down two or three honest responses you could use to set a boundary with someone when you wouldn't be able to give them adequate attention.

4. Assertive Techniques Every Minister Can Use

Due to the nature of our work as ministers, there will always be people asking for things from us. This is one of the primary reasons we need our own intimate relationships. God, our spouse and close friends are places we can go to be "filled up" from the drain of the daily grind in ministry.

However, it's also helpful to learn a few techniques for letting others know what we can and cannot do, will and will not do, want and do not want, believe and do not believe. Scripture encourages us to let our "yes" be "yes" and our "no" be "no" (James 5:12). This is not only true for keeping our word but also for being clear in our communication with others.

The techniques presented here have just as much power to help as they do power to harm. The attitude of our heart when applying them will determine the difference. It will be important to check our motive before putting any of these techniques into practice.

THE PASSIVE-ASSERTIVE-AGGRESSIVE CONTINUUM

Imagine an old-fashioned scale, with a plate on either end for weighing items against each other. Placing a heavy object on one end with nothing on the other tips the balance to one extreme. However, placing an item of equal weight on the other plate returns "balance" to the scale.

Passivity and aggression are like those two weights. Being passive is allowing the world to force us into its mold. Those who react passively tend to avoid responsibility by ignoring it, operating by the motto "Live and let live." As a result, some become doormats that others step on at will.

At the other extreme, being aggressive is an attempt to force the world into *our* mold. Those who react aggressively tend to avoid responsibility by blaming others, operating by the motto "Do unto others *before* they do unto you." They sometimes also step on others as a means for getting what they want from life.

Scripture teaches us to not conform to the world's pattern but rather be transformed by renewing our mind (Romans 12:2). It encourages us not toward aggression or passivity but toward purposeful action—making internal mind and heart changes that lead to changes in our external behavior. This is called *assertiveness*.

To be assertive is to live in balance, taking responsibility for where we are. It involves letting others know who we are and what we are willing to do and not do from healthy boundaries that flow out of a clear sense of calling.

Which of the two extremes do you struggle with more: passivity or aggression? What do you suppose accounts for this?

CONFLICT "DO'S": PREREQUISITES FOR ASSERTIVENESS

Three things are essential to effectively utilize the assertive skills presented here. First, we must be willing to *treat other people with respect*.

Regardless of our viewpoint, we should recognize other people as human beings with a right to their own opinions. We can't let someone's differing viewpoint (even if we consider it the "wrong" view) blind us to the image of God in them. Second, we must seek to *understand before seeking to be understood*. This prevents us from reacting with emotion in the heat of the moment. It will many times also win us the right to be heard. Third, we must be *willing to be upfront and honest* about our own views, needs and feelings. Expecting others to read our mind or interpret our body language leaves too much to chance. We can be respectful, understanding and direct. If we can do these things, the following techniques can be quite helpful.[6]

Making Requests to Others

Making a request greatly minimizes the chance that the other person will respond defensively out of a sense that we are attempting to manipulate them. Making requests involves a six-step process: (1) identifying who owns the problem, (2) describing the problem, (3) stating the consequences, (4) describing our feelings, (5) pausing and (6) making a direct assertion.[7] Let's take a look at each step using two different scenarios. First is an executive assistant in a parachurch ministry whose supervisor neglected to tell her about a big meeting. The second is a senior pastor dealing with a rumor from a lay leader. In our two scenarios, the second one has the authority for corrective action and the first one does not. Making a request can be useful in both situations.

If we desire something from another person, we can use words that communicate our recognition that we own the situation we're trying to resolve or improve. Consider beginning the conversation with a phrase such as "*I have a problem.*" Next we briefly describe the nature of the problem in the simplest terms possible. For example, "I have a problem. *When you called that staff meeting without telling me . . .*" or "I have a problem. *When you made that comment to Brother Johnson last weekend . . .*" It's important to avoid all-or-nothing language, such as "you always" or "you never." It's also helpful to avoid derogatory language such as "when you went around me" or "when you gossiped." Including these types of descriptive words will only make it less likely they will want to help us with our problem.

After giving a brief description, state the consequence that has already occurred, could have occurred or possibly still may occur as a result of the problem. For example, "I have a problem. When you called that staff meeting without telling me, *many people came to me asking for details about the meeting and I couldn't give them an answer.*"

---

[6]These are only models and aren't the only method for resolving each situation.
[7]Alan Garner, *Conversationally Speaking* (New York: McGraw-Hill, 1997), pp. 121-36.

Or "I have a problem. When you made that comment to Brother Johnson last weekend, *it required me to meet with eight people this week to help them understand the truth about the music minister's resignation.*"

At this point, we can share how the consequences have or could have personally affected us. For example, "I have a problem. When you called that staff meeting without telling me, many people came to me asking for details about the meeting and I couldn't give them an answer. *I felt embarrassed.*" Or "I have a problem. When you made that comment to Brother Johnson last weekend, it required me to meet with eight people this week to help them understand the truth about the music minister's resignation. *Because the reasons for his departure were a private matter, I felt betrayed. I'm also disappointed that his confidentiality was violated.*"

Inserting a brief pause after sharing our personal consequences (perhaps five to fifteen seconds) allows the gravity of the situation to sink in for the other person and allows them time to reflect on our words. It will also cause us to appear stronger and make the other person more likely to work with us toward resolution. Sometimes the other person will break the silence and suggest how to resolve the issue without our having to share with them a direct assertion (step six) of what we want them to do.

We don't have to be afraid of the silence. Instead, we can quietly ask God to accomplish what only he can and give the Holy Spirit time to convict their heart. If the other person is next to speak, they will likely share their true feelings about the matter, positive or negative. Either way, this is valuable information toward conflict resolution.

Depending on how the pause plays out, we may need to assert directly what we want the other person to do. This will be necessary if the other person did not respond during the silence, if they merely defended themselves or if their suggested resolution was unacceptable. Sample direct assertions might be, "I have a problem. When you called that staff meeting without telling me, many people came to me asking for details about the meeting and I couldn't give them an answer. I felt embarrassed. *Please touch base with me first when you are planning to call any special committee meetings.*" Or "I have a problem. When you made that comment to Brother Johnson last weekend, it required me to meet with eight people this week to help them understand the truth about the music minister's resignation. Because the reasons for his departure were a private matter, I felt betrayed. I'm also disappointed that his confidentiality was violated. *I would like for you to make a public apology at our next business meeting.*"

The request should ask for a specific change rather than something general or vague ("I would appreciate it if you would set things straight"). It is also better to be direct rather than hinting at what we would like to see done ("People need to hear the truth from you in a public forum, don't you think?").

Some people find it helpful to rehearse communication skills with a spouse or friend, using scenarios from their ministry or their imagination to practice this model. Who might be a "practice buddy" to help you learn the art of requesting?

NEGOTIATING A "WIN-WIN"

When we must negotiate with another person to attain a mutual result, we want to do our best to avoid a "win-lose" arrangement. If the relationship is important to us, "win-lose" is a bad outcome because it may sour the relationship and potentially cause more harm than it's worth—even if we're on the winning side.

In all negotiations there are two viable options: "win-win" and "no deal."[8] Active/reflective listening skills help us to determine what the other person (or group) wants, making a win-win result—the preferred outcome—more likely. What do they want to accomplish? What result will they be happy with in the end? We can confirm that we truly understand the other party's goals by clearly reflecting back to them a summary statement (reflective listening). If we're still off-base, we can continue listening and reflecting until they agree we have clearly understood their concerns. Only then can we be certain they'll be willing to listen to our concerns and objectives.

Once both parties have demonstrated clear understanding of each other's goals, we can ask ourselves, "Is there a solution that would satisfy both parties?" This is a time for brainstorming and thinking outside the box. Here's a classic Negotiating 101 illustration: Two sisters are arguing over who gets the last orange in the fruit bowl. Neither is willing to lose it to the other. Their mother wisely asks why each of them wants the orange. "I want some orange juice with my breakfast," huffs the younger sister. Her older sister complains, "I need the rinds for a recipe I'm baking."

If the mother had not wisely sought to understand the reason each child wanted the orange, she would likely have come up with only a limited number of solutions: the older sister would get the entire orange (win-lose), the younger sister would get the entire orange (lose-win), or each would have received only half the orange (lose-lose). Identifying the girls' desires for the orange reveals an "outside

---

[8]Stephen R. Covey, *The Seven Habits of Highly Effective People*, 1st ed. (New York: Free Press, 1989), p. 207.

the box" solution: the younger sister can first squeeze out the juice, leaving the rind for the older sister's baking recipe.

While some situations will require significant time, thought and patience to find an acceptable win-win, other situations may never yield a win-win solution. In such cases, it's best to agree to "no deal." If no win-win could have been found in our illustration, the mother could have simply kept the orange from both sisters. When applied to our ministry, such a response recognizes our integrity as being more important than agreeing to something that either is inconsistent with our calling or has the potential to damage a good working relationship. "No deal" is agreeing to disagree and leaving things at status quo.

Think about a situation in the past when you attempted to negotiate something with another person or group. What was the issue? What did you want and what did the other side want? What was the result?

Looking back, what was (or might have been) a win-win solution to the problem?

RESPONDING TO CRITICS

Everyone has critics. When critics refuse to share their misgivings with us, we may want to initiate using the "making requests" process mentioned earlier. Yet when others do approach us directly with their criticisms, it's helpful to have models by which we may respectfully respond without compromising our position or opinion.[9]

The first step in responding to a critic is (as always) to use active and reflective listening to determine the exact nature of their concerns. If we understand that we have erred, we can immediately own up to our mistake—regardless of whether they own up to any mistakes on their part—and suggest a means for correcting the issue. This is the nature of true biblical confession and repentance.

But what should we do when our critic is wrong or merely holds a differing viewpoint? Consider someone who says, "People don't think you really care about this ministry." First ask for the details of their criticism. Critical comments using broad generalities make it difficult to get a handle on the real issue. We might consider asking a few questions: "*Who* are the people you've spoken with who are saying that?" "*What* specific things have I done that led to your interpretation?" "*When* did you first hold such an opinion?" "*Where* do you

---

[9]Garner, *Conversationally Speaking*, pp. 87-120.

see evidence that suggests I don't care?" "*Why* do you think I wouldn't care about the ministry?" "*How* would you suggest I change to demonstrate that I do care?"

Once we understand their criticism, the next step is to agree with them! This might sound strange, but giving such a response will short-circuit their negativity and often leave them without ammunition for attack (which sometimes is the only purpose for their criticism, anyway). There are two ways to agree with them: (1) agree with the kernel of truth in their statements or (2) agree with their right to an opinion.

Frequently, people will bring to our attention something having a kernel of truth but that has been taken to a wrong conclusion. In such cases, we can restate and *agree with the truth*. We may then either say nothing to the rest of it or share with them a more accurate conclusion. For the critic who says, "You think spending money on our facilities is more important than spending it on salaries," we might respond with "You're right, I do think a well-maintained facility is important" while ignoring the erroneous conclusion about staff salaries. For the critic who says, "You scrapped VBS this year when lots of families wanted to bring their kids to it," you might respond by saying "Yes, I did cancel VBS, but we didn't have enough volunteer support to ensure the children's safety."

Agreeing with a critic's *right to an opinion* is especially helpful when we know our critic isn't going to change their mind. We maintain our own opinion without feeling compelled to convince them of something different and we avoid the conflict. A response to the complaint about ministers' salaries might be, "I respect your opinion, but staff salaries and facility development are different budgetary categories and need to be considered separately." The other person learns that their opinion has been heard, yet leaves our decision uncompromised.

Sometimes a decision must be made to move forward on a matter, but it can't be made with total certainty. Once we've made our decision, it would do more harm than good to admit such uncertainty to our critics. Agreeing with a critic's right to an opinion can be helpful here. Simply responding, "I understand your reasoning for not wanting to cut VBS, but we did what we thought best," without further explanation, might be completely appropriate.

WHEN ALL ELSE FAILS: THE BROKEN RECORD
Some critics simply want to engage in a verbal tennis match. As long as we're willing to volley the argument back over the net by continuing to debate the issue, they will continue to play. In such cases, the *broken record* technique can be an effective way to break the cycle. The broken record is simply repeating what we've already said—

exactly or very nearly as we have already said it—over and over again until our critic stops with their criticism. Consider the following hypothetical dialogue:

Sally: "I don't think you should have cancelled VBS this year. Lots of people were looking forward to it."

Minister: "I understand you feel many people were looking forward to it, but without enough volunteers we can't ensure the children's safety."

Sally: "But what about all the parents who had planned to bring their children?"

Minister: "I understand you feel many people were looking forward to it, but without enough volunteers we can't ensure the children's safety."

Sally: "What am I supposed to tell my children?" (We're finally closer to the real motive here!)

Minister: "I understand it will be uncomfortable for you to tell your children they won't be going to VBS this summer, but without adequate volunteers we can't ensure the children's safety."

In the short run, such critics may be more upset with us. But if we have respectfully applied these skills, even if they still disagree with our opinion, many critics will come to respect us for standing on our convictions.

Reflect on a time when you were confronted about something. Replay in your mind how the conversation unfolded. What role did agreement with your critic play?

How might you have handled the critique differently? Create an alternate response to your critic's challenge using one of the models presented here.

Wrap-Up: Foundation Stone 6— People Skills

Reflecting on all you've learned in this foundation stone, use the space below to record your most important takeaways.

Which of your relationships are most in need of repair or proactive maintenance? List them here. Place a check beside each person for whom you believe personality differences play a role in your conflict.

_____ ☐		_____ ☐	
_____ ☐		_____ ☐	
_____ ☐		_____ ☐	

Which communication model (Active Listening, Reflective Listening, Making Requests to Others, Negotiating a "Win-Win," Agreeing with the Kernel of Truth, Agreeing with Their Right to an Opinion, The Broken Record) might improve each of these relationships? How might they help? (Be specific.)

Name   *Model(s) to consider*   *Reasoning*

Return to the personal self-care plan on pages 98-99 to consider any modifications to your purpose statement. Change the statement in light of any insights the Holy Spirit has given you as you've reflected on people skills. If no change is needed, reinforce your statement by copying it as is into the space provided.

LEADERSHIP SKILLS

Setting Ministers Apart from the Rest of the Sheep

The church was picturesque as I (Brad) arrived in the parking lot. Sitting in my car for a moment, I gathered my thoughts and prayed. The lawn had neatly manicured flower beds dotted with decorative annuals and shrubbery. The outside of the church revealed nothing of what was happening inside.

Walking across the pavement, I opened the front door and noticed several people standing in the foyer. After being greeted warmly and exchanging introductory pleasantries, I was escorted to a small conference room. A half-dozen people had gathered around the table, each representing a segment of the elected leadership. The toll of their circumstance wore on their countenance as they were forcing the termination of their senior minister. I listened attentively as they shared from their heart moments of tears interspersed with expressions of anger.

Some blamed the minister, a few blamed themselves, and still others blamed circumstances. When one of them blurted out, "It's his leadership," I asked, "What do you mean?" The responses from the group were vague until someone finally said, "His style of leading doesn't take into account working *with* us in this church."

1. Transformative Leadership

While the introductory story is true, it's also representative of many others. Lack of an appropriate leadership practice often plays a significant role in forced exits from ministry.

Being an effective leader requires us to be *transformative*—willing to continuously be remade from the inside out by the power and direction of the Holy Spirit. This means we will need to be humbly open to God's constant reshaping. It also means transforming our practice when necessary to provide the most effective influence.

In the mid-1980s, Hasbro introduced the ever-popular Transformers toys. With the movement of a few parts, an airplane could become an amphibious escape vehicle. A few more turns and it might transform into an artillery vehicle. In the hands of a creative child, the Transformers could morph into whatever was needed most. While each toy had its limitations, all were able to shift back and forth among a variety of manifestations.

Transformative leaders in ministry are able to change their style of influence given the life moment of the ministry organization. Transformative leadership is a necessary component of what it takes to succeed in tenured ministry. Organizations sometimes outgrow leaders because the leaders fail to transform, unable to work out of more than one style of leadership.

A quick perusal at our favorite bookseller yields an abundance of leadership titles touting the latest leadership techniques. While we can glean some insight for our ministry from such books, we ought to remember that these success stories are from the practice of leadership within a specific environment. Their context or situation may or may not be similar to ours. We will still want to develop a competency in the practice of a variety of leadership styles suitable for our own unique ministry context.

Write down the names of a few people you consider great leaders. What characteristics make them great in your opinion?

How helpful would these characteristics be applied to your current ministry setting?

Being an effective leader requires us to be **transformative**—*willing to continuously be remade from the inside out by the power and direction of the Holy Spirit.*

THE LEADERSHIP QUOTIENT

The interaction of our personality, practice of integrity and place of ministry is what we refer to as our *leadership quotient*. Effective leaders take into account all three components when developing a leadership style that will have maximum impact.

Personality

Our *personality* is a part of who we are as individuals. Each personality type approaches leadership a bit differently. While the powerful hammer might take on projects head-first without fear or reservation, the precision tape measure might first ensure all the details are accurately cared for. Personality affects our default method of operation and how we tend to interact with others.

Some personalities are naturally more people friendly than others. A more charismatic personality is fun to be around and more pleasant to spend time with. But even gregarious ministers can't depend solely on the strengths of their personality to lead. Leadership developed on personality alone will be more shallow, shorter-lived and less transparent. Many people (and even entire ministries) burn out and eventually abandon charismatic leaders in pursuit of one with more genuine depth of character.

While seeking to rely on the positive characteristics of your personality, you will want to honestly address your negative characteristics as well. Recall your personality blend from page 193. With which natural strengths and weaknesses from your personality type do you identify as most applying to you (see appendix E)?

Personality Blend:

Strengths:

Weaknesses:

I (Brad) recently played golf with a guy who'd been attending our church for the past couple of months. During the conversation, he shared his struggle with being in front of people. To his surprise, I shared that I become nervous every time I speak before a crowd. He responded, "I never would have known." As an adaptable duct tape personality, I'm actually quite happy observing from the back row and not speaking a word. Yet at the church, my position as senior pastor doesn't allow for that. I have to be intentionally conscious of my need to interact with confidence to compensate for my natural tendency. Otherwise, people might mistake my actions as aloofness.

No matter our personality, we'll at times have to compensate for certain natural tendencies. It's good to be mindful of both the value of our personality to our organization as well as the perceptions of the people we serve.

Practice of Integrity

Our *practice* is the unique way we live out our ministry. While imperfect at best, we as ministers desire to practice a life of integrity. In the last few decades, we've watched megabusinesses and megaministries collapse because the integrity of their leaders gave way to varying degrees of indiscretion.

Our integrity will shape the way we lead. A ministry practiced with integrity will slowly multiply in influence over the long-term—though not always over the short-term. Lots of crowds and buildings have been built simply to crumble at the exposed lapse of integrity in the lives of ministers. General Ronald R. Fogleman, former chief of staff of the United States Air Force, once said:

> Leaders who have the appearance of substance but lack internal integrity won't have the strength to make it through the tough times. In the military, commanders with a veneer of integrity cannot build organizations capable of withstanding the unique challenges of military life, much less the trials of combat.[1]

Ministry for leaders lacking integrity is simply another act in the performance of holiness—walking, talking, dressing, acting and responding in the clergy way. Unfortunately, some religious communities create a set of established "spiritually correct" behaviors that actually discourages real integrity in leadership. This is done by placing hyperfocus on a half-dozen or so "super sins" and effectively ignoring the rest. Those successful at abstinence from the super list are publicly praised as models of integrity—regardless of how far off the mark the rest of their lives might be.

Christian leaders need to be honest about the inherent challenges of our faith. There was only one sinless person; he died to make up for where our integrity falls short. Integrity isn't so much about how close to some human measure of perfection we achieve as it is about relying on God's strength to live out a walk congruent with our internal desire for godliness. Integrity is having the humility to admit we're imperfect before God and, when necessary, to confess specific imperfections privately or publicly—even if we lose our position of organizational leadership in the process. Such a walk will more deeply impact others than any far-reaching ministry void of such authenticity. When we choose to be who we are in Christ—nothing more and nothing less—we demonstrate to people that Jesus is real and isn't just some mask we wear.

Ask the Holy Spirit to reveal areas of your life that may presently lack integrity. Use the space below to jot down your insights.

Integrity isn't so much about how close to some human measure of perfection we achieve as it is about relying on God's strength to live out a walk congruent with our internal desire for godliness.

---

[1]Donald Phillips, *Lincoln on Leadership* (New York: Warner Books, 1992), pp. 55-56.

What steps might you take to restore integrity to these areas?

Place of Ministry

Each different *place* of ministry adheres to differing values and impacts how we ought to provide leadership there. Rural, urban and suburban settings will embrace three different sets of expectations. We will likely be ineffective if we attempt to take one template and superimpose it onto every ministry in every setting, expecting the same results.

Describe your current ministry environment and its geographical context.

What is your position or ministry function within the organization?

As best you can, describe the general expectations others have of you and your position, both ministry associates and those to whom you minister.

Briefly describe the demographics of those to whom you minister (age ranges, nationalities, typical socioeconomic status, marital status, culture/subculture, etc.):

   As a pastor, I (Brad) have had the opportunity to serve four wonderful congregations. The first church I served was a start-up mission church in a suburban setting. This situation required a hands-on approach and a generalist style of management with no other ministerial personnel to lean on. The second church was an established church of twenty years. Because this church had endured a difficult transition prior to my arrival, it required a ministry of healing and vision-casting. Other personnel were already in place, including people to care for the building and grounds. The third church was a 125-year-old county-seat first church in a rural setting, requiring yet a different set of skills. The church I currently serve is over eighty years old with a rich history of influence in its community, a city adjacent to Houston, Texas. At all four places of ministry, different sets of expectations existed. The demands of each location called for an approach somewhat unique to that congregation.

When some ministers relocate to a new ministry setting, they drag their baggage with them. It is presumptuous at best and spiritually toxic at worst to blindly transplant the same style of leadership, programs, methodologies and teachings from one ministry location to the next without regard for its particular location and people.

Those of us with teaching responsibilities should seriously consider not repeating messages out of convenience, even if they're given to completely different audiences. If we're simply in the habit of repeats, we miss the opportunity to hear God speak to us regarding a fresh message for ourselves and for the audience at hand. We can challenge ourselves to seek God's message for that moment and for that particular audience. Passion abounds in teaching from the fresh winds of what God is teaching us in our intimate relationship with him.

A rich metaphor for ministry leadership is that of the shepherd. The psalmist describes the character of a shepherd who knows his personality, practice and place as it relates to leadership (Psalm 23). The sheep are not in want because the shepherd knows them and their personalities intimately, understanding and caring for their unique needs. He loves them and gives them rest. His practice of integrity earns their trust as the shepherd guides them and restores their soul. He knows how to lead them to the right places, causing them to graze in lush pastures. He knows his sheep and his sheep know him.

People grow to trust competent leadership. In time, the folks in our flock will welcome us to walk with them through the dark valley of suffering and hard times. Our presence and our ministry will be a comforting and stabilizing factor in their lives.

Considering the material presented here, create your own working definition of leadership.

How do your own personality, practice of integrity and place of ministry affect your overall leadership ability, both positively and negatively?

What adjustments could you make with regard to the components of your leadership quotient to become more effective in your role?

It is presumptuous at best and spiritually toxic at worst to blindly transplant the same style of leadership, programs, methodologies and teachings from one ministry location to the next.

2. Dealing with Change in Ministry

We live in a complex age. Our environment is forever adjusting, with new technologies revolutionizing communication and productivity in the marketplace. Effective ministry must proactively adapt to its ever-changing, culturally diverse environment.

Sometimes we confuse our changeless God with the need for a changeless style of ministry. While the mission and message of the church should remain steadfast, ministry strategy (the delivery vehicle for the gospel's changeless message) must adapt to meet a changing environment. Successful leadership cooperates with change by taking advantage of new tools and methodologies for the advancement of the organization's unchanging mission.

CHANGES IN SOCIETY AFFECTING LEADERSHIP

Everywhere we look, cultural and societal change is obvious. It might be easier to point out what hasn't changed than what has, and we're experiencing it today at an accelerated rate as compared with previous generations. This rapid shifting requires our ability to adapt and navigate our organizations through such changing times. Of particular interest for the minister are the rapid changes in technology, consumerism and ethnicity, as well as the arrival of the postmodern generation.

Technology

A significant factor driving change in leadership is the great blessing (and potentially frustrating curse) of ever-changing technology. Even some traditional churches with strong liturgy have begun adding large screens and even plasma televisions, replacing hymnals and enhancing sermons. The Internet has revolutionized the way we minister, with more of us using it as our primary research tool for newsletters, sermons and publications. The high cost of print and postage has many ministries opting for colorfully interactive e-newsletters.

This is also the age of the mobile office. With a cell phone, laptop and Wi-Fi, we can complete a project while having coffee at our favorite coffee shop or catch up on e-mails while we're waiting for a flight. E-mail and other Internet-based communication tools provide instant connection to coworkers, employees and ministry partners. Only a few short years ago, I (Brad) could have gone several days without being online. Today, it's not uncommon for me to spend two hours a day initiating and responding to e-mail communication.

Consumerism

The demands of consumers are altering the fashion by which ministry operates and functions. Just one generation past, churches were on every city corner and served as community-based organizations. People joined a church based on denomination and neighborhood location. Today church attendees in metropolitan areas visit any number of locations in search of a ministry to meet specific felt needs—sometimes with little concern over location, denomination or doctrine. Some worshipers pass any number of churches to reach the church of their preference.

Ethnicity

A more mobile society has encouraged a greater ethnic diversity in most metropolitan areas. Such shifts in the ethnic composition call for strategic change in the way ministries relate to their community. In the days before Disney World, Orlando was a small, segregated, conservative community. Many families growing up there had lived in Orlando for generations. In fact, I (Brad) was born in the same Orlando hospital where both my parents were born. In the years since Disney World opened, a tremendous influx of ethnic diversity has changed the face of the community.

The community where I now minister is in the heart of the petrochemical industry. Baytown (Texas) has experienced a significant population shift, from a predominantly Anglo community to a community almost equally proportioned between Hispanic and Anglo.

What cultural changes have occurred within your ministry's community in the past twenty years? How about in just the last five years?

What current trends do you notice in your ministry context? How do you see them affecting your approach to ministry in the near future?

How might you begin now preparing your ministry and key ministry leadership for such a transition?

The Postmodern Generation

Whereas previous generations preferred a hierarchical approach to leadership, the current one prefers working in teams:

Certain characteristics of this postmodern world support a team-based ministry in two ways. First, they suggest new models for leadership that strike me as more biblically and theologically sound than the leadership models traditionally used in congregations. Through these models, the postmodern culture actually encourages good reforms in the church. Second, because the people whom we seek to reach with the Gospel are, like most people, heavily influenced by the social culture, team-based ministry fits well with their ideas and their experiences.[2]

The younger generations gravitate toward organizations that embrace and engage in participative leadership and shy away from rigid hierarchical organizations. If they don't have a say, they may well not participate. Ministries embracing such change will likely thrive; it remains to be seen what will happen for those that don't.

What is the current generational mix of your ministry? What different expectations of leadership do you notice within the various generations you serve?

Do you instinctively lean more toward a hierarchical or participative leadership approach? What challenges has that orientation presented for you?

How might you adapt your leadership approach to more effectively work with the generational mix within your ministry?

CHANGE MANAGEMENT

Change is one of the biggest challenges to effective ministry leadership. For changes within the organization to be accepted, our rationale as leaders must resonate within the hearts of the people making the journey with us. The compelling reason for many will be fueled by spiritual discontent, an inward understanding that something in the present must give way for a better future. When leaders are accused of creating change for the mere sake of change, it may be that the leader failed to communicate the need clearly or that their people don't yet feel adequate spiritual discontent with the way things are.

---

[2]George Cladis, *Leading the Team-Based Church* (Seattle: Jossey-Bass, 1999), p. 17.

We would be wise to never embark upon change alone. A common mistake made by leaders is to unilaterally initiate change. After all, we're the leader—right? Yes and no. While we may be the leader in position, we're not necessarily the ministry's most strategic influencer. We need the help of others to create and sustain the process with us, whether the change is simple or comprehensive.

In my second pastorate, I (Brad) wanted to make a change in our Sunday evening schedule. For twenty years, the congregation had a Sunday evening worship service. I was convinced the best use of our time would be to move our visitation program to Sunday night because more folks appeared to be home on Sunday nights in our community than any other night of the week. This turned out to be a major undertaking. I learned to spend time sharing my vision with my influencers, both individually and collectively. With key leadership in support, a recommendation was brought before the church for approval. I could have stood before the congregation to make my case for the change. Instead, a senior leader (perhaps the most influential man in the church) stood in his stately fashion, saying he wanted to make a motion to move our visitation program to Sunday night. The motion passed without dissent.

Now this didn't just happen. I had spoken with this leader weeks before the meeting and asked him if he'd consider making this motion. Believing this was a good decision for the church, he agreed. His influence encouraged the ministry at large to embrace the change. As I went about sharing my dream, one of the more influential men in the congregation stood with me—and that made a world of difference. Change management can be labor-intensive, but when approached strategically it's time well spent.

There are several important details to remember as we facilitate change. First, we must know our people. This includes knowing their personal dreams, passions and especially any identifiable spiritual discontent. Second, change is often resisted—even by some who really know it's for the best. Especially in well-established organizations, people are often creatures of habit. Third, change will in some way happen whether we want it to or not. Even mature organizations that try to hold on to the past by digging in their heels will eventually change. Organizations unwilling to embrace change at some level will change in the ultimate sense—they will die. Fourth, we must communicate, communicate, communicate, keeping the vision, purpose and direction in front of people day in and day out.

Is there any discernible spiritual discontent in the people you lead? If so, what changes might positively address such discontent?

How will you know when they are ready for change?

3. Leadership Styles: What's in Your Wardrobe?

God gives each

minister the raw

material necessary

to provide good

leadership and then

helps us to fashion

that material into

functional outfits for

the work of our

unique ministry.

Hence leaders are

both born and

made.

Many of us have a wardrobe filled with outfits for a variety of occasions, from suits and dresses for a fancy party down to the most comfy casual jeans for lying around the house. Some people enjoy getting dressed up; it's when they are in their element. Others won't be comfortable until they've put on their favorite old T-shirt and pair of sneakers. While there are a few occasions we might not have exactly what we need, most of us have options. And although some of what's in our closet may feel uncomfortable and not fit all that well, we could (and would) wear it in a pinch.

Styles of leadership are much like the styles of clothing in our wardrobe. God gives each minister the raw material necessary to provide good leadership and then helps us to fashion that material into functional outfits for the work of our unique ministry. Hence leaders are both born and made. Our approach to leadership, then, involves identifying our natural strengths and recognizing our inherent weaknesses. We most likely will gravitate toward one style as our default, or "best fit." Other styles will be found in our wardrobe but will fit with varying degrees of comfort. One or more styles may not fit at all and, consequently, won't even be found in our wardrobe.

No single style of leadership can provide adequate leadership over the lifetime of an organization. Therefore, a key component to leadership is determining which styles are necessary for a particular time and place. Where voids exist, we'll want to either embrace such styles ourselves or be prepared to delegate leadership in those areas to someone else.

MODELING

Regardless which leadership styles we use in ministry, it's important for all ministers to model their styles in front of those they lead. Leadership through modeling is demonstrated through a life lived consistently with the values we profess: "Follow my example, as I follow the example of Christ" (1 Corinthians 11:1).

Many of the best lessons ever taught were never spoken audibly. St. Francis of Assisi was reported to have said, "Preach the gospel always, and if necessary, use words." Modeling is authentic and flows from the heart rather than a well-rehearsed stage presence. Modeling is also transparent, so those we serve can see us as we truly are on the inside (Ephesians 4:24). While we will interact with those we serve at varying levels of intimacy, each person should be able to observe our successes and failures (and how we work through them). This allows them to gain encouragement and hope by them. Modeling isn't just good theory but is demonstrated in our day-to-day routine.

The level of our credibility will be in direct proportion to the quality of our modeling. When we attempt to portray ourselves as something we're not or as practicing something that we're actually not practicing, we're no longer modeling but acting. Such lack of authenticity, transparency and demonstration will eventually be seen for what it is. Ministries and their leaders are destroyed when their credibility is tarnished or lost. Most will recall a prominent television ministry that claimed if viewers sent a prayer request with a monetary donation a prayer partner would pray for them. It was later discovered that the ministry's mailroom protocol was to remove the check from the envelope and discard anything else—including prayer requests. No one ever prayed for the requests. This practice was eventually disclosed on a network news program. Not only did this ministry suffer, their public actions caused a ripple-effect loss of credibility for countless other Christian ministries.

When we attempt to portray ourselves as something we're not or as practicing something that we're actually not practicing, we're no longer modeling but acting.

How many times have we made a promise only to fail to meet the expectation? It may appear trivial to us, but not necessarily to others. Ministry leaders are notoriously delinquent in fulfilling their financial obligations. Recently we heard about a minister who publicly "praised God" because the bank decided not to pursue him for the difference between the money he owed on his repossessed automobile and its actual value. Evidently, the minister felt no sense of responsibility for his debt. Nonprofit ministries are increasingly conducting preemployment criminal background and credit checks because they know a minister's background speaks to their character. Where there are shady pasts in one area of life, there's a greater likelihood they'll exist in another. By contrast, Jesus calls us to let our word be as good as done (Matthew 5:37).

Modeling is not an attempt to be perfect. There will be times we'll live out our faith life well and plenty of times when we won't. But when we fall short, Christlike modeling deals with the shortcoming directly and honestly rather than trying to cover it up.

How do you currently model well? In what areas is there room for improvement?

What changes could you make for your modeling to more authentically reflect your personal faith?

With the understanding that every style of leadership must be modeled before those we lead, let's now try on five of the leadership styles commonly found among ministry leaders. This will help us determine which styles are "in our wardrobe," which are our "best fit" and which are simply "not our style."

"FIELDMASTER" ADVENTUREWEAR

The *Fieldmaster* style of leadership is modeled by ministers who see themselves as guides to the next level God has in store for the ministry. Ministers who sport this leadership style see clearly the trail marked out for an organization, create a field map to get to the end and bring as many people as possible along for the journey. They are able to clearly articulate a future while engaging others in a strategy to realize it. Joshua led the people into the Promised Land, having intimate knowledge of it because he'd been there. As Joshua sent two men to spy out the Land, he planted a vision in their minds when he specifically told them to stop and look over Jericho. Joshua's vision of the future was compelling because he already had a vision for where he was leading them.

This style of leadership requires a dream, a God-supplied direction for the ministry. God will give such vision to these ministers because it's the fuel on which they operate. The dream can be as simple as a procedure or policy change, or something as complex as establishing a permanent missionary presence in a hostile foreign country. However, even God-sized dreams are achieved one step at a time, just as there were stages and smaller victories that eventually accomplished Joshua's possession of the Promised Land. Once the dream can be simply articulated, it's usually shared individually with one or more key influencers within the ministry. As these influencers prayerfully consider and spread the dream through smaller and then larger group settings, ownership of the dream is realized by the core of the ministry community.

While it's most commonly modeled in new-start ministries, this style is also helpful for giving new or renewed direction to declining or stagnant organizations. Yet the minister using this style must exercise care to not lose focus of the present while helping others envision the future. Ministry leaders who spend all their time in the future can get too far ahead of their people, which can lead to conflict, especially if the leaders are perceived as overlooking needs or opportunities in the here-and-now. Such leaders must take time to enjoy what God is doing today with the people they influence as they maintain a clear view for the future vision.

Describe any personal experience you've had with this leadership style.

Would you describe this style as being one "in your wardrobe," your "best fit" or "not your style"? Why?

BLUE-COLLAR WORKWEAR

Blue-collar leadership is modeled through collaborative process. Such leaders roll up their sleeves and actively get others involved in the work of ministry. This group process solicits input from as many different perspectives as possible. Say, for example, a mission organization is considering relocation. This style of leadership might create a team of six people responsible for researching the options and formulating a strategy for the relocation. Each team member will have equal input, with their recommendations presented to the board for consideration. The team's success requires cooperation from every member.

Churches that operate with a congregational style of government demonstrate such leadership in a larger context, with each person in the congregation having one vote. Each voice is valued and has the opportunity to be heard as the leader seeks consensus from a majority of the participants.

Rumors and conflict arose in the early church when both Grecian and Hebraic Jews were disgruntled about the way the apostles were handling the distribution of food (Acts 6:3). In response to the complaints, the apostles determined that the task required a team of people devoted to it. They could have chosen for themselves the seven to serve the overlooked population. Instead, they invited the church to participate in the decision-making process. This allowed everyone not only ownership of the situation but also a sharing of future responsibility for their success.

Ministries targeting younger generations typically thrive on collaboration and value the opportunity for input. Giving people a certain amount of opportunity to participate in organizational decision-making often creates enthusiasm within an organization. Leaders who employ the blue-collar workwear style of leadership often invest greater time with people and utilize stronger people skills than do those who model other leadership styles. They are also willing to allow others to do some of the work of ministry—even if their methods or results aren't the way the leader would have done it personally. This style is effective in organizations recovering from conflict or tragic loss, creating a natural environment of open dialogue and building new trust between leaders and followers. This style also creates the greatest buy-in for change in an organization.

One caution for leaders wearing this style is to remember that not all decisions can be made with everyone participating in the process. Such leaders will want to clearly communicate ahead of time which decisions will be made by the group and which ones will be made by leadership alone.

Describe any personal experience you've had with this leadership style.

Would you describe this style as being one "in your wardrobe," your "best fit" or "not your style"? Why?

CORPORATE BUSINESSWEAR

The *corporate* style of leadership emphasizes helping others develop skills for becoming what God has called them to be, both individually and as a corporate member of the body of Christ. This style is characterized not only by individual training but by team development within the organization. Believing in the individuals and the organization being developed, such leaders see the undeveloped talent in those they lead—helping them identify and achieve their personal goals within the organizational context. Jesus told Peter and Andrew that he not only saw their raw talent but would use it to mold them into "fishers of men" (Matthew 4:19). Not only did Barnabas boldly see Paul's potential when others feared him (Acts 9:26-27), he was willing to invest time into Paul by coaching him in ministry for an entire year (Acts 11:25-26). Paul would later model this same style of leadership as he developed Timothy.

A caution for the corporate businesswear style of leadership is that the leader can become so wrapped up in developing others that they jeopardize their own personal growth. Such leaders must be as intentional about their own development as they are their people's.

Describe any personal experience you've had with this leadership style.

Would you describe this style as being one "in your wardrobe," your "best fit" or "not your style"? Why?

DINNER PARTY FORMALWEAR

The *dinner party* style of leadership models more concern for the quality of relationships than with individual tasks or accomplishments. Priority is placed on the unity and harmony of those within the organization as well as their emotional, physical and spiritual well-being.

The value of this style is found in the power of well-connected relationships focusing on the worth of the individual. People want to know they are valued more than the goal they're trying to achieve. This style can be very helpful in conflict situations. Jesus reconciled relationships among his disciples after James and John's mother created a stir by asking that her sons be given the most powerful positions within the kingdom (Matthew 20:24-28). Jesus refocused them back toward humility and servitude, bringing the disciples into harmony. However, such leaders must be careful not to allow harmony among members to completely overshadow the stated goals of the organization.

Describe any personal experience you've had with this leadership style.

Would you describe this style as being one "in your wardrobe," your "best fit" or "not your style"? Why?

EMERGENCY RESPONDER UNIFORMWEAR

The *emergency responder* style is the most directive form of leadership and works best in times of crisis. Whether the crisis is inside or outside of the organization, this style effectively leads others to safety. During an internal crisis, the leader might model a new direction and pace—challenging the accepted culture and practices of an organization. Nehemiah was the right leader at the right time for the inhabitants of Jerusalem, who were distraught over the destruction of their great city (Nehemiah 2:11-18). The people were only able to focus on the crisis; their own survival created blinders to their true condition. Nehemiah became a fresh set of eyes, able to see and deliver a message of hope. He also identified himself as one of them, as if to say, "We're in this together. It's time to rebuild!" Nehemiah engaged and challenged the internal influences of the people to help them create a new future.

Such leaders also tackle external crises, during which there isn't time to practice other leadership styles without risking damage to both the organization and its individual members. In times of real crisis, someone has to take charge and steer toward safety. I (Brad) can't help but remember the crises in our community from hurricanes Katrina and Rita. Our church responded to thousands of people who arrived in our community overnight after Katrina hit the Gulf Coast. Decisions had to be made quickly and in coordination with various governmental and relief agencies. We had to adopt an emergency responder leadership style to engage this circumstance. With Rita approaching the Gulf Coast just a few short weeks later, our community was issued a mandatory evacuation order. The safety of our members and their evacuation plans were our primary concern. Within twenty-four hours, our leadership team checked on each member to ensure everyone had a way out of town.

Paul modeled this style of leadership in the midst of a storm at sea by not only calming the passengers but getting them ready for an imminent shipwreck (Acts 27:27-36). He offered limited comfort while giving clear direction as many of the men began to abandon the boat, instructing them to remain on board for their safety.

One cautionary note about this style of leadership: a leader cannot constantly lead an organization wearing the emergency responder style without eventually being experienced as controlling. While there certainly are times and circumstances that call for such a directive style, an organization will not thrive long-term under such constant leadership.

Describe any personal experience you've had with this leadership style.

Would you describe this style as being "in your wardrobe," your "best fit" or "not your style"? Why?

Place a check in the corresponding box of the styles that are in your wardrobe (that is, you either sometimes wear or have worn in the past but they're not a best fit for you), wear often as your best fit, or are not your style (that is, you either have never worn or presently don't wear).

Leadership Style	Best Fit	In My Wardrobe	Not My Style	Comments
Fieldmaster Adventurewear				
Blue-Collar Workwear				
Corporate Businesswear				
Dinner Party Formalwear				
Emergency Responder Uniformwear				

THE RIGHT STYLE FOR THE JOB

Every organization has acceptable practices and expectations unique to its own culture. Some ministry settings also have subcultures with separate cultural practices and expectations. Effective leaders have an understanding of both the overall practices as well as the subcultural practices. Likewise, they recognize that they may have to take on differing styles to successfully lead both.

While our strongest leadership will come through our best fitting styles, another style may be what the organization needs to move into the next phase of God's overall plan. A traditional church setting (even an average-sized one) often exhibits a wide variety of subcultures. Laying out a long-range vision for a particular organization might require a minister to wear a blue-collar collaborative style among several subcultures, a corporate style with the younger people in the church to mature them for the future and a dinner party style to reconnect senior adults who feel alienated by the new vision—all the while modeling a faith-walk before the entire congregation and providing Fieldmaster leadership to keep them excited about the direction of the ministry.

What cultural expectations exist within your organization?

How are decisions generally made within the organization? Who are the primary decision-makers?

What style(s) of leadership does the overall culture respond to most effectively? How does it match up with your best-fit leadership style?

In what ways might you make some "alterations" to lead more effectively?

For each of the various subcultures within your organization, answer the following: How would you define this subculture? What (if any) unique expectations does this group possess? To what style(s) of leadership might they respond most effectively? What alterations might allow you to lead them more effectively?

Subculture 1: _____
Unique Expectations: _____
Most Effective Leadership Style: _____
Possible Leadership Alteration: _____

Subculture 2: _____
Unique Expectations: _____
Most Effective Leadership Style: _____
Possible Leadership Alteration: _____

Subculture 3: _____
Unique Expectations: _____
Most Effective Leadership Style: _____
Possible Leadership Alteration: _____

Subculture 4: _____
Unique Expectations: _____
Most Effective Leadership Style: _____
Possible Leadership Alteration: _____

Determining what style is best for modeling in a specific situation can be challenging. In many ways, leadership is a learning process. Leading an organization over the long term requires leaders to grow alongside the organization. Certain seasons in the life of an organization may require us to change out of our naturally best-fitting style. Transformative leaders see this as opportunity for both personal and professional growth.

4. Other Ingredients for Effective Leadership

As previously discussed, transformative leaders are open to God's re-shaping in their own lives. This includes an awareness of our leadership quotient (the interaction between our personality, practice of integrity and unique place of ministry), the changes in leadership (the changing methods by which we might deliver God's unchanging message) and the various styles available to us in our leadership wardrobe. Here are a few other common ingredients for effective leadership in ministry.

LOVE: THE REASON WE CARE

No matter our best-fit ministry style and particular ministry environment, we must have a love for both God and God's people (Matthew 22:37-39). We won't have much desire for leading people we don't love. They'll see through such lack of desire too. When a two-way love relationship exists between minister and people, each has a greater tendency to believe the best in the other, give the benefit of the doubt and even overlook the other's shortcomings (1 Peter 4:8). Regularly prioritized intimacy with God will also yield an ever-renewing love for those to whom he has called us to minister.

Frustration can exist between ministers and those they lead if they've never truly made the decision to love each other. Such love is often built one experience at a time over time. Loving people means being actively engaged in their lives. We can't afford to allow the demands of ministry to separate us from people. Even if we know we've been called to a particular ministry for a short-term assignment, we can resist the urge to short-change them by remaining detached and uninvolved.

Expressing love can be done through phone calls, passing comments, personal notes and random demonstrations of kindness. It's also expressed by living as if we plan to spend our entire lives right where we are. Some ministers live too far down the road from their current ministry placement. We can trust God to speak clearly when it's time to move on. Meanwhile, our job is simply to be faithful to his calling on our lives today. If we live with permanence in mind, it will change the way our people relate to us.

Our ability to love is also born out of personal brokenness and

We can trust God to speak clearly when it's time to move on. Meanwhile, our job is simply to be faithful to his calling on our lives today.

deep surrender. Brokenness comes when we realize we're unable to do something on our own. The year 1994 will be a year that I (Brad) will always remember. It represented the best and worst moments of my life. In 1990, just two months after my daughter was born, I left the ministry both burned out and disillusioned. For a couple of years, I worked for our family's business before venturing out on my own. In hindsight, I made the mistake of becoming an owner-operator of a fast-food franchise. Almost a year to the day, I locked the restaurant's doors for the last time; a dream had died. Over the ensuing months, I walked under an almost unbearable load as a husband, father and supposed breadwinner. With an enormous obligation and no income, failure felt final. If I cried once, I cried a hundred times. Not only was I physically and emotionally broken, I felt spiritually defeated. I found myself at a point of compelling surrender to Christ because there was simply no other place to go.

In picking up the pieces, I discovered compassion. Had I not walked through that valley, I wouldn't have learned how to deeply love a congregation. Through brokenness, God taught me compassion—renewing my sense of calling into the ministry and equipping me to truly love the people I serve.

In what ways might your love for God have grown cold in recent days?

In the past, what things tended to stir your passion for God? How might those things help you today regarding your response to the question above?

How do you demonstrate your love for those you serve?

What ways have you stopped demonstrating love recently? Why did you stop?

Read 1 Corinthians 13:4-8:

> *Love is patient, love is kind. It does not envy, it does not boast, it is not proud. It is not rude, it is not self-seeking, it is not easily angered, it keeps no record of wrongs. Love does not delight in evil but rejoices with the truth. It always protects, always trusts, always hopes, always perseveres. Love never fails.*

Which aspects of love do you express regularly toward others in your ministry? Which are typically absent?

What can you do to more consistently and completely show love to the people you shepherd?

VISION: DREAMING FOR THE FUTURE

Dreaming about our ministry's future happens alongside our helping the organization achieve the vision it owns in the here and now. While ministers with a Fieldmaster leadership style thrive on dreaming, all ministers have the capacity for a certain level of vision. While many books on ministry leadership discuss the components of vision, we prefer to focus on the *process* of vision—from birth to incubation to presentation to commitment to realization.

God is ultimately the Creator of all dreams and gives *birth* to the vision needed to see the dream toward maturity. During a time of *incubation*, we ask God to give us direction. As we share the dream with a mentor or a few trusted friends, we give them permission to speak truth into us. We can then prayerfully sit with their feedback, listening for God's direction.

Next is the *presentation* of the dream with small groups of key people. Depending on the organizational and decision-making structure of the ministry, this might be a small group of board or vestry members or key lay leaders. We share the passion behind the dream and ways they can become involved in shaping the dream. We incorporate their feedback into how we might practically achieve the dream. We listen for people willing to put their hands to the plow— men and women who are either willing to work to make it happen or influencers who will embrace the dream as their own and help communicate it to others.

Once the dream has taken on general acceptance among the decision-makers of an organization, the leader moves the dream toward reality by bringing it before the governing board or congregation for endorsement and *commitment*. Standing by our side, major influencers or lay leaders affirm the dream publicly, allowing others to feel, "This is our dream and our leader. We'll be a part of this together." The dream has become a corporate vision moving toward *realization*. Communicating the vision regularly keeps it fresh before the people.

What dream has God given you for your ministry? At what stage is the dream (birth, incubation, presentation, commitment, realization)?

What might your next step be in taking the dream toward realization?

CONFLICT RESOLUTION

Ministry is often filled with conflict. Jesus endured seemingly end-less conflict, from the religious leaders to his own disciples. Transfor-mative leaders know the difference between peacekeeping and peacemaking. *Peacekeeping* is the effort to maintain an environment of nonconflict. It's the strained attempt to ease escalating pressure. Peacekeeping doesn't deal with issues but only focuses on keeping peace for the moment.

Unaddressed conflict can destroy ministry vitality and longevity. When leaders fail to address conflict in a constructive manner, it will have a ripple effect on the entire ministry. We may be forced to leave, stacking the deck against our future opportunity for success. We have a moral responsibility to engage conflict not only for the sake of cur-rent ministry but also for the effectiveness of leaders who follow us.

Peacemaking, on the other hand, doesn't focus on present tranquil-ity but is directly interested in seeking resolution to the issues that created the conflict in the first place. Conflict resolution through peacemaking often has a short-term cost but yields a tremendous long-term benefit. In his book *The Peacemaker*, Ken Sande teaches the "PAUSE" principle as a practical acronym for proactively approach-ing others to resolve conflict: Prepare yourself for the conversation; Affirm the other person's dignity and worth; Understand the inter-ests of the other person; Search for creative solutions; and Evaluate options as objectively and reasonably as possible.[3] Once reconcilia-tion has taken place, Sande also suggests each partner make "four promises" to each other as a way to avoid rehashing the same issues in the future: (1) I will not dwell on this incident; (2) I will not bring up this incident again and use it against you; (3) I will not talk to oth-ers about this incident; and (4) I will not allow this incident to stand between us or hinder our relationship. These peacemaking princi-ples will help us not only to resolve conflict in a biblical way but also to keep bitterness from creeping into our ministry.

---

[3]Ken Sande, *The Peacemaker*, 3rd ed. (Grand Rapids: Baker, 2004), pp. 267-68.

List any areas of conflict you're presently facing in the following areas:

 Within personal relationships?

 With other ministry leaders?

 With people you lead?

Of these, what do you perceive would be the cost of peacemaking rather than peacekeeping?

How might Ken Sande's principles be helpful in the above situations?

TEAM-MINDED MINISTRY

"A team is a small number of people with complementary skills who are committed to a common purpose, performance goals, and approach for which they hold themselves accountable."[4] Whether our organization uses committees, is board-driven or operates using a relatively informal group process, a team-minded environment values other people and their input. Efficient teams utilize no fewer and no more members than are required for the goal and are composed of people with differing yet complementary giftedness and relational qualities.

To facilitate a team-minded environment, members need to feel ownership of the purpose and goal for the organization. Some form of accountability should also exist to keep each member of the team dedicated to the task at hand. While employees are compensated for their effort, ministry teams are often built solely from volunteers. In such cases, we might create another system of accountability within the team, whether by using recognition, special privilege or some other form of incentive.

Another component to promote effective teamwork incorporates trust built over time. Trust exists when team members can depend upon and confide in each other without fear of ridicule or retribution. When members feel free to confide, they don't worry about being misinterpreted, sabotaged or quoted out of context. Team mem-

---

[4]Jon R. Katzenbach and Douglas K. Smith, *The Wisdom of Teams: Creating the High Performance Organization* (New York: Harper Business School Press, 1994), p. 45.

bers speak freely among the group, with their input remaining inside the group. Trust is established when team members follow through with stated expectations, including being on time for meetings and contributing their fair share of the work.

Creativity in ministry ventures prevents stagnation in the same old rut. Team members are free to express their creative ideas regardless of how "outside of the box" they may seem. I (Michael Todd) love to brainstorm. While I can sometimes generate ten times the ideas of others, 80 to 90 percent of them may be so far outside the box as to border on the ridiculous. However, as a result of my methods I will sometimes generate a highly creative but workable idea that no one else might have ever considered. Groups that squelch such creativity rarely benefit from such members.

Sharing the adventure of ministry with others provides camaraderie for the minister and mentoring and training opportunities for others. Although Jesus was often alone when refueling or spending time with the Father, he typically ministered alongside at least one of his disciples. His priority in team-minded ministry was the vehicle for countless moments of dialogue and shared ministry opportunity.

What areas of ministry are you currently doing alone?

How might a team-minded approach prove beneficial for you or for those you lead?

What might be the first step toward making such a transition a reality?

Wrap-Up: Foundation Stone 7— Leadership Skills: Implementing a Transformative Self-Care Plan

While the study of leadership is a discipline of theories and concepts, transformative leadership is leadership put into practice. It's a dynamic process rather than a cookie-cutter recipe, a continual process that requires regular monitoring and investment. In short, the heart of transformative leadership is the practical application and practice of the seven foundation stones.

The regular practice of these foundation stones is life-changing. Application of these concepts is critical to our personal and professional success. If we're going to safeguard our life and ministry, it will be because we worked to develop and mature each of these principles into our daily lives.

The seven foundation stones come together to form our own tailor-made transformative self-care plan. We don't have to worry about "getting it right"; the only way to not get our self-care plan right is not to create one. Any plan can serve as a starting place, allowing its application and our real-world experience to give us valuable feedback on how to make helpful modifications over time.

INTIMACY

Review the application questions from foundation stone 1, including the wrap-up exercise at the end (p. 64).

What are you doing to nurture your intimate relationship with God?

What are you doing to nurture your intimate relationship with your spouse?

Write down the names of three-to-five same-gender friends with whom you are pursuing a deeper relationship. Next to each, write down their current level of intimacy (1-5) and your likely next step to promote greater intimacy in that relationship.

Name   *Intimacy Level (1-5)*   *Likely Next Step*

Whatever it takes, make time in your schedule to engage each of these important relationships in your life. Don't become so busy that you miss out on them. The enemy will tell you that you're too busy and that it's not really all that important. But each of these friendships can help you maintain proper focus in your life and ministry. Transformation is often facilitated through such close relationships.

CALLING

Review the application questions from foundation stone 2, including the wrap-up exercise at the end (pp. 97-99). Also, review the most recent version of your personal purpose statement (p. 99). Take a few minutes to pray through what you've learned about leadership skills, along with any additional insights the Holy Spirit may have given you. Rewrite your statement in the space provided on p. 99, making whatever modifications you feel are appropriate. Then, copy the most current version of your personal purpose statement here:

What are the implications of your revised personal purpose statement on your ministry in your present context?

What evidence can you point to that might indicate you should consider leaving your current position or location? What evidence do you see that might indicate you should stay?

Consider writing your personal purpose statement inside the front cover of your Bible, reviewing it periodically. It serves as a plumb line for your life and ministry direction. Transformative leaders who are confident in their calling are more protected from being derailed by stuff they're not called to do.

STRESS MANAGEMENT

Review the application questions from foundation stone 3, including the wrap-up exercise at the end (pp. 137-38).

What safeguards are you presently working on in the following areas:

Spiritual:

Relational:

Emotional:

Physical:

If you're having difficulty on one or more safeguards, use this space to brainstorm modifications that might improve their effective application:

    Ineffective Safeguard   *Possible Modification*

Productivity isn't so much defined by the amount of stress you can handle as it is how well you handle the stress you have. Proactively working a stress-management plan prevents stress from turning into distress, which ultimately leads to bad decision-making, burnout and possible unhealthy behavior.

BOUNDARIES

Review the application questions from foundation stone 4, including the wrap-up exercise at the end (pp. 168-69).

What boundaries are you presently seeking to implement or improve on in the following areas:

   Your Ministry:

   Your Family:

   Your Friends:

   Yourself:

   God:

If you're having difficulty on one or more boundaries, use this space to brainstorm ideas that might improve their effective application:

    Ineffective Boundary   *Possible Modification*

Boundaries protect and promote what's most important to us, especially our calling and our intimate relationships. Because ministry can place unhealthy expectations on both you and your family, healthy boundaries allow for strategic development of transformative leadership practices.

RE-CREATION

Review the application questions from foundation stone 5, including the wrap-up exercise at the end (pp. 187-88).

What excuses do you still tend to use to justify avoidance of or deficiency in re-creation?

Update the list of "restful" activities you created on the wrap-up page. Which ones are you regularly prioritizing at this time? Which ones are neglected?

Regularly prioritized	*Mostly neglected*

What might you do to give greater focus to those neglected?

What re-creation plans are you presently working on in any of the following areas? What's the next step toward your destination in each?

	Re-creation	*Next Step*
Physical		
Mental		
Emotional		
Spiritual		

The practice of re-creation is most reflected by the scheduling of such activity into your routine. By building rest, recess and renewal into your calendar, you "re-create" greater stamina to pursue your calling and your important intimate relationships.

PEOPLE SKILLS

Review the application questions from foundation stone 6, including the wrap-up exercise at the end (p. 219).

Update the status of your list of "difficult people" from page 219.

What have you done or what are you actively doing to improve these relationships?

How can you practice listening skills to improve your ministry to others?

Which assertiveness techniques might you benefit from practicing? How might you go about doing this?

LEADERSHIP SKILLS

Review the application questions thus far in this foundation stone. Reproduce the following matrix from page 237:

Leadership Style	Best Fit	In My Wardrobe	Not My Style
Fieldmaster Adventurewear			
Blue-Collar Workwear			
Corporate Businesswear			
Dinner Party Formalwear			
Emergency Responder Uniformwear			

What areas of personal growth or changes might need to occur to improve your overall leadership effectiveness?

What steps can you take in the following areas?

Love:

Vision:

Conflict resolution:

Team-minded ministry:

The transformative leadership approach is demonstrated by loving, knowing, guiding and caring for those under our care. To know our people and our organization, we will want to commit to a long-term perspective—even if we know our time there is limited.

A LEADERSHIP APPROACH FOR LIFE

A transformative approach to leadership takes a holistic and lifelong attitude toward influence. We won't be effective in leading an organization if we aren't ourselves in the process of transformation. Transformative leaders are constantly growing. Some growth areas will be less challenging for us than others. The seven foundation stones help us identify which of our growth areas are in greatest need for improvement, allowing us to begin work in the most critical area.

The men from Issachar were transformative leaders because they "understood the times and knew what Israel should do" (1 Chronicles 12:32). With great wisdom, they understood the bigger picture and made decisions accordingly. They possessed the ability not only to interpret the times but also to put an appropriate transformative plan into practice. That kind of wisdom is a lifetime pursuit.

Even the largest of transformative plans are executed one step at a time. With that in mind, describe the very next step you might take in carrying out any facet of your self-care plan:

This is where you should begin. Know that we are cheering you on toward long-term effectiveness in your ministry calling. The Lord will be your Fieldmaster guide at every twist and turn along the journey. Faithfully following his leadership will result in a more successful and satisfying ministry than you ever thought possible.

> Now to him who is able to do immeasurably more than all we ask or imagine, according to his power that is at work within us, to him be glory in the church and in Christ Jesus throughout all generations, for ever and ever! Amen. (Ephesians 3:20-21)

APPENDIX A
Feelings List

Sometimes ministers are unaware of their feelings about people and situations. Increasing our awareness of our own feelings empowers us to take better responsibility and appropriate action for our situation.

What follows are two lists. The short list can be helpful as a quick reference tool. The longer list is more comprehensive and can be beneficial for discovering finer "shades" of meaning to our feelings. Both lists can also help identify "root" feelings that are deeper than the feelings we are aware of on the surface.

ABBREVIATED LIST

Happy	Loving	Strong	Angry	Confused
appreciative	accepting	able	aggravated	conflicted
content	benevolent	authentic	annoyed	divided
excited	caring	bold	bitter	hypocritical
glad	connected	brave	critical	indecisive
peaceful	friendly	confident	defensive	overwhelmed
playful	intimate	energetic	envious	stuck
pleased	kind	enthusiastic	frustrated	stumped
safe	patient	independent	impatient	undecided
sociable	romantic	intelligent	infuriated	unsure
thankful	sympathetic	positive	mad	
		resilient	prejudiced	
		safe	sarcastic	

Hurt	Sad	Scared	Weak
abused	contrite	afraid	bored
afflicted	depressed	alarmed	dumb
betrayed	grieved	anxious	embarrassed
blamed	guilty	flustered	exhausted
criticized	hopeless	mistrusting	fake
disliked	lonely	nervous	helpless
ignored	low	reluctant	hindered
mistreated	mellow	shy	ineffective
wronged	numb	suspicious	insecure
	unsatisfied	threatened	out of control
	upset	worried	tempted
			tired

COMPREHENSIVE LIST

Happy	Loving	Strong	Angry	Confused	Hurt	Sad	Scared	Weak
accepted	accepting	able	aggravated	absorbed	abandoned	alienated	afflicted	anemic
affectionate	admiring	adequate	aggressive	agonized	abused	alone	afraid	ashamed
alive	adoring	adventurous	agitated	ambivalent	accused	apologetic	alarmed	bent down
animated	agreeable	alert	annoyed	anguished	afflicted	badly	anxious	blocked
appreciative	altruistic	ambitious	appalled	anxious	battered	blue	apprehensive	bored
at ease	amorous	articulate	arrogant	apathetic	betrayed	broken-hearted	awed	broken
attractive	aroused	assertive	belligerent	awkward	blamed	bummed out	bashful	burdened
bright	benevolent	authentic	bitter	baffled	brutalized	closed	cautious	challenged
bubbly	brotherly	authoritative	blunt	baited	bullied	contrite	edgy	cheapened
cheery	caring	bold	bugged	bewildered	cheated	crushed	fearful	clumsy
comfortable	charitable	brave	callous	bothered	condemned	dark	flustered	confined
content	close	buoyant	cantankerous	careless	criticized	dejected	frantic	constrained
contented	committed	capable	combative	concerned	crowded	depressed	frightened	cowardly
curious	compassionate	clever	contemptuous	conflicted	despised	desolate	harassed	crippled
dashing	connected	competent	contrary	confused	destroyed	despairing	hesitant	defeated
delighted	considerate	competitive	cranky	crazy	discarded	desperate	horrified	defective
easy-going	cooperative	confident	critical	dazed	disgraced	despondent	horror-stricken	defenseless
ecstatic	cordial	conscientious	cross	disillusioned	disliked	detached	hysterical	deficient
elated	courteous	courageous	cruel	disorganized	distrusted	devastated	immobilized	demoralized
encouraged	cuddly	creative	cynical	disoriented	dominated	disappointed	insecure	dependent
euphoric	dedicated	daring	deceitful	distracted	doubted	discouraged	intimidated	deprived
excited	devoted	dedicated	defensive	divided	duped	dismayed	jittery	diminished
exhilarated	friendly	determined	defiant	doubtful	excluded	displeased	jumpy	discouraged
expectant	generous	driven	demanding	fragmented	forced	dissatisfied	menaced	dumb
fascinated	gentle	durable	destructive	hypocritical	forsaken	distraught	mistrusting	embarrassed
festive	gracious	eager	disagreeable	inconsistent	harassed	distressed	nauseated	exasperated
fulfilled	harmonious	effective	disgusted	indecisive	hard-pressed	disturbed	nervous	exhausted
funny	hospitable	energetic	distrustful	indifferent	hated	down	offended	exposed
giddy	infatuated	enterprising	enraged	inquisitive	ignored	dreadful	on edge	fake
giving	intimate	enthusiastic	envious	jolted	imposed upon	dull	panicky	fatigued
glad	involved	faithful	frustrated	jumbled	injured	empty	pensive	foolish
gratified	kind	fearless	furious	overwhelmed	insulted	gloomy	petrified	fragile
groovy	neighborly	forgiving	grouchy	paralyzed	manipulated	grieved	protective	frail
hopeful	nurturing	free	grumpy	perplexed	mishandled	grim	quaking	gullible
humorous	passionate	gallant	hard-hearted	puzzled	mistreated	guilty	quivery	helpless
inspired	patient	healthy	harsh	shocked	misunderstood	heartbroken	reluctant	hindered
intrigued	polite	helpful	hateful	speechless	opposed	heavy	ridiculous	humiliated
jovial	romantic	heroic	hostile	stuck	ostracized	hollow	self-conscious	immature
joyful	sacrificial	honored	impatient	stumped	overlooked	homesick	shaken	impaired
jubilant	seductive	important	incensed	stunned	persecuted	hopeless	shaky	impotent
light	sexy	independent	inconsiderate	stupefied	pressured	hurt	sheepish	imprisoned

Happy

lighthearted
liked
lively
loving
majestic
moved
natural
nonchalant
optimistic
peaceful
peppy
playful
pleasant
pleased
privileged
receptive
refreshed
rejuvenated
relaxed
safe
satisfied
sentimental
serene
settled
silly
sociable
soft-hearted
special
spirited
spontaneous
sunny
supported
tender
thankful
thrilled
treasured
vivacious
warm
zappy
zestful

Loving

submissive
supportive
sympathetic
thoughtful
turned on
understanding

Strong

industrious
infallible
influential
inspired
intelligent
invincible
loyal
manly
mature
noble
omnipotent
positive
potent
powerful
pretty
proud
reassured
reliable
resilient
respectful
responsible
rigorous
robust
safe
secure
selfless
skillful
solid
stable
sure
tenacious
tough
triumphant
true
uninhibited
virtuous
vital
whole
willing
wise
youthful

Angry

inconvenienced
indignant
infuriated
insensitive
insulting
irreverent
irritated
jealous
judgmental
livid
mad
manipulative
mean
mouthy
nasty
obstinate
outraged
peeved
perturbed
pissed
prejudiced
quarrelsome
rageful
rebellious
resentful
revengeful
riled up
rude
ruthless
sarcastic
seething
selfish
sore
spiteful
stingy
stubborn
ticked off
uptight
vicious
vindictive
worked up
wrathful

Confused

surprised
swamped
taken aback
tormented
tortured
trapped
troubled
uncertain
uncomfortable
undecided
unsure
surprised
swamped
taken aback
tormented
tortured
trapped
troubled
uncertain
uncomfortable
undecided
unsure

Hurt

provoked
rebuked
reprimanded
repulsed
restrained
ridiculed
thwarted
used
victimized
wronged

Sad

isolated
joyless
left-out
lethargic
lifeless
limp
lonely
lonesome
lost
low
mellow
miserable
mournful
neutral
numb
pathetic
pessimistic
pitiful
reserved
resigned
separated
shabby
sorrowful
sorry
suicidal
sulky
sullen
tearful
uneasy
unhappy
uninterested
unloved
unpleasant
unresponsive
unsatisfied
unsociable
upset
useless
weepy
woeful
worthless

Scared

shy
skeptical
squeamish
startled
suspicious
tempted
tense
tentative
terrified
threatened
timid
uneasy
unsure
wary
worried
shy
skeptical
squeamish
startled
suspicious
tempted
tense
tentative
terrified
threatened
timid
uneasy
unsure
wary
worried

Weak

impulsive
inadequate
incapable
incompetent
ineffective
inept
inferior
inhibited
insecure
irresponsible
lazy
lifeless
lost
needy
obsolete
out of control
overwhelmed
passive
powerless
puny
restless
run down
sickly
sluggish
small
stupid
tempted
timid
tired
unimportant
uninspired
unprepared
unqualified
unsettled
unstable
unworthy
useless
vulnerable
washed out
weary
worn out

Appendix B

Christian Counseling Resources and Related Ministries

Individual and Marital Counseling Resources
American Association of Christian Counselors (www.aacc.net)
Association of Marriage & Family Ministries (www.amfmonline.com)
Christian Association for Psychological Studies (www.caps.net)
Focus on the Family (www.family.org)

Sexual Issues: General (Individual and Marital)
American Board of Christian Sex Therapists (www.sexualwholeness.org)

Sexual Issues: Compulsivity/Addiction
Bethesda Workshops (www.bethesdaworkshops.org)
Exodus International (www.Exodus-International.org)
Faithful and True Ministries (http://faithfulandtrueministries.com)
National Coalition for the Protection of Children and Families (www.nationalcoalition.org)

Support Groups
Celebrate Recovery (www.celebraterecovery.com)
Living In Freedom Everyday (www.freedomeveryday.org)

APPENDIX C
The Holmes-Rahe Life Stress Inventory

The Social Readjustment Rating Scale[1]
Mark down the point value of each of these life events that has happened to you during the previous year. Total these associated points. Then add up all your points to find your score.

Life Event	Mean Value
1. Death of spouse	100
2. Divorce	73
3. Marital separation from mate	65
4. Detention in jail or other institution	63
5. Death of a close family member	63
6. Major personal injury or illness	53
7. Marriage	50
8. Being fired at work	47
9. Marital reconciliation with mate	45
10. Retirement from work	45
11. Major change in the health or behavior of a family member	44
12. Pregnancy	40
13. Sexual Difficulties	39
14. Gaining a new family member (i.e., birth, adoption, older adult moving in, etc.)	39
15. Major business readjustment	39
16. Major change in financial state (i.e., a lot worse or better off than usual)	38
17. Death of a close friend	37
18. Changing to a different line of work	36
19. Major change in the number of arguments w/spouse (either a lot more or a lot less than usual regarding child rearing, personal habits, etc.)	35

[1]Thomas Holmes and Richard Rahe, "Holmes-Rahe Social Readjustment Rating Scale," *Journal of Psychosomatic Research* 11 (1967): 213-18.

20. Taking on a mortgage (for home, business, etc.)   31

21. Foreclosure on a mortgage or loan   30

22. Major change in responsibilities at work (e.g., promotion, demotion)   29

23. Son or daughter leaving home (marriage, attending college, joined military)   29

24. In-law troubles   29

25. Outstanding personal achievement   28

26. Spouse beginning or ceasing work outside the home   26

27. Beginning or ceasing formal schooling   26

28. Major change in living condition
    (new home, remodeling, deterioration of neighborhood or home, etc.)   25

29. Revision of personal habits (dress manners, associations, quitting smoking)   24

30. Troubles with the boss   23

31. Major changes in working hours or conditions   20

32. Changes in residence   20

33. Changing to a new school   20

34. Major change in usual type and/or amount of recreation   19

35. Major change in church activity (i.e., a lot more or less than usual)   19

36. Major change in social activities (clubs, movies, visiting, etc.)   18

37. Taking on a loan (e.g., car, appliance)   17

38. Major change in sleeping habits (i.e., a lot more or a lot less than usual)   16

39. Major change in number of family get-togethers   15

40. Major change in eating habits (a lot more or less food intake,
    or very different meal hours or surroundings)   15

41. Vacation   13

42. Major holidays   12

43. Minor violations of the law (traffic tickets, jaywalking, disturbing the peace, etc.)   11

Less than 150 points: relatively low amount of life change and low susceptibility to stress-induced health breakdown in the next two years.

150 to 300 points: 50 percent chance of a major health breakdown in the next two years.

More than 300 points: 80 percent chance of a major health breakdown in the next two years.

Appendix D
Balanced Breathing Exercise for Relaxation

When we are relaxed or sleeping,[1] there is a natural rhythm to our breathing: the stomach slightly protrudes, the rib cage expands, and the shoulders lift slightly at the end of the cycle. When under stress, the natural rhythm of breathing is disturbed. We may hyperventilate by breathing rapidly and shallowly, or we may breathe too slowly and create hypoxia or hypoventilation. In either case, the natural hydrogen-ion concentration (pH) level of the blood (normally 7.40) is disturbed. If the pH level increases sharply through hyperventilation, it causes respiratory alkalosis (where carbon dioxide is increased and oxygen decreased).

The effects of hyperventilation are quite common: dizziness, weakness, nervousness and concentration difficulties. Effective results can be achieved through balanced breathing, restoring the natural pH condition and relieving nervousness or anxiety.

STEPS TO BALANCED BREATHING
Sit comfortably but straight with your feet firmly planted on the floor just slightly in front of your knees. The weight of your head and neck should be resting firmly on the spinal column, hands resting on your lap, eyes closed, garments loosened.

Inhale for three seconds, hold for twelve seconds, and exhale for six seconds. Repeat this procedure five times for a total of six rounds.

At the end of the sixth cycle, exhale explosively and sit quietly for a minute or so, allowing your breathing to return to normal.

Practice this exercise frequently until you can visualize the resulting relaxation even before you begin. The more you practice the exercise, the better the results will be. Balanced breathing is an emergency technique to help with highly stressful situations. This technique may be modified for use while doing most anything, including driving a car or walking down the hallway at work (with your eyes open, of course). While the results will be lessened, many people nonetheless find it to be a very helpful and practical intervention.

---

[1]Kenneth B. Matheny, "Psychological Change Strategies," summer 1994, Georgia State University, Atlanta, Georgia, p. 35.

Appendix E
Personality Strengths Inventory

This inventory is a resource from Dennis L. Howard, Family Care Center, Fort Wayne, Indiana (www.VitalityCareInst.org). Used with permission.

POWERFUL HAMMER

Strengths in Check

___Leader
___Takes charge
___Eager
___Assertive, confident
___Firm
___Enterprising
___Competitive
___Daring, enjoys challenges
___Problem solver
___Vigorous, productive
___Bold
___Purposeful, goal-driven
___Decision maker
___Adventurous spirit
___Force of character, strong-willed
___Independent, self-reliant
___Unconquerable
___Persistent
___Action-oriented
___Determined

Strengths Carried Too Far

___Too direct or demanding
___Pushy
___Overbearing
___Unyielding, too blunt
___Takes big risks
___Cold-blooded, uncooperative
___Avoids relations
___Too busy
___Overlooks feelings—do it now!
___Insensitive
___Imbalanced, workaholic
___Unthoughtful of others' wishes
___Impulsive, restless
___Stubborn
___Inflexible
___Bossy
___Avoids seeking help

VERSATILE SWISS ARMY KNIFE

Strengths in Check

___Confident, charming
___Open-minded
___Persuasive
___Enthusiastic
___Takes risks
___Visionary
___Motivator
___Energetic
___Very verbal
___Promoter
___Friendly, mixes easily
___Enjoys popularity
___Fun-loving
___Likes variety
___Spontaneous
___Enjoys change
___Creative, goes for new ideas
___Group-oriented
___Optimistic
___Initiator
___Infectious laughter
___Inspirational

Strengths Carried Too Far

___Cocky, proud, tries hard to impress
___Gullible
___Pushy
___Overbearing, overcommits
___Dangerous, foolish
___Daydreamer
___Manipulator
___Impatient
___Puts foot in mouth
___Exaggerates
___Shallow relationships
___Too showy
___Too flippant, not serious
___Too scattered, disorganized
___Not focused
___Lacks follow-through
___Unrealistic, misses details
___Bored with "process"
___Obnoxious
___Phony

ADAPTABLE DUCT TAPE

Strengths in Check

___Sensitive
___Loyal
___Calm, even-keeled
___Avoids confrontation
___Enjoys routine
___Warm and relational
___Moderate
___Generous
___Cheerful
___Accommodating
___Cautious humor, considerate
___Adaptable
___Sympathetic
___Thoughtful
___Nurturing
___Patient
___Tolerant
___Good listener
___Peacemaker

Strengths Carried Too Far

___Easily hurt
___Misses opportunities, overtrusting
___Lacks enthusiasm
___Pushover
___Misses honest intimacy
___Stays in rut, complacent
___Not spontaneous
___Few deep friendships
___Codependent, passive
___Unwilling to risk
___Can be taken advantage of
___Patronizing
___Indecisive, compromising
___Overly cautious
___Loses identity, vacillates
___Holds on to others' hurts
___Enabling
___Weak convictions
___Attracted to hurting people
___Stuffs feelings

PRECISION TAPE MEASURE

Strengths in Check	**Strengths Carried Too Far**
___Reads all instructions, deliberate	___Afraid to take risks
___Accurate, cautious	___Critical
___Consistent	___Lacks spontaneity
___Controlled	___Too serious
___Reserved	___Stuffy
___Predictable	___Lacks variety
___Practical	___Not adventurous
___Factual	___Picky
___Conscientious	___Controlling, inflexible
___Well-disciplined, orderly	___Negative toward new opportunities
___Discerning	___"Paralysis of analysis"
___Detailed	___Loses big-picture view
___Analytical	___Smothering, nosey
___Inquisitive	___Strict, perfectionistic
___Precise	___Pushy
___Persistent	___Boring
___Scheduled	___Stubborn, oversensitive
___Sensitive	___Self-absorbed
___Introspective	___Gullible
___Receptive	___Reluctant, overcautious
	___Rigid, unrealistic

APPENDIX F
Contributors from CareGivers Forum

Charley and Beverly Blom (www.geneseehome.org). Genesee Home is a renewal retreat center in Taylorsville, California, for pastors and spouses.

Steve and Patti Cappa (www.marbleretreat.org). Marble Retreat in Marble, Colorado, offers eight-day intensive psychotherapy for Christian ministers and all believers who are burdened or troubled.

Bill and Anita Ellenberger (www.faithfulpath.com). Faithful Path is a mentoring, speaking and consulting ministry in Tyrone, Pennsylvania, serving ministers, churches and seminaries.

Dale and Marlene Frimodt (www.thebarnabasministries.org). Barnabas Ministries (Omaha, Nebraska) provides encouragement, counseling and consulting for pastors, church leadership, missionaries and other Christian leaders.

Ed and Teresa Gray (www.heartlandbiblicalcounseling.org). Heartland Biblical Counseling offers grace-based biblical counseling by licensed therapists in La Mesa and San Diego, California, with special consideration for pastors and missionaries.

Andrew and Nancy Hagen (www.pastorsretreatnetwork.org). Pastors Retreat Network offers five-day retreats in Oconomowoc, Wisconsin, for pastors and pastor couples.

Denny Howard (www.vitalitycareinst.org). Vitality Care Institute/Family Care Center in Fort Wayne, Indiana, equips those serving in ministry and other "care giving" vocations in the process of gaining and maintaining personal vitality.

Herb and Kathy Miller (www.faithmountain.org). Faith Mountain Ministries offers restorative retreats in Rosedale, West Virginia, for pastors, missionaries and Christian families.

Ted and Linda Pampeyan (www.leadershiprenewal.com). Leadership Renewal Center offers life coaching retreats near Fresno, California, for Christian leaders and their spouses.

Nathan and Jane Phillips (www.battlefieldministries.org). Battlefield Ministries, Inc. (Rome, Georgia) offers counseling, marriage retreats, family workshops and romantic adventures.

Gary and Georgia Pinion (www.encouragementdynamics.com). Encouragement Dynamics (Richland, Washington) is a ministry of encouragement, restoration, motivation and education focused on the needs of pastors.

Tom and Barbara Salter (www.barnabasfactor.com). Barnabas Factor offers retreats of rest and rejuvenation for pastoral families on beautiful Lake Tahoe, California.

Charles and Colleen Shepson (www.fairhavenministries.net [Tennessee]; www.fairhavenministries.org [British Columbia]). The Shepsons are internationally sought-after speakers and authors, and founders of Fairhaven Ministries in Roan Mountain, Tennessee and Vernon, British Columbia, Canada.

Dennis Siebert (www.mtlakealliance.net). Dennis is assistant pastor of Alliance Missionary Church, Mountain Lake, Minnesota.

Dick and Dee Sochacki (www.barnabas-ministries.com). Barnabas Ministries of Michigan is an encouragement and resource outreach to hurting clergy and their wives.

Cal and Linda Swanson (www.fairhavenministries.net). Fairhaven Ministries is a retreat and counseling center in Roan Mountain, Tennessee, for Christian workers.

APPENDIX G
For Further Reading

INTRODUCTION

Arterburn, Stephen. *The Twelve Step Life Recovery Devotional.* Wheaton, Ill.: Tyndale House, 1991.

Biehl, Bobb. *Mentoring: Confidence in Finding a Mentor and Becoming One.* Nashville: Broadman & Holman, 1996.

Hendricks, Howard G., and William D. Hendricks. *As Iron Sharpens Iron.* Chicago: Moody, 2000.

Kent, Carol. *Becoming a Woman of Influence.* Colorado Springs: NavPress, 2006.

London, H. B., Jr., and Neil B. Wiseman. *Pastors at Greater Risk.* Ventura, Calif.: Gospel Light, 2003.

Mahaney, C. J. *Humility: True Greatness.* Portland, Ore.: Multnomah, 2005.

Murray, Andrew. *Absolute Surrender.* Minneapolis: Bethany House, 2003.

FOUNDATION STONE 1: INTIMACY

Bentall, David C. *The Company You Keep: The Transforming Power of Male Friendship.* Minneapolis: Augsburg, 2004.

Brestin, Dee. *The Friendships of Women.* 2nd rev. ed. Colorado Springs: Life Journey, 2005.

Brestin, Dee, and Kathy Troccoli. *Falling in Love with Jesus.* Nashville: Nelson, 2002.

Chapman, Gary. *Covenant Marriage: Building Communication and Intimacy.* Nashville: Broadman & Holman, 2003.

Rosenau, Doug, and Michael Todd Wilson. *Soul Virgins: Redefining Single Sexuality.* Grand Rapids: Baker, 2006.

Smalley, Gary. *Secrets to Lasting Love.* New York: Fireside, 2000.

Thomas, Gary. *Sacred Marriage.* Grand Rapids: Zondervan, 2002.

———. *Sacred Pathways.* Grand Rapids: Zondervan, 2002.

Weber, Stu. *All the King's Men: Strength in Character Through Friendships.* Portland, Ore.: Multnomah, 2006.

Wright, H. Norman. *Communication: Key to Your Marriage.* Ventura, Calif.: Regal, 2000.

FOUNDATION STONE 2: CALLING

Allen, Blaine. *Before You Quit: When Ministry Is Not What You Thought.* Grand Rapids: Kregel, 2001.

Blackaby, Henry T., Henry R. Brandt and Kerry L. Skinner. *The Power of the Call.* Nashville: Broadman & Holman, 1997.

Bratcher, Ed, Robert Kemper and Douglas Scott. *Mastering Transitions.* Portland, Ore.: Multnomah, 1991.

Cionca, John R. *Red Light, Green Light.* Grand Rapids: Baker, 1994.

Crowell, Rodney J. *Musical Pulpits: Clergy and Laypersons Face the Issue of Forced Exits.* Grand Rapids: Baker, 1992.

Cullinan, Alice R. *Sorting It Out: Discerning God's Call to Ministry.* Elgin, Ill.: Judson Press, 1999.

Guinness, Os. *The Call.* Nashville: W Publishing Group, 1998.

Hightower, James E., Jr., and W. Craig Gilliam, *Time for Change: Re-visioning Your Call.* Bethesda, Md.: Alban Institute, 2000.

Johnson, Ben Campbell. *Hearing God's Call.* Grand Rapids: Eerdmans, 2002.

Ludwig, Glenn E. *In It for the Long Haul: Building Effective Long-Term Pastorates.* Bethesda, Md.: Alban Institute, 2002.

Prime, Derek, and Alistair Begg. *On Being a Pastor.* Chicago: Moody Publishers, 2004.

Rubietta, Jane. *How to Keep the Pastor You Love.* Downers Grove, Ill.: InterVarsity Press, 2002.

Trent, John, Rodney Cox and Eric Tooker. *Leading from Your Strengths.* Nashville: Broadman & Holman, 2004.

FOUNDATION STONE 3: STRESS MANAGEMENT

Faulkner, Brooks R. *Burnout in Ministry.* Nashville: Baptist Sunday School Board, 1981.

Faulkner, Brooks, and Guy Greenfield. *The Wounded Minister.* Grand Rapids: Baker, 2001.

Foster, Richard. *Celebration of Discipline.* 25th anniv. ed. San Francisco: HarperSanFrancisco, 1998.

Hart, Archibald. *Adrenaline and Stress.* Rev. ed. Dallas: Word, 1995.

MacDonald, Gordon. *Restoring Your Spiritual Passion.* 3rd ed. Godalming, England: Highland, 2004.

Minirth, Frank. *How to Beat Burnout.* Chicago: Moody Publishers, 1999.

Sande, Ken. *The Peacemaker: A Biblical Guide to Resolving Personal Conflict.* Grand Rapids: Baker, 2004.

Swenson, Richard. *The Overload Syndrome: Learning to Live Within Your Limits.* Colorado Springs: NavPress, 1999.

———. *Margin: Restoring Emotional, Physical, Financial, and Time Reserves to Overloaded Lives.* Colorado Springs: NavPress, 2004.

Thomas, Gary. *Authentic Faith: The Power of a Fire-Tested Life.* Grand Rapids: Zondervan, 2003.

FOUNDATION STONE 4: BOUNDARIES

Cloud, Henry, and John Townsend. *Boundaries.* Rev. ed. Grand Rapids: Zondervan, 2002.

Covey, Stephen R. *The Seven Habits of Highly Effective People.* 15th anniv. ed. New York: Free Press, 2004.

Curtis, Brent, and John Eldredge. *The Sacred Romance: Drawing Closer to the Heart of God.* Nashville: Thomas Nelson, 1997.

Laaser, Mark R. *Healing the Wounds of Sexual Addiction.* Grand Rapids: Zondervan, 2004.

Rosenau, Doug, and Michael Todd Wilson. *Soul Virgins: Redefining Single Sexuality.* Grand Rapids: Baker, 2006.

Scazzero, Peter, with Warren Bird. *The Emotionally Healthy Church.* Grand Rapids: Zondervan, 2003.

FOUNDATION STONE 5: RE-CREATION

Dennis, Jay, and Marilyn Jeffcoat. *Taming Your Private Thoughts.* Grand Rapids: Zondervan, 2002.

Edwards, Tilden. *Sabbath Time: Understanding and Practice for Contemporary Christians.* Nashville: Upper Room, 1992.

Gemignani, Michael C. *Spiritual Formation for Pastors.* Elgin, Ill.: Judson Press, 2002.

Hinson, E. Glenn. *Spiritual Preparation for Christian Leadership.* Nashville: Upper Room, 1999.

Jones, Kirk Byron. *Rest in the Storm: Self-Care Strategies for Clergy and Other Caregivers.* Elgin, Ill.: Judson Press, 2001.

Melander, Rochelle, and Harold Eppley. *The Spiritual Leader's Guide to Self-Care.* Bethesda, Md.: Alban Institute, 2002.

Muller, Wayne. *Sabbath: Finding Rest, Renewal, and Delight in our Busy Life.* New York: Bantam, 2000.

Oswald, Roy M. *Clergy Self-Care.* Bethesda, Md.: Alban Institute, 1991.

Sisk, Ronald D. *The Competent Pastor: Skill and Self-Knowledge for Serving Well.* Bethesda, Md.: Alban Institute, 2005.

Ulmer, Kenneth C. *Spiritually Fit to Run the Race: Personal Training Manual for Godly Living.* Nashville: Thomas Nelson, 1999.

Whitney, Donald S., and Don Whitney. *Spiritual Disciplines for the Christian Life.* Colorado Springs: NavPress, 1991.

FOUNDATION STONE 6: PEOPLE MANAGEMENT

Baron, Renee. *What Type Am I? Discover Who You Really Are.* New York: Penguin, 1998.

Bozeman, Jeanine Cannon, and Argile Asa Smith. *Interpersonal Relationship Skills for Ministers.* Gretna, La.: Pelican, 2004.

Garner, Alan. *Conversationally Speaking: Tested New Ways to Increase Your Personal and Social Effectiveness.* Columbus, Ohio: McGraw-Hill, 1997.

Leas, Speed B. *Discover Your Conflict Management Style.* Bethesda, Md.: Alban Institute, 1998.

Littauer, Florence. *How to Get Along with Difficult People.* Eugene, Ore.: Harvest House, 2006.

———. *Personality Plus: How to Understand Others by Understanding Yourself.* New ed. Oxford: Monarch, 2007.

Mason, Paul, and Randi Kreger. *Stop Walking on Eggshells: Taking Your Life Back When Someone You Care About Has Borderline Personality Disorder.* Oakland, Calif.: New Harbinger, 1998.

Maxwell, John C. *The Winning Attitude: Your Key to Personal Success.* Nashville: Thomas Nelson, 1992.

Meier, Paul, and Robert L. Wise. *Crazy Makers: Getting Along with the Difficult People in Your Life.* Nashville: Thomas Nelson, 2001.

FOUNDATION STONE 7: LEADERSHIP SKILLS

Allender, Dan B. *Leading with a Limp: Turning Your Struggles into Strengths.* Colorado Springs: Waterbrook, 2006.

Anderson, Leith. *Leadership That Works: Hope and Direction for the Church and Parachurch Leaders in Today's Complex World.* Minneapolis: Bethany House, 1999.

Arbinger Institute. *Leadership and Self-Deception.* San Francisco: Berrett-Koehler, 2002.

Badaracco, Joseph L., Jr. *Leading Quietly.* Boston: Harvard Business School Press, 2002.

Barna, George. *Leaders on Leadership: Wisdom, Advice, and Encouragement on the Art of Leading God's People.* Ventura, Calif.: Regal, 1997.

Blackaby, Henry, and Richard Blackaby. *Spiritual Leadership.* Nashville: Broadman & Holman, 2001.

Cladis, George. *Leading the Team-Based Church.* Seattle: Jossey-Bass, 1999.

Csorba. Les T. *Trust: The One Thing That Makes or Breaks a Leader.* Nashville: Nelson Business, 2004.

Eskelin, Neil. *Leading with Love.* Grand Rapids: Revell, 2001.

Farris, Lawrence W. *Ten Commandments for Pastors New to a Congregation.* Grand Rapids: Eerdmans, 2003.

Finzel, Hans. *The Top Ten Mistakes Leaders Make.* Wheaton, Ill.: Victor Books, 1994.

Forman, Rowland, Jeff Jones and Bruce Miller. *The Leadership Baton.* Grand Rapids: Zondervan, 2004.

Galford, Robert M., and Anne Seibold Drapeau. *The Trusted Leader.* New York: Free Press, 2002.

Galloway, Dale. *Leading with Vision.* Boston: Beacon Hill, 1999.

———. *Building Teams in Ministry.* Boston: Beacon Hill, 2001.

Galloway, John. *Ministry Loves Company.* Louisville, Ky.: Westminster John Knox, 2003.

Geoffrion, Timothy C. *The Spirit-Led Leader.* Bethesda, Md.: Alban Institute, 2005.

Greenleaf, Robert K., and Larry C. Spears. *The Power of Servant Leadership.* San Francisco: Berrett-Koehler, 1998.

Hansen, David, and David L. Goetz. *The Power of Loving Your Church.* Minneapolis: Bethany House, 1998.

Herrington, Jim, Robert Creech and Trisha L. Taylor. *The Leader's Journey.* Seattle: Jossey-Bass, 2003.

Hybels, Bill. *Who You Are When No One's Looking.* Downers Grove, Ill.: InterVarsity Press, 1987.

Johnson, Dwight L. *The Transparent Leader.* Eugene, Ore.: Harvest House, 2001.

Katzenbach, Jon R., and Douglas K. Smith. *The Wisdom of Teams.* New York: Collins, 2003.

Kinnaman, Gary D., and Alfred H. Ells. *Leaders That Last.* Grand Rapids: Baker, 2003.

Kotter, John P., and Dan S. Cohen. *The Heart of Change.* Boston: Harvard Business School Press, 2002.

Malphurs, Aubrey. *Being Leaders.* Grand Rapids: Baker, 2003.

———. *Building Leaders.* Grand Rapids: Baker, 2004.

Maxwell, John C. *Developing the Leader Within You.* Nashville: Thomas Nelson, 1993.

———. *Developing the Leaders Around You.* Nashville: Thomas Nelson, 1995.

———. *The 17 Essential Qualities of a Team Player: Becoming the Kind of Person Every Team Wants.* Nashville: Nelson Business, 2002.

McCormick, Blaine, and David Davenport. *Shepherd Leadership.* Seattle: Jossey-Bass, 2003.

Norton, Robert, and Richard Southern. *Cracking Your Congregation's Code.* Seattle: Jossey-Bass, 2001.

Rock, David. *Quiet Leadership: Six Steps to Transforming Performance at Work.* New York: Collins, 2006.

Sande, Ken, and Kay Moore. *Peacefakers, Peacebreakers, and Peacemakers.* Garland, Tex.: Hannibal Books, 2005.

Stanley, Andy. *The Next Generation Leader.* Portland, Ore.: Multnomah, 2003.